FAR FROM
A DONKEY

Also from Brassey's

DAVID
Mutiny at Salerno
An Injustice Exposed

VERRIER (Ed)
Agents & Empire
Anglo-Zionist Intelligence Operations 1915–1919
Brigadier Walter Gribbon, Aaron Aaronsohn and the NILI
Ring

ZADKA
Blood in Zion
How the Jewish Guerrillan drove the British out of Palestine

FAR FROM
A DONKEY

—•◆•—

The Life of
General Sir Ivor Maxse
KCB, CVO, DSO

JOHN BAYNES

Brassey's
London • Washington

First English Edition 1995

UK editorial offices: Brassey's Ltd, 33, John Street, London WC1N 2AT
UK Orders: Marston Book Services, PO Box 87, Oxford OX2 0DT

North American Orders: Brassey's Inc, PO Box 960, Herndon, VA 22070.

John Baynes has asserted his moral right to be identified as the author of this work.

Library of Congress Cataloging in Publication Data
available

British Library Cataloguing in Publication Data
A catalogue record for this book is available from the British Library

ISBN 1 85753 185 X Hardcover

Typeset by M Rules
Printed in Great Britain by Bookcraft (Bath) Ltd

Contents

———•◆•———

Peacetime Soldiering

The First World War

Last Army Appointment and Retirement

List of Plates

———— •◆• ————

List of Maps

———— •◆• ————

A Brief Note on the Title

———•◆•———

The use of the word 'donkey' in the title of this book comes from a popular perception of British generals in the First World War as 'donkeys' driving the 'lions', who were their soldiers, into endless, disastrous battles.

The matter is treated by John Terraine in his book *The Smoke and the Fire: Myths and Anti-Myths of War 1861–1945*, Sidgwick & Jackson (1981). In support of the destruction of this myth he refers first to a reported conversation to be found in the front of Alan Clark's book *The Donkeys*, published by Hutchinson in 1961:

> LUDENDORFF: 'The English soldiers fight like lions.'
> HOFFMANN: 'True. But don't we know that they are lions led by donkeys.'
> (Falkenhayn, *Memoirs*).

Terraine then goes on to quote two letters which throw light on the facts behind this quotation:

First Letter

> I have been sufficiently curious to enquire further into the source of this quotation. Assuming that Falkenhayn, Hoffman [sic] and Ludendorff were the German generals of those names in World War I, I have sought the assistance of the librarians of the Imperial War Museum and the Library for Contemporary World War literature in Stuttgart, and I have received replies from both, to the effect that the reported conversation could not be traced in any books connected with those names which had been examined.
>
> An enquiry to the publishers of *The Donkeys* could be met only by a

reference back to the printed statement in the book. . . . A letter addressed to the author which the publishers' representative undertook to forward to him remains unacknowledged.

(J C SHARP ESQ., Birmingham: letter in *The Daily Telegraph*, 16 July 1963.)

Second Letter

In Francisque Sarcey's *Le Siège de Paris*, published by Nelson in 1871, on page 57, are quoted the words of the London *Times* about the French soldiers who had been completely defeated by the Prussians in 1870: "Vous êtes des lions conduits par des ânes!"

(D G LIBBY ESQ., London SW15, letter in *The Daily Telegraph*, 19 July 1963.)

A more recent direct approach to Alan Clark has been swiftly and courteously replied to. He states that: 'The quotation was given to me by Basil Liddell Hart. (I worked with him for 2 years while I was preparing *The Donkeys*).'

It is probable that the lions led by donkeys assessment has been applied in other cases beyond those mentioned above, and is something of an old 'chestnut' in the field of military commentary.

Preface with Acknowledgements

———— •◆• ————

I first met Tony Maxse in a friend's house near my home in Wales in 1992. I knew about his grandfather, General Sir Ivor, because of many references to the Maxse papers in books I had read about the First World War, and also because of the frequency with which the General's name appeared in Major General Eric Sixsmith's book *British Generalship in the 20th Century*. As a one-time ADC to Sixsmith, a fellow Scottish Rifleman, it was an obvious duty to study the book: this I did with more pleasure than his son Edmund whose comment on returning a copy of the proofs to his father was reported to be: 'Well, it's a pretty dry biscuit, but I don't think there are any weevils in it!'

Following some discussion with Tony during the following months the idea of writing Ivor's biography was born, and Brassey's in due course gave me a contract to tackle it. Tony Trythall agreed to undertake the preliminary editing himself, and to him and Caroline Winterbottom his assistant, thanks must first be given for their constant encouragement and help. Before going on to mention others who have assisted with work on the book, the enormous contribution of Tony Maxse must be explained. Without the benefit of his research over many years into his grandfather's papers, and his skill in handling his word processor to produce the typescript, this book might still be floundering along short of even the half-way stage.

Many people have provided advice or assistance in one way or another, and I would like to thank the late Colonel Paul Adair; Correlli Barnett; Mrs J M Blacklaw of the MOD Library; Professor Brian Bond; Major C P Bowes-Crick of the Royal Regiment of Fusiliers; Alison McCann and the reading room staff at the West Sussex Record Office; Lieutenant

Colonel M J Evetts; Earl Haig; P H Liddle; Mrs P J Methven of the Liddell Hart Centre for Military Archives; Andrew Orgill of the RMA Sandhurst Library; Mary Sheffield; Peter Simkins and Nigel Steel of the Imperial War Museum; John Terraine; J F Russell of the Scottish National Library; Professor T H E Travers; Major G Wemyss; Major S B Whitmore.

For permission to quote extracts of more than 100 words from their works I am indebted to: John A Hutcheson, Jr, for quotations from *Leopold Maxse and the National Review, 1893–1914*; Ivry, Lady Freyberg for quotations from the late Paul Freyberg's biography of his father, *Bernard Freyberg, VC*; General Sir Anthony Farrar-Hockley for quotations from *Goughie*; and finally General Sir David Fraser for quotations from *Alanbrooke* and *In Good Company* as well as valuable advice and assistance.

Authorities Consulted

Unpublished Sources:

Maxse papers at the West Sussex Record Office (WSRO), Chichester.
Maxse papers at the Imperial War Museum.
War Diaries at the Public Record Office, Kew.
Haig's papers at the National Library of Scotland.
Letters and Documents still in the possession of the Maxse family.

Prologue

———•◆•———

In spite of bringing the First World War to a victorious conclusion, and in the final year playing the major part, the British Army and its leaders have often been portrayed as inferior to their adversaries in most military activities. The image of the British general as a pompous, incompetent bungler, callously sending his troops to be slaughtered by a more skilful foe, has become fixed in all too many minds. This book records the long life of a man of a different stamp, and the title has been purposely chosen to help dispel the concept of all our generals being 'donkeys'.

That there were some inefficient senior officers in the army cannot be denied, just as there are inefficient people in responsible posts in all walks of life. The curse has been placed on the generals because of the loss of so many lives during the four years of war. They have become the scapegoats on whom the tribulations of the whole nation have been laid, though in truth all these tragic deaths were inevitable once war had been declared on Germany and its allies. However much they came to hate it by 1918, the people of Britain were, almost without exception, full of enthusiasm for the war in 1914. It was a freely taken decision by the whole country to enter a conflict with formidable opponents, in which it should have been obvious that terrible battles of attrition would have to be fought, and dreadful destruction suffered, before either side could claim victory.

If this premise is accepted, it must be asked what sort of person was required to lead those who served in the nation's armed forces through the vale of tears entered so readily, and alas so recklessly. Nobody has described better the qualities of mind and character required of such a leader than Field Marshal Earl Wavell, who fought at the front in the First World War and bore great responsibilities in the Second.

1

Lecturing at Trinity College, Cambridge in 1939 on 'Generals and Generalship' he gave 'as the first essential of a general, the quality of robustness, the ability to stand the shocks of war', going on to expand on this requirement:

> Delicate mechanism is of little use in war; and this applies to the mind of the commander as well as his body; to the spirit of an army as well as to the weapons and instruments with which it is equipped. All material of war, including the general, must have a certain solidity, a high margin over the normal breaking strain.[1]

When suggesting the mental abilities needed he put first *le sens du praticable*, or common sense allied to 'a really sound knowledge of the "mechanism of war", i.e. topography, movement, and supply'. In respect of the principles of strategy, he pointed out that these 'can be apprehended in a very short time by any reasonable intelligence.' At this stage he might have quoted from *The Merchant of Venice* the well-known lines which start 'If to do were as easy as to know what were good to do . . .'.[2]

Ivor Maxse, the subject of this biography, is of special interest because he was not only robust enough to hold important commands right through the War from 1914 to 1918, but he was one of the generals who, amid the fog of war, taught his subordinates to go a long way towards doing 'what were good to do'. This was due in large measure to his unusual originality and drive as a communicator, which made him a remarkably effective trainer of officers and men at all levels. Although his period as a commander during the First World War will be the main concern of those reading this book, there is much to relate about the rest of his long life, which is not only important in giving an insight into his conduct during the war years, but is of considerable interest in itself.

Notes

1 WAVELL, Field Marshal Earl, *Soldiers and Soldiering* (Cape, 1953) p. 16.
2 WAVELL, p. 21.

The Early Years

1
Childhood and First School, 1862–77

————— •◆• —————

When Frederick Ivor Maxse, always known simply as Ivor, was born in London in December 1862 it was not hard to imagine for those who first saw him as a baby that he might enjoy a long life, but they could hardly have envisaged the changes that would take place in the world before he died just over 95 years later in January 1958. He lived almost long enough to sense the first stirrings of the spirit that would make the 1960s such an iconoclastic period in British social history, and so different from the 1860s in which he had spent his formative years. Although Ivor was to grow up into an original thinker, and often find himself at variance with conventional opinion on numerous subjects, he was inevitably influenced in many ways by the attitudes prevalent in the social milieu into which he had been born. He grew up in what might be called the enlightened sector of the upper class, among people who moved comfortably in intellectual circles, but who were also strongly influenced by the views of the formidable body known as 'society', of which Winston Churchill wrote in 1930 in *My Early Life*:

> It was a brilliant and powerful body, with standards of conduct and methods of enforcing them now altogether forgotten. In a very large degree every one knew everyone else and who they were. The few hundred great families who had governed England for so many generations and had seen her rise to the pinnacle of her glory, were interrelated to an enormous extent by marriage.[1]

Growing prosperity founded on international trade, inventive industry, and improving agriculture created conditions in Britain that gave birth to the Victorian concept of the inevitability of progress in human affairs.

That the 1860s were peaceful years for Britain in comparison with the previous decade helped give credence to such optimistic beliefs. During the 1850s the armed forces had seen much active service in the Crimean War (1854–56), the Anglo-Chinese War (1856–58) and the Indian Mutiny (1857–58), but in the 1860s there was little for them to do and for the next 30 years or so, their involvement would be restricted to minor skirmishes.

While life at home in Britain was dissimilar enough from modern times, the difference in respect of the United Kingdom's place in the world beyond its own shores was even more striking. Though Germany and the USA would become strong enough to challenge it in due course, it was in the 1860s still firmly at the top of the world power league. The majority of the population rejoiced in this supremacy among all other nations. It was based on three factors: on being ahead in industrial inventiveness and its application to manufacturing; on trade-generated wealth; and on the Royal Navy's mastery of the oceans, leading to control of the routes along which so much of the trade passed. Linked to these factors was that great source of pride: the Empire 'on which the sun never set'. In the 1860s what was to become known as the scramble for Africa had not begun, and few voices were ever raised, as they were later in the century, to suggest that the imperial role was anything but beneficial to the countries controlled by the British whether as settlers or as colonists: either in the countries which had become, or were becoming, self-governing dominions, or in the colonies where the populations were merely governed by officials who came and went. Most important in yet a further category was India, where stories of the atrocities committed during the recently ended Mutiny confirmed the opinion that strong rule by an impartial British government was necessary to civilise such apparently barbarous natives. Throughout Britain, though real knowledge about the Empire might be hazy, it was regarded as providing an opportunity for British values to be spread around the world while offering excellent opportunities for trade at the same time – in short good works allied to good business, and so wholly commendable.

Following this brief glance at some of the elements which shaped young Ivor Maxse's early years, it is time to look at his family background. His surname was probably derived from the village of Maxey in Northamptonshire. A family spelling their name in that way was prominent in Essex in the 17th century, while the alternative of 'Maxse' has been discovered in parish records in London as early as 1575. Ivor's own line was descended from John Maxse of Bristol, a rich West India merchant who died in 1808. His son James sold his inherited shipping interests and devoted his energies to his favourite sports of fox-hunting and sailing. He was a big man who rode fine, heavyweight hunters, and was long remembered in the Quorn country as showing 'how sixteen stone should o'er a country go'. In sailing circles he was equally well known, and was a founder member of the Royal Yacht squadron. In 1828, James married Lady Caroline Berkeley, eldest daughter of the fifth Earl of Berkeley, by whom he had four children: two sons and two daughters. He died in 1864, leaving an estate of £300,000, which would be something over £12 million at the present time. Lady Caroline lived on until 1886, one of her grandchildren recalling that 'she kept a considerable measure of mental and physical activities right into extreme old age'.[2]

The second son of James and Lady Caroline was Frederick Augustus, Ivor's father. He was born in 1833, a year after his older brother Fitz. Although Fitz was to have a distinguished career, first as a soldier and later as a colonial governor, his marriage when a young man to a Viennese actress shocked his parents, who eventually transferred the weight of their affection to Frederick, though the brothers themselves remained on good terms.

After schooling in England, and for a short time in Paris, Frederick entered the Royal Navy at the age of 13. Following tours of duty on the South American and Mediterranean stations he became a lieutenant in 1852. Next came a posting to the West Indies, but he was back in time to be appointed an acting flag-lieutenant to Admiral Lord Lyons on the outbreak of the Crimean War. Arriving in the theatre of war he was attached to Lord Raglan's personal staff as naval aide-de-camp. Soon afterwards he was commended for gallantry after a dangerous 15-mile ride carrying despatches from Raglan to Lyons following the battle of the Alma. Later he was present at the battle of Inkerman, and witnessed the charge of the Light Brigade at Balaclava, where Fitz took part as an ADC to the commander, the notorious Earl of Cardigan. When Lord Raglan died in 1855, Frederick was one of the officers deputed to escort his body back to Britain. He then returned to the Mediterranean in command of a steam corvette, and later became one of the youngest captains in the Royal Navy. The promise of a distinguished naval career, however, was not fulfilled, as he retired from active service onto half-pay in 1867 at the age of 34. He attained flag rank in 1875 only by virtue of seniority: though he was from then on always referred to as 'The Admiral', within his family as well as outside it, he never served actively in that rank. In 1861, while still serving, Frederick married Cecilia Steel, the daughter of an Indian Army general. There were four children of the marriage: Ivor born in 1862; Leopold James, always just Leo, in 1864; Olive Hermione in 1866; and Violet Georgina in 1872. In spite of the children it was not a happy marriage and in 1877 they agreed to live apart. Violet was to record later that her father and mother 'were wholly incompatible, and the real miracle was not that they had separated, it was that they had stayed together for sixteen years'.[3] In the same book as these words appear, entitled *My Picture Gallery, 1886–1901*, Violet described two effects of their separation on the young Maxses. On the one hand, in spite of the devotion shown by both parents, and their efforts to mitigate the results of the trouble between them, the children were unhappy. 'The division, separation, the never seeing our parents together, nor hearing them talk to each other, the differing views about our lives they held, all these were a terrible burden for us.'[4] On the other hand, the unhappiness made the children very close to each other. Violet also explained that '. . . you have no conception of the tremendous intimacy in which we all lived at the time of our growth. Our divided home seemed to bring us closer as we went from our brilliant, beautiful, witty mother to our thoughtful, active father whose intimate friends were an exhilaration in themselves'.[5]

It was the thoughtful aspect of the Admiral's nature which brought him into conflict with the outlook and opinions of most of the people in the social circles into which he had been born, and among whom he had served in the Royal Navy. His disillusionment with these circles began in the Crimea. The bungling and incompetence which he had witnessed during the war affected him deeply; the sufferings of the appallingly ill-administered British army sent there he blamed on aristocratic lethargy and incompetence in the government. Later, on leaving the navy, he saw the results of the same inefficiency on the lives of the poor at home. It was this that led him to take up radical politics, and he is quoted as saying:

> I was brought up to the tune of 'Rule Britannia' and 'Britons never shall be slaves,' . . . What made me an active politician was, when I came to live on shore, observing the conditions of the English agricultural labourers, I found that a large number of Britons *were* slaves – slaves to artificial oppressive circumstances – for the maintenance of which the governing classes stood, in my eyes, responsible; and upon the discovery of this I determined that, if during the whole of my life I could carry but a simple handful of earth towards the foundation of a better society, that handful would I carry.[6]

To achieve the carrying of 'his handful of earth', Frederick Maxse attempted to enter parliament, first contesting the borough of Southampton as a radical Liberal in the general election which brought Gladstone and the party to power in December 1868. This venture was unsuccessful, as was a further attempt to represent the Tower Hamlets constituency in the east end of London in 1874. His problem is succinctly summed up in his entry in the *Dictionary of National Biography*, where it is suggested that 'the certain idiosyncrasies which made his character an interesting study . . . unfitted him for modern political life'.[7]

At once idealistic and impulsively on the side of the underdog, Frederick was also an aristocrat with a considerable private fortune following his father's death in 1864. While contemptuous of what he regarded as the failings of the members of his own class, he continued to share many of their prejudices. Among the eccentricities which set him apart from most of his contemporaries were his abhorrence of alcohol, his vegetarianism, and his unconcealed scorn for Christianity. Against these unconventional opinions can be set his standing on women's suffrage and land reform in Ireland, where his opposition to granting both was as fierce as that of any high Tory. In the latter case, he admitted the suffering of the Irish peasants under the existing system of landownership, but felt that reform could only lead to chaos: a point of view no doubt derived from his naval officer's regard for discipline and good order as even more beneficial than liberty.

Due to his aristocratic background, his naval rank, and his wealth, he was at home in the most exalted circles, 'being so familiar with the Prince of Wales', according to the Liberal politician John Morley, that he 'habitually' tried to 'persuade him that a Republic is the only decent form of government'.[8] Because of his political opinions, however, he tended to make his firmest friends in other social areas. Amongst the intellectuals were Matthew Arnold, the scholar and poet, son of the famous Thomas, one-time headmaster of Rugby; Sir Lesley Stephen, the agnostic writer and historian, perhaps best remembered as the father of Virginia Woolf and Vanessa Bell; and closest of all, the once renowned but now largely forgotten novelist George Meredith, whom he met in 1859, when he was twenty-six and still an up-and-coming serving officer. It is generally assumed that the hero of Meredith's novel *Beauchamp's Career* was based on his study of Frederick Maxse's character:

> He had taken up arms; he had drunk of the questioning cup, that which denieth peace to us, and which projects us upon the missionary search of the How, the Wherefore, and the Why Not, ever afterward. He questioned his justification, and yours, for gratifying tastes in an ill-regulated world of wrongdoing, suffering, sin, and bounties unrighteously dispensed . . . and reached results amazing to his instincts, his tastes, his training, not less rapidly and naturally than tremendous.[9]

His friends in the sphere of politics included many influential Liberals. Among these was John Morley, to whom he introduced in 1873 a rising, young radical from Birmingham called Joseph Chamberlain. Because of his love of France he was often in Paris, and there 1872 he was introduced by Louis Blanc to Georges Clemenceau, who became his close friend for the rest of his life, and the friend of his children as well. Although best known as the great Prime Minister of France at the end of the First World War, with the nickname 'The Tiger', Clemenceau was in fact a radical who had played an active part in the Paris Commune as a young Mayor of Montmartre just a year earlier in 1870–71. Nearly 20 years after this first meeting, Frederick gave a dinner party in his London house to introduce Clemenceau to Joe Chamberlain, from which sprang another important friendship.

The four Maxse children spent more time with their father than with their mother, and in the free-thinking, enquiring, intellectual climate of his house were encouraged to do or say more or less what they liked, as long as anything they tackled was given their full attention and energy. They were expected to mix freely with their father's friends and to hold their own in discussions with them. In an article, 'Victorian Freedom', written in her old age his daughter recorded, 'The arguments of authority were never used at all. Nor were we told we were too young to understand anything, nor that wiser, better people had thought differently from us – we were left to find these truths out for ourselves.'[10]

Given the encouragement of these views, the relationship between the children was in constant ferment:

> These four children of Admiral Maxse had been nurtured in world politics from the cradle. They had learned to tear the heart out of new books, to seize upon new ideas with frenzied partizanship, and to discuss with passionate arguments hurled across the breakfast table the social, political and literary questions of the hour. . . . A newcomer could only listen and hope words so contentious would not lead to blows. Such alarms were indeed groundless; the wordy storms engendered no bitterness, they were the breath of life to the Maxse family.[11]

Before moving on from Ivor's family to the study of his own life, a resumé of the lives of his brother and sisters is necessary. Leo, born in 1864, was educated at Harrow and Cambridge, with a spell between school and university living in Paris to perfect his French. In 1893, with the encouragement and financial backing of £1500 from the Admiral, he purchased a monthly journal called the *National Review* which survived until the 1950s and was for many years one of the most influential organs for the expression of conservative opinions, on political and general subjects, throughout much of the English-speaking world. Leo was a furiously energetic editor, and attracted articles from a wide range of leading figures who saw the magazine as a good medium through which to express their views. Members of the family were also frequent contributors, and when Leo fell ill in 1929, dying in 1932, it was his sister Violet who took the editor's chair; joined, incidentally, by Ivor's wife as literary editor, as will unfold later.

Violet was born in 1872. She married in 1894 Lord Edward Cecil, nicknamed 'Nigs', a younger son of the Marquis of Salisbury. He died in 1918, and in 1921 she married Lord Milner, celebrated and admired in his day as a great imperial pro-consul, but treated less kindly, and perhaps less fairly, by modern historians. Between Leo and Violet came Olive, born in 1866. Although a gifted musician she was shy and diffident, and somewhat overshadowed by her brothers and sister, who were of anything but a retiring disposition. Throughout Ivor's youth his most permanent base was at Effingham Hill in Surrey, the home of his grandmother, Lady Caroline. Apart from the to-ing and fro-ing between the two separated parents, his father's penchant for moving house kept the children from becoming too settled in one place. On Lady Caroline's death the Admiral sold her house and built one for himself on part of the estate called Dunley Hill. This had 17 bedrooms and was cared for by 40 servants. At the time, he owned two more substantial houses, one near Eastbourne and one in London at Wetherby Gardens, South Kensington. His property and building deals were not always financial successes, and through them he contrived to dissipate most of the substantial inheritances that came to him, although behaving carefully and abstemiously in his own private life. The first school that Ivor was sent to was a small preparatory boarding school run by a Mr Lake at Witherden near Caterham, Surrey. Some letters to his father from this period survive, one from the school dated 7 April 1875 when he was 12.

> There is great excitement in the school because we are going to have some athletic sports next week. All the boys are practising running and jumping as much as they can and this morning we are most of us very stiff, I could hardly walk downstairs this morning. Mr Lake, Mrs Burton, Mr Guilmore and Patinson are going to give prizes and we would like to have another one to make up.
>
> P.S. Best love to Leo, hope he is well now.

Another one, written a year later, shows how he had adopted his father's political viewpoint, though the somewhat advanced comments on this are followed with more normal requests from a 13-year-old:

> I am very pleased to hear the great victory of the Radicals, in the *Weekly Dispatch*, (which I generally read). It praises Gambetta very much indeed. The French master at school is a monarchist and is greatly mortified when I show him the Repubilcan scenes. The weather is very bad. When you come, please bring me another collar stud from the Palais Royal and I am very greatly in need of pocket handkerchiefs.

Near the end of the Christmas holidays in January 1877 he described a piece of rural engineering carried out at one of his father's properties at Holly Hill, Southampton:

> Yesterday morning it was fine and we agreed to go down and drain the kiln copse of its bogs and ponds; Sam, George and Leo elected me foreman and we commenced work. . . . We finished the whole of the work this morning, and have left the water flowing rapidly from the copse to the river. I have also drained the road and a little of the stable field through the same channel and I am sure that altogether it will be very useful work.

Ivor left Mr Lake's school at the end of the Easter term 1877 in order to start at Rugby the following term.

Notes

Letters quoted from Maxse to his father can be found in West Sussex Record Office, (WRSO) file 208.

1 Churchill, Winston, *My Early Life* (Odhams Press, 1930), p. 38.
2 Milner, Viscountess, *My Picture Gallery 1886–1901* (John Murray, 1951), p. 8.
3 Milner, p. 1.
4 Milner, p. 1.
5 Milner, p. 3.
6 Davidson, J M, *Eminent British Liberals In and Out of Parliament* (Boston, 1880) pp. 268–9 (Quoted by Hutcheson, John, in *Leopold Maxse and the National Review, 1893–1914* (Garland, New York, 1989), p. 266.
7 Article on F A Maxse in *Supplement* (1909) to *Dictionary of National Biography*, p. 1029.
8 Hirst, F W, *Early Life and Letters of John Morley* (London, 1927), Vol 1, p. 252.
9 Meredith, George, *Beauchamp's Career* (World's Classics, 1950 edition) p. 135.
10 Milner, Viscountess, 'Victorian Freedom' in the *National Review*, CXVIII, No 707 (Jan., 1942) pp. 59–63.
11 Gore, John, *Mary Maxse, 1870–1944* (Rolls House, 1946), p. 33.

2

Rugby School and the Royal Military College, Sandhurst.

———•◆•———

Ivor was 14 when he arrived at Rugby at the start of the summer term in 1877. Why the Admiral chose this particular school for his eldest son cannot be known, but it is possible that his friendship with Matthew Arnold, son of the famous headmaster Dr Thomas Arnold, may have had some influence on his decision. Due to the Doctor's efforts during his tenure of office from 1828 to 1841, Rugby had become one of the most successful schools in the country, its fame being increased by the publication in 1857 of Thomas Hughes' book *Tom Brown's Schooldays*.

Anyone remembering the episode in the book where Tom is framed by Flashman so that he is caught poaching, and the beating which followed, may be surprised to discover that 20 years after the book came out conditions at Rugby had changed little, as shown by Ivor's first letter to his father dated 3 May 1877:

> . . . I should be very grateful for anything in the way of something to eat for breakfast and tea, as a cake or any kind of potted meat. Please tell Leo I have not yet been able to go out birds nesting once yet for two or three reasons. Firstly because I am afraid of trespassing where I ought not, the consequence of which would be a 'sixth licking' or some hundred lines to write out. A 'sixth licking' means three or four hard cuts on one's naked back by three or four different sixth form boys.

He wrote frequently to his father throughout his time at Rugby, with a freedom unusual for a public schoolboy of the period, whose letters might be expected to have been more reticent and stilted. When a member of the Arnold family had died in 1878 they had a painted window put in the school chapel in his memory. Ivor was scornful of the people who had subscribed £300 towards it, ending his letter of 18 May 1879 by recording that: 'The window has been put in – what a waste of money!'

Being keenly interested in education, both in a general sense and in respect of his own son, the Admiral was not entirely happy about the Rugby syllabus. Among the family papers, there is a weekly time table for one of the forms which shows the 22 periods to be allocated to subjects as follows: Classics – 11; Maths – 4; French – 2; Science – 2; Bible – 1; History – 1; English – 1. With it is the draft of a letter dated 15 October 1878 from the Admiral to the Headmaster complaining about Ivor being taught too much Greek, and suggesting that the curriculum should include more science and history. The tone of the letter is polite but it does suggest that if there are no changes he might remove his son from the school. This did not happen, although when Ivor left at the end of the summer term in 1880 he was younger than the normal leaving age at the time. His report of a nasty case of bullying may have been a factor. A letter of 4 May told of a group of three boys who had, as he reported:

> . . . determined to get all the power of the house in their hands. They have formed an agreement by which they all act together. If one takes a dislike they all agree to make him their common enemy. I am the first victim of this cowardly law. Two days ago they smashed every ornament in my study and a good many pictures. I am unable to sit there at all – the breakfast room is my refuge.

Mr Whitelaw, his housemaster was quick to take action on discovering what had happened, and wrote the next day to the Admiral:

> The ill treatment and annoyance which your son is suffering came to my knowledge this morning. I saw three of the Sixth at once and told them it must cease. They will tell me this evening whether they undertake to stop it without my intervention.

In the end the intervention of not merely the housemaster, but of the headmaster, was required to deal with the matter. Whether or not this had a bearing on the decision that Ivor should leave at the end of the term cannot be known, but it would seem likely, since in those days 17½ was considered young to leave a public school. Boys often stayed on to 19 and the group who had persecuted him were probably at least a year older than he was.

The main reason why the teaching at Rugby was still so firmly based on the classics was the influence of the famous Dr Thomas. He had achieved a classical double first during his Oxford days, as well as editing Thucydides and writing a three-volume history of Rome while headmaster, and his great reputation ensured that such subjects would be the core studies at his school long after his own day. Though Ivor could not show his disapproval of the curriculum as freely as his father at the time, he was later to express it most forcibly. In a book published in 1905, about which more will be said in a later chapter, he wrote:

> In truth we have none of us received any solid groundwork of practical instruction, and those who desire to acquaint themselves with the world in which they live have to pick up the elements of history, geography and money matters after their school days are over. By this method we usually remain amateurs in all the walks of life, unaccustomed to sustained mental effort and constantly displaying ignorance of rudimentary facts. . . .
> Look where you will, in the Army, in Parliament, in the leading professions, in our railways, and in our business houses, you will see a number of excellent amateurs struggling ineffectually with technical problems. They make admirable subordinates and shine most especially in their behaviour to native populations in India, the Sudan, Egypt and other places. But when it becomes necessary to excel in a particular line, to go one better, to get out of a groove and be something of a specialist, the Englishman is disinclined to leave the beaten track. Such ideas were discountenanced in the old school-days as cranky and tending to divide a boy from his fellows. He was trained to be a gentleman, not an expert, and it does not occur to him to try to be both. Moreover, he lacks the necessary groundwork of modern history, languages, geography and science, which are painfully acquired after the age of twenty-five. So he sticks to the school standard which was good enough for him and his compeers. Thus it comes to pass that mediocrity, if it but bear the accepted hall mark, must pass muster amongst us and is promoted to positions which demand capacity and special training.[1]

The Admiral, having encouraged his son to look with a critical eye at the syllabus he had been taught at Rugby, in taking him away from school took steps to ensure that in one respect he would not share a major failing of most young Englishmen of his day, namely a hopeless inability to speak any other language. Being strongly Francophile he was determined that Ivor should be fluent in French. To this end he arranged for him to live with a family at Angers in the Loire valley, where he attended language classes as well as learning from conversation with the family. Although achieving the desired degree of fluency and becoming fond of the country and many aspects of French life, Ivor was not greatly impressed by the people he met in Angers, writing to his father on 9 December 1880:

> My great drawback here is want of exercise; the French take absolutely no exercise except a mild walk with a cigar, and after that they imagine they are tired. A short journey in a railway carriage, say about 30 miles, quite knocks some people up – M. Audra for instance. In this department particularly, the people are a very slack race, they have no go in them, neither physical or political.

In the same letter he mentioned the intention he had now formed to take the entrance examination for the Royal Military College, Sandhurst (RMC) the following July, with a view to becoming a regular army officer. He suggested that if he failed to get into the army he would have to 'go out to the colonies and pick up something there'. But he remained confident of success in the exam – or at least claimed to be, stating that . . . 'it won't be necessary – I hope the July exam will finish me off?' To help him prepare for the exam the Admiral hired a young man called Bernard Wise as a tutor who came out to Angers to join Ivor for a period of intensive study. Wise was an Australian who had come to study at Oxford, and was to give similar coaching to Leo three years later when he was working for entry to King's College, Cambridge. Eventually Wise returned to follow a successful political career in Australia, finishing as Attorney General in the central government.[2]

After sitting the exam, Ivor went to stay with his Uncle Fitz, the Admiral's elder brother who was now Governor of Heligoland. This small rocky island, lying 36 miles off the mouth of the River Elbe, had been taken by Britain from the Danes in 1807 as part of the operation to prevent Napoleon obtaining possession of the Danish fleet. It was formally ceded to Britain in 1814 during the Congress of Vienna, and in 1890, nine years after Fitz ended his tour as Governor, was to be handed over to Germany in exchange for the African islands of Zanzibar and Pemba.

Fitz had entered the army in 1849 by purchasing his commission as an ensign in the Grenadier Guards. In the fashion of the times, for those able to afford the price, he bought advances in rank as vacancies occurred in other regiments. In this way he spent short periods in the 13th Light Dragoons and the 21st Foot, later Royal Scots Fusiliers. By 1854 he was back in the Brigade of Guards as a captain in the Coldstream, in which regiment he rose to become a major the following year at the age of 23, giving him the rank of lieutenant colonel in the army, under the system which still existed of officers in the Guards holding a higher rank than their regimental one in the army as a whole. Knowledge of his uncle's complicated, though far from unusual, career may have had a bearing on Ivor's actions during his own army service.

On 9 August 1881 Ivor wrote to his father from Heligoland:

> I am expecting every day a telegram from you announcing the result of the exam. Please telegraph immediately you know it; also please prepare grandmama in case I fail. She does not know how hard the exam is and will think I did not work for it.

Fortunately this 'groundwork' with Lady Caroline proved unnecessary, as he passed the exam, coming 27th out of 105 successful candidates.

In September he started his one-year course at the Royal Military College, and his letter of the 8th shows that he fitted into the Sandhurst routine without trouble:

I like Sandhurst very much and everyone else seems to like it too. The reveille sounds down the corridors at 6.30 a.m. and we have to be at first study at 7.00. Breakfast from 8.00 to 8.30. Parade or drill from 9 to 10.00 and then indoor work and practical outdoor from 10.15 to 2 p.m. without stopping – that is rather a long pull. Lunch from 2 to 2.30 and then either parade or gymnastics for an hour during the afternoon. That is all the work we have. Mess is at 7.30 and the lights must be out at 11 p.m. That is a sketch of the weekday.

We are not allowed to wear plain clothes except in going on visits or for long walks. There are hundreds of other small regulations: but I don't remember them now. Please send me a lamp – any oil or liquid can be used and all the lamps have paraffin. The light from the gas is really wretched. I can't read or write by it.

While in no way rebellious in respect of his ordinary daily duties, Ivor retained a strong degree of scepticism about one aspect of the Sandhurst regime, which he described in a letter to his father dated 5 March 1882. It shows how much the Admiral's opinions had influenced him in his attitude to religion:

That repulsive Church Parade is just over: it is the one thing I dislike on Sunday. I really believe that if it was not for the glitter of swords and red tunics and the pleasure of hearing a good band, which did enliven me a little this morning by playing a piece from 'Patience' (the Heavy Dragoon song), no one who is not obliged to be on parade would be there. The last notes of 'Patience' having died away, we march into church. At the end of the service we had a sickening piece of British Jingoism – the Parson in solemn tones began a servile eulogy of Her Gracious Majesty's life, extolling all the 'divine' qualities and consummate statesmanship in conducting the affairs of this vast empire, etc. Every word was received with audible satisfaction. Of course I am very glad indeed that a would be assassin has been thwarted and I am also very glad that the Queen has escaped, more glad than I should be if an ordinary subject had done the same, for I know that she is a most excellent nonentity in politics; but the praise of her 'divine' quality by a man placed in the pulpit to tell the 'truth' is rather too bad.

It is hardly the sort of letter that anyone with a stereotyped vision of a Victorian Sandhurst cadet would expect to read.

Eight subjects were taught to the cadets; military administration, military law, tactics, fortification, military topography and reconnaissance, drill, gymnastics and riding. His final report in August 1882 showed that he received good pass marks in all these subjects, but none in the 75%

category required to be awarded a distinction. His conduct was recorded as: 'Fair, but inclined to be unpunctual and careless.'

Perhaps as an insurance against failure at Sandhurst, the Admiral arranged for Ivor to be admitted to the Inner Temple. On 8 June 1882 the commandant, Colonel Middleton, gave grudging permission for him to go up to London to eat a dinner in the Temple Hall, and on 10 June the Admiral provided a £100 deposit for his admission. Nothing more came of the venture and Ivor finished the Sandhurst course satisfactorily. Shortly after the passing out parade, Ivor and three friends, among them Bernard Wise, went for a holiday to the United States. They took cheap 'intermediate class' tickets on the SS *Wyoming* and sailed from Liverpool at the end of July. They found their cabin clean though short of storage space, but the sanitary arrangements were on a par with the catering, which Ivor explained in a letter written, soon after sailing, on 30 July 1882:

> The worst part of the business is the feeding and our little intermediate mess room is quite overcrowded and as the company is not the most select I have ever had to sit down with, I can't say that the meals are very enjoyable. One plate for all things, one knife and fork and everybody shoving their knives into the salt, etc, are minor evils we must put up with.

A second letter from the SS *Wyoming*, dated 7 August reports:

> I would give anything for a bath: the sea is so clear, so near and so tantalising! but it might as well be 100 miles off. . . .
> We got a bath at last – but rather a curious one. Crutwell discovers they wash the lower deck every night at 10.30 pm with a hose and salt water. So Crutwell and I undress in our cabin and go forth naked along the deck. The sailors are only too pleased to squirt us and we enjoy our bath immensely. We return dripping wet to the cabin much to the disgust of Wise and Giles who are asleep already and object to being splashed. However Crutwell threatens to get into bed with Wise, who promptly dries up. We have this nightly bath every day.

In spite of these discomforts the four remained 'in capital spirits', which they retained following their arrival in New York. On 10 August they were at sea again, this time on their way to Georgia on board the Ocean Steamship Company's *City of Columbus*. In his letter of that date Ivor told of their first night at the St Nicholas Hotel in Broadway, and explained why they were now travelling south by ship:

> We had intended to go south by rail but on enquiry found the steamers to be much more comfortable and much cheaper so at 3 p.m. on Wednesday we found ourselves lounging in easy chairs under an awning; clothed in the minimum amount of garments permitted by civilisation

and inhaling the best cigarettes procurable. The scene viewed from the deck of a steamer built as the Americans alone can build sumptuous boats with engines that consume their own smoke, and with a dozen stewards ready to administer to your every want, was thoroughly appreciated by us after an 'intermediate' passage across the Atlantic. We expect to arrive in Savannah tomorrow morning and thence go by steamer to St Simons Island.

Ivor thoroughly enjoyed his first visit to the United States, and was to return there with equal pleasure on three further occasions. After he and his friends arrived home later in August they waited for the notification of their appointments to their regiments. On 9 September 1882 Ivor was commissioned into the Royal Fusiliers, and in due course reported to the regimental depot in the Tower of London.

Notes

Letters from Maxse to his father can be found in WSRO, files 208, 211.

1 Maxse, Colonel F I, *Seymour Vandaleur* (National Review, 1905), pp. 5–6.
2 Hutcheson, John A Jr., *Leopold Maxse and the National Review, 1893–1914* (Garland, New York, 1989), p. 15.

First Commissioned
Service

3

Service with the
Royal Fusiliers – 1882–91

———•◆•———

The Tower of London was the home of the Royal Fusiliers, the 7th of Foot, from the day the Regiment was formed by James II in 1685 during the Monmouth rebellion. It was based on a nucleus of the two independent companies already stationed in the tower with the task of guarding the guns belonging to the King's artillery train, the forerunner of the Royal Artillery, many of which were kept there. It was the early role of protecting the Royal Artillery trains which led to the new regiment being armed with flintlock muskets, referred to by the French word *fusils*, and so becoming known as the Royal Fusiliers. At that time most infantry were armed with matchlock muskets, which were dangerous weapons to handle in close proximity to the open barrels of gunpowder carried by the artillery. For this reason the regiments primarily employed to escort the guns were the first to be armed with *fusils*. In due course, as this escort role became less important, some companies were armed with a new weapon, the exploding, hand-thrown bomb or grenade, which forms the design for the cap badges and insignia of all the fusilier regiments in the British Army.

During the Crimean War the 1st Battalion won five Victoria Crosses, and two years after the war came to an end, a 2nd Battalion was formed in 1857 as a permanent entity due to the army's expanding imperial commitments. The regiment operated from then on following a system whereby one battalion served abroad in various stations around the empire, while the other one stayed in Britain. The foreign service battalion was kept at full strength, while the home based one trained drafts to be sent out to it. This pattern became general throughout the infantry of the line following the reorganisation of the army in 1881, when all regiments were given a two-battalion structure. At this point the Royal Fusiliers had their secondary title of 'City of London Regiment' officially confirmed.

The pay of a second lieutenant when Ivor joined was £95 a year, rising to £112 for a lieutenant, and £200 for a captain. To exist in the least expensive infantry regiment, a private income of at least £100 a year was essential, while in a relatively affluent one like the Royal Fusiliers several officers were given allowances more like the £250 provided for Ivor by the Admiral. His uniform cost around £200. For 1995 equivalents these sums should be multiplied by at least 40. Private contributions in even more expensive circles could rise to £400 a year minimum in the footguards, and up to £700 in some cavalry regiments, where uniforms might cost up to £1000.

On joining, Ivor was warned for service with the 2nd battalion in India. It had gone out there in 1873 and so was over half way through a normal 15-year tour. Having been involved in the Afghan campaign of 1879–80, where it took part in the siege of Kandahar and a private soldier won the Victoria Cross, the battalion moved a long way from the North West Frontier in 1881 to a station at Bellary, on the Malabar Coast, some 600 miles south of Bombay. Here, on 20 September 1882, celebrated in the Royal Fusiliers as 'Alma Day', and shortly after Ivor's commission was gazetted, the 571 members of the battalion entitled to medals for their part in the Afghan campaign were presented with them on a full-dress parade. About the same time, on orders from the Commander-in-Chief in India, the army changed from wearing white clothing into Khaki dyed uniform, of which other ranks were provided with two suits. This was not popular with many regiments, who felt that khaki made them look like Indian sweepers and gradually, while retaining it for field training, they moved back into white for formal occasions.

On 8 December 1882, Ivor sailed from Southampton on board the troopship HMS *Serapis*. A letter from Suez dated 28 December told of his objection to wrangling over prices in the bazaar in the few hours that he and some others had earlier spent at Port Said before entering the canal. A fortnight later they docked at Bombay. A letter of 15 January 1883 told of his arrival with the 2nd Battalion at Bellary. After spending two days in Bombay he set out on the 30-hour rail journey south to his new home, a trip which he explained 'really is a short journey in India'. He ended with the comment: 'I have only been here 2 days and can tell you little as yet. The fellows are nice and gentlemanly but don't seem very energetic.'

This last sentence gives a foretaste of what was to become the theme of many of his letters during the six years he eventually spent in India. Eight months later in September he was writing: 'Days go by with very little change, and what is worse with very little to do, however willing one is to

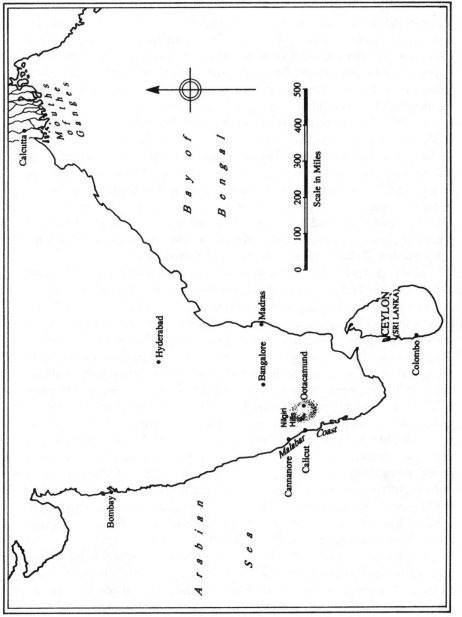

SOUTH INDIA

do a great deal.' This slothfulness was a feature of military life in India, and other places with hot, enervating climates, which was often commented upon by contemporary visitors to the tropics. Coupled with the archaic, unimaginative local army training cycle of the times it made Ivor increasingly dissatisfied with his service in what he felt was a hopeless professional backwater. There were, however, compensations, largely of his own creation. One, shared with nearly all his brother officers, was the opportunity to enjoy many forms of sport; the other, in which few of his fellows took any interest, was the study of the surrounding country and the people who lived there.

The main forms of sport were connected with horses, and consisted of polo, racing and hunting. Without these interests he recorded that, 'Bellary would be a truly awful place,' but polo three times a fortnight and his duties as whipper-in to the small pack of hounds kennelled in the Fusilier stables, with which they hunted jackals and foxes twice a week, provided spice in an otherwise unappealing way of life. Other sports to be enjoyed were small and big game shooting. For the former there were plenty of opportunities along the Malabar coast, with snipe and duck the main quarry. To find bigger game he went further afield.

One of his tasks in his first year was to learn Hindustani. He took pains over this and also extended his interest in the language to include the customs and way of life of the local people. In due course he combined his curiosity about the native population's ways with his enthusiasm for snipe shooting in a long article he submitted for publication in *Blackwoods Magazine*. It was sent to the editor on his behalf by the Admiral, but returned with a note to say he already had too much similar material about India. However, it gives an insight into Ivor's interests at the time.

The title is *Notes from Malabar*. The first part begins by describing the geography of the Malabar coast, explaining how the moist climate and fertile soil makes the existence of the peasant farmers who form the majority of the population so much easier and more prosperous than that of the *ryots* living on the drier plains further north. In discussing the natives and their customs he points out that they were civilised in the days when the ancient Britons were wearing woad, and he is contemptuous of English attempts to 'civilise' Indians. He has no time for missionaries, and objects strongly to their efforts to make natives wear unsuitable 'Christian' clothing.

The second part tells of a day's snipe shooting, starting before dawn with a journey through backwaters in a dug-out canoe to the place where he meets his *shikari*, known as Buddum Coolie. He explains that the services of this elderly man are essential for a successful day's sport, and describes how he takes Ivor to the right places to find the birds, as well as his skill at retrieving them when shot. The story ends with an account of the journey home in the evening in the canoe, extolling the beauty of the sunset over the marshes along the sea shore.

At the end of 1883 the battalion marched to a training camp at Bangalore. The standard routine for such marches in India was followed, travelling about 10 miles each day in the early morning from one camp site to another, arriving before the sun became too hot. The battalion plus its baggage train made up a huge column. Just before setting out Ivor wrote home from Bellary on 21 November to say: 'I am getting all my camp kit ready – it will consist of a small tent, camp bed, chair, bath and a few flannel shirts. The Government will not carry a single thing for us so we have to get our own bullock carts.' Back in Bellary early in 1884 he was writing with plans for another journey, but this time a longer one and on leave. 'I am going with Captain Ives', he wrote on 18 February, 'to the most beautiful and most invigorating country in the whole world – Cashmere (Kashmir) in the midst of the Himalayas for six months.' Though slightly surprising that he should be granted this leave after little more than a year's service with the regiment, it was not unusual for officers to be granted such opportunities as long as their intended project was arduous and adventurous. With so much of the day-to-day routine in barracks controlled by NCOs it was easy to spare young officers for long periods. In laying on the trip there was much to learn about administration, in particular arranging the journey on ponies and on foot, accompanied by a gang of coolies, from the railhead at Rawalpindi through Murree and Srinagar to their allotted shooting grounds. Once there, Ivor had useful experience of living rough, as his letter to his father of 4 June 1884 recounted:

This is a grand life even with its many drawbacks. I know you would enjoy it thoroughly. I returned to camp from the upper end of my nullah (valley) this morning after being nine days away – no bed, chair or table for nine days! I had good quarters under a big overhanging rock and my servant and cooking things up there. We had some rather nasty weather – thunder, snow and rain and I did little in the shooting line – one ibex 26". I had a dreadfully bad night one of the days. I had followed three good looking buck up a branch nullah, having previously sent all my bedding up another nullah which I expected to reach at night. I had to sleep quite in the open with only a single blanket over me. It was perfectly clear and starlit night but didn't it freeze! I was quite cold all night and the cold tea in my bottle was hard frozen in the morning.

Returning to the softer climate of the south, he heard that the battalion was to move in December to Cannanore on the coast, with a company detachment at Calicut. Reporting this to the Admiral he wrote that: 'I don't think it can be a worse place than Bellary though I have always heard that it is less healthy.'

Leaving Bellary on 4 November, the battalion marched to Cannanore, arriving on 15 December 1884. Towards the end of 1885 Ivor's thoughts were again preoccupied with leave. In his letter of 11 October he told how his application had been signed by his colonel and had been forwarded to the local general. He went on to say: 'I do hope that during my year at home I will be able to work something in the way of a staff appointment or the prospect of one in the future. "Existence" in Bellary or Cannanore is all very well for one's first three years; it won't do for a lifetime.' The generous allocation of a year's leave was granted to officers after three years' service in all tropical stations. His application having been approved, Ivor travelled from Cannanore to Bombay in early November with a draft of 60 time-expired other ranks returning home, who were housed in a holding depot until a suitable ship arrived to take them. He found a berth on a troopship for himself and arrived at Portsmouth in December, a month before Lady Caroline died at Effingham Hill while he was there for Christmas. The diary he kept during 1886 shows him constantly on the move, starting in February with a visit to Hanover to stay with his Aunt Augusta, the Austrian widow of his Uncle Fitz, who had died in 1883. Here he took daily German lessons and was much amused by watching the numerous army officers in the streets, all in uniform, carrying swords and constantly saluting each other. A short stay in England on his return in March was followed by a month in Paris. Back home in May he attended a two-month 'garrison class' at Shorncliffe in Kent where he studied fortification, tactics, topography and military law in preparation for the promotion exam to captain, which he passed with 'no problem', though it would be some time before a vacancy in that rank would arise in the regiment. The second half of July was passed once more in Paris. In early September he was at Effingham Hill for partridge shooting. His father had sold the house and part of the 900-acre estate, and was planning to build a new house on the hill known as Dunley Brow in the 382-acre section of land he had retained. On 23 September Ivor sailed from Liverpool for a long visit to Canada and the United States.

On 3 October he wrote from Quebec, commenting that '250 miles of a grand blue river and a picturesque old world city, seen from the deck of a steamer are better left to the imagination!', rather than being inadequately described by him. Moving to Detroit he was fortunate to be given a week's duck and snipe shooting on the 36,000-acre section of the St Clair marshes on the shores of the lake of that name lying to the east of the city. Next came a visit to the town of Buffalo at the other end of Lake Erie where he was most hospitably entertained for a week in November by a Mr John Glenny and his wife, with a visit to the Niagara Falls. At the end of the month he was in New York, staying at the Union League Club. Through his father's contacts he was introduced to the Winthrop and Vanderbilt families, thus coming to know the grandest people in New York society. He also visited Buffalo Bill's Wild West show and met the impresario himself: a meeting which was to be significant in his life many years later. However, as his leave was nearing its end his thoughts were turning once more to his profession and future. A letter to the Admiral dated 28 November included the comment that 'I am sure you have done all you can to try to save me from going back to India', and then went on to say that he was tempted to leave the army and go into business in America. However, it ended with an admission that in the end he would have to return to his regiment. Since he was, as he put it, 'of an energetic nature and want some real hard work', he could at least take out a stock of books and try to learn something to overcome the fact that he found himself 'painfully ignorant'.

Sailing from New York on 4 December, Ivor was at home for Christmas and then in February 1887 set off once again for India, travelling overland to Venice to catch the P & O liner *Cathay*, which landed him in Bombay on the 28th of the month. The day after his arrival he was told in a letter from his commanding officer that he was to report to his battalion headquarters, which had now moved to Wellington, in the Nilgiri Hills near Ootacamund. Here he finally arrived in early March after a four-day boat trip down the coast from Bombay to Beypore, followed by an 80-mile ride overland, bringing with him two Arab polo ponies purchased in Bombay.

Ivor was fortunate to be posted to battalion headquarters in the hills, since some detachments remained in low-lying bases along the coast at Cannanore and Calicut. The area around 'Ooty', as Ootacamund was always known, was one of the most beautiful and healthy in India, and on 13 March he was happy to write: 'This is a charming place with a beautiful climate – at night a two blankets on one's bed temperature.' In the same letter he mentioned the coming arrival of his brother Leo, who was at the time travelling around the world after leaving Cambridge. Leo would sleep in his dressing room and live with him in the mess. Ivor ended with a comment about the cost of serving in this popular and very social station: 'No one who has less than £150 a year beyond his pay could live here out of debt.'

During the next two years, before the battalion returned to England, Ivor's regular letters were full of news of polo, his ponies and racing. In August 1888 he acted as secretary of a three-day race meeting at Wellington, and won six races himself. He also hunted regularly with the 'Ooty' hounds, and went in search of big game. An article on *A Bison Hunt in India* was published in the *St James's Gazette* in 1888. But in spite of all these interests and amusements he remained fundamentally dissatisfied with his life. Under pressure from the Admiral to explain himself, he replied in a letter from Wellington on 30 August 1888, after news of the battalion's forthcoming return home had been received:

You asked me of myself and what I would wish. My first wish is to get out of this cursed India, where I never feel well in spirits or in body. At the same time I will confess that I have had the best of everything which is to be got out here. As to the future, I like my regiment and have got on well in it but to anyone who is the least ambitious a line regiment is a terrible drag.

The last consideration was a matter to which he referred on several occasions at this time, and before long was to lead to a big change in his career.

The Royal Fusiliers sailed from India on 2 March 1889 in HMS *Serapis*, the same troopship in which Ivor had come to India in 1883, and arrived home on 28 March, having encountered unusually bad weather in the Mediterranean. Their first station was in Citadel Barracks, Dover.

Garrison life in Britain did not differ greatly from India in respect of military training and routine duties. The annual musketry course was fired in early summer, and manoeuvres were held in the autumn. In the winter officers were encouraged to hunt and shoot, and there were opportunities for long periods of leave. Ivor's continuing dissatisfaction with his career prospects kept appearing in his letters, coupled with concern about financial matters. While appreciating the fact that his father's allowance of £250 a year, plus various presents from time to time, made him better off than officers in many line regiments, he still found his income as a subaltern inadequate, though on becoming a captain in the near future things would improve. He attached a list of his expenses for a year to a letter dated 23 July 1889:

Monthly Mess Bill at £15 plus subscriptions, extra duty pay to servant, etc	£200
The keep on one's pony, shoeing, groom, etc	50
Travelling expenses	60
Dress (uniform, civilian clothes, boots, laundry)	40
Club subscriptions	25
Incidental expenses (tobacco, books, racquets, etc)	50
TOTAL per year	£425

He noted that his mess bill was below average as he drank little wine.

Concern about his financial state cannot have been too serious as he spent a month's leave during November and December based at a hotel in Malmesbury in order to hunt with the Duke of Beaufort's hounds. Possibly one of the Admiral's presents helped with this!

During 1889 the opening moves were made towards achieving a transfer into the Brigade of Guards. Sympathetic to Ivor's military ambitions, the Admiral approached General Sir Arthur Fremantle, a personal friend who had originally served in the Coldstream Guards, to see if there might be a vacancy in that regiment for his son. Although Fremantle wrote on 29

May 1889 to say that there was 'no chance', Ivor and his father were not put off, and turned to Mr A Tull, an army exchange agent. Tull's agency was one of a few still existing as relics of the days when commissions could be purchased, a practice which had come to an end in 1871. Its activities were now reduced to arranging transfers of officers between regiments, and within regiments between those who were anxious to serve with battalions abroad and their normally richer brother officers who wanted to stay at home

Finding a suitable Coldstreamer with whom to effect an exchange proved a slow process. However, after a disappointment early in 1890, when Tull 'jumped the gun' in one case and gave Ivor premature assurance of success, a satisfactory transfer *was* arranged the following year with Captain Douglas Hamilton. The Admiral paid the necessary £2,200 to Hamilton – some £88,000 in 1995 terms – and on 23 May 1891 the *London Gazette* carried the official notice of Ivor's posting to the Coldstream Guards.

Notes

Letters quoted from Maxse to his father can be found in WSRO, file 208, 211.

4

Settling into the Coldstream Guards, 1891–96

—— • ◆ • ——

Ivor received a warm welcome from members of his new regiment. The Colonel of the Regiment at the time was General Lord William Seymour, who was sufficiently pleased about the exchange to go so far as to pass on some items of his own Coldstream uniform to him. Captain Lambton, adjutant of the 2nd Battalion, to which he was posted, wrote in a friendly vein shortly before Ivor joined: 'It is not likely to take you for any guard duties till 1 July, so you will have plenty of time to get accustomed to our ways. You will come in for a second go of training as we go down to Pirbright in August.'

In 1891, there were only three regiments of footguards: the Grenadiers, with three battalions, and the Coldstream and Scots, with two each. The Irish and Welsh Guards were not yet formed. One Coldstream battalion, the 1st, was stationed in Dublin, while the 2nd was based in Wellington Barracks, London. All other battalions of the Brigade were also quartered in London, apart from one nearby at Windsor. Although elements of the Brigade had served in Africa in 1884 and 1885, during the unsuccessful attempt to relieve General Gordon in Khartoum, and in the brief campaign at Suakin on the Red Sea coast, no active service was to come their way again until 10 years later. The entirely home-based way of life of Ivor's new battalion followed a set pattern which provided limited encouragement to its members to give original thought to their profession except during the periods when moved away from London for field training. Most of the time a London-based battalion was involved with 'public duties', which included Royal guards in London and Windsor, State ceremonial occasions such as the opening of Parliament, Guards of Honour for visiting dignitaries, and provision of a picquet at the Bank of England each night. As in present times, the Queen's Birthday was celebrated each year with the Trooping the Colour ceremony, and officers were also on duty at Royal levées.[1] Such training for war as was carried out took place at the field training area at Pirbright in Surrey, with access to the nearby ranges at Bisley, as mentioned in Lambton's letter. Apart from shooting, including annual classification, and marching, tactical exercises took place. Signallers were trained and took part in the annual tests run for the whole army. Company commanders were held responsible for the efficiency of their men, and the keen ones were able to train them in a way which was not easy when on public duties in London.

The duties of a captain while in London were not onerous, and he was expected to be on leave for several months each year. When required for duty, he was provided with quarters in Wellington Barracks, but there was no officers' mess such as was provided at the Tower of London, or in stations away from the city, and he was expected to make his own arrangements for his meals. No better picture of this way of life can be found than that painted by Osbert Sitwell in his book *Great Morning*.[2] Although he served as a Grenadier some 20 years after Ivor joined the Coldstream, his descriptions of life in the Brigade exactly suit the earlier period, especially in connection with time spent guarding Buckingham Palace and St James's, with a base in the precincts of the latter:

So far as I know, though it has been for so long one of the spectacles most familiar to inhabitants of London, and most loved by visitors, little has been written about the Changing of the Guard: to the crowd, the performers in the ceremony cease to exist when they have marched away: and so I propose to give for a page or two an account of the very individual life led by the officers on this duty, who, after the manner of monks, albeit for twenty-four hours only, are immured in the seclusion of a brick building from which, though situated in the very centre of the capital, you can scarcely hear the passing of traffic. . . . The oncoming guard was on duty until relieved twenty-four hours later. During this space of time, the officers had to remain in the part of St James's Palace allotted to them – an inner section, built of stout, dark brick, more nearly recalling, save that there were no trees, part of some college or close than the centre of a palace: this haven they were not allowed to leave, except for tours of duty and inspection, when they visited the sentries at Buckingham Palace and Marlborough House, and except for a few minutes in the afternoon when they were permitted if they wished, to walk across to the Guards Club or the Marlborough Club, then both situated within a stone's throw in Pall Mall. (All officers serving in the Brigade joined automatically the Guards Club, though not the Marlborough.) As the Ensign had to go on a tour of inspection at 2 a.m. it made a long day for him, and life in the guardroom with its view of lead flats and dingy crenellations, though it possessed an air, and seemed the very core of St James's, became a little monotonous and might, indeed, have grown insupportably to resemble a prison, had it not been for the munificence of King George IV, who had directed that, after his death, an annual sum should be paid to the officers on guard. It was not enough to defray the whole of the expense, but it certainly enabled them to entertain their friends to dinner in a handsome manner, and, in consequence, the long room, in the evening, with its table arranged with silver trophies, and its food, celebrated for its excellence, as no doubt that gourmet, King George IV, would have wished, became a place where many distinguished – and undistinguished – people could pass a most pleasant evening.[3]

Apart from guard duty and the short spell of training at Pirbright in August, Ivor had plenty of time to follow his own interests during 1891. At Christmas he arranged and took part in a show for the battalion which was described as 'a choice selection of songs and comedy, accompanied by battalion drummers'. He hunted throughout the winter, and in March 1892 rode in the Coldstream regimental point-to-point, held in Cheshire in order to be of easy access for members of the 1st Battalion to come over with their horses from Dublin. In April he was a member of the six-man Coldstream team which took part in the annual point-to-point contested by the three regiments of footguards, this year held near Oakham in Rutland across a country described with rapture in *The Brigade of Guards Magazine* published in May 1892:

> The arrangements were made by Lord Lonsdale and if one travelled throughout the length of England, a more perfect course could not be found. From the starting post, at Ashwell Kennels, to the finish, on a hill beyond Barleythorpe, near Cold Overton, not a single ploughed field was to be seen – a veritable sea of grass, and where all the names of surrounding places are historical to fox-hunters: Ranksborough Gorse, Owston Wood, &c. A truly glorious country, grass everywhere, magnificent large fields and fences, the latter jumpable almost everywhere, the going magnificent, though inclining to the hard side, and what more could be desired. Three and a half miles, straight as the crow flies, not a flag necessary, and with the winning post indicated by a flag hoisted on a wooden pagoda (built for the Purpose), visible everywhere, the line was as perfect as arrangement and forethought could make it.[4]

Unfortunately Ivor, described in the magazine as having 'been thrusting along in grand form', was 'cannoned' into by the falling horse of a fellow Coldstreamer as they neared the end of the race. This mishap nearly brought him down and lost him his leading place, so that he finished 13th out of the 18 competitors rather than near the head of the field. The Grenadiers won with 77 points, the Coldstream were second with 73, and the Scots Guards third with 40.

In July 1892 the 2nd Coldstream set out on a four-day march to Ash Vale, near Aldershot, to take part in army manoeuvres. Overnight halts were made at Hounslow and Cobham on the way. At the end of the manoeuvres the battalion moved from Wellington Barracks to the Tower of London, where they were stationed alongside the depot of Ivor's old regiment, the Royal Fusiliers. A change from regimental duty came early the next year with a letter from the old family friend General Sir Arthur Fremantle, who wrote on 5 February 1893 to say: 'I am to have the command in Scotland from February '93 with two paid ADCs – would you like to be one of them?'

Ivor accepted the offer, and joined the newly appointed GOC-in-C, Scotland, at the headquarters of Scottish Command in Edinburgh, later the same month. Fremantle's connections with the Maxse family went back almost 40 years to the time of the Crimean War, when he transferred into the Coldstream Guards on purchase from the 52nd Light Infantry in 1854, at the same time as Fitz joined them from the 21st North British Fusiliers. During that war he also established his friendship with the Admiral. The regimental nickname 'Chummy' gives a clue to Fremantle's cheerful character: he was also what his contemporaries would have called a 'bit of a wag', referring to Ivor in his letters to the Admiral by such names as 'Cock Robin' or 'Sir Ivory'. He proved a pleasant master to serve, and Ivor stayed with him for 18 months. After a year in Edinburgh he moved with Fremantle to Malta on the general's appointment as Governor of the Island. In September 1894 he returned home for a period of leave before joining the 2nd Coldstream in Dublin towards the end of the year.

It was during this leave that he first met the Honourable Mary Wyndham, who in due course was to become his wife. As she was always known by family and friends as 'Tiny', she will be called that from now on in this book. The unusual afternoon that she and Ivor spent together after their first meeting is described in an account of it he wrote many years later for inclusion in the privately printed biography *Mary Maxse, 1870 to 1944*, by John Gore. The story starts with mention of a lunch party in Eaton Square given by Tiny's aunt, the Dowager Lady Mayo, after which the party moved to Olympia to watch Buffalo Bill's 'Wild West Show':

> I suggested to Miss Wyndham that it was dull merely to sit in the stalls and that I knew Buffalo Bill himself in the United States; and that I could easily propose to him that two of us, she and I, should occupy Bill's 'Deadwood Coach' which was to be the main item in the afternoon's programme. This was reluctantly agreed to by Lady Mayo and I arranged the jaunt with Buffalo Bill behind the scenes. He said there was room for four in the coach and we enlisted Guy Campbell and Miss Evelyn Bulkley-Johnson to fill the coach from amongst our lunch party.
> The 'Deadwood Coach' was a ramshackle affair with wooden seats

and cracked boards as a floor. It was to be driven by wild horses round and round the show ring and to be attacked and captured by wild west desperadoes on horses. All this occurred whilst I and Guy Campbell fired blank cartridges out of the windows from ancient blunderbusses to the applause of crowds of spectators. The dust was appalling, but Miss Wyndham enjoyed the fun and the episode remained vivid in our memories though years passed before we discussed it together.[5]

It was shortly before Ivor met Tiny that Violet had married Lord Edward Cecil, or 'Nigs' as he was known, in June 1894 at St Saviour's Church, Chelsea. The names of those who signed the register show the power of the circles into which the family was now closely drawn. The list includes, as well as the Admiral and Mrs Maxse, three Prime Ministers and two other famous political figures. From the Conservative ranks came Lord Salisbury, now Violet's father-in-law, and Arthur Balfour, while from the Liberal fold there were H H Asquith, John Morley, and Joseph Chamberlain. The wedding had an impact on an important political figure across the channel as well. During 1893 Violet had been studying painting in Paris, and had been in constant touch with the great family friend, Clemenceau. In a translation of a letter he wrote to her a week before the wedding there is an expression of his feelings: 'It seems to me that a handsome Englishman has appeared, impeccable, correct, who is stealing me of my daughters. I find him horrible since he deprives me of the charming visits I used sometimes to receive in the evenings.' However he ended the letter with all his good wishes, and 'je vous embrasse de tout mon coeur'.[6]

Ivor only served with the 2nd Battalion in Dublin for a few months before returning to join the 1st Battalion in London in February 1895. In June of the following year he was posted to the Guards Depot at Caterham. Unlike the infantry of the line, whose regiments all had their own small individual depots, the three regiments of footguards ran a combined one for the basic training of their recruits. The main advantage of this system was the speed at which complete squads could be assembled for training, avoiding the problem common to individual depots of recruits hanging about with little to do while waiting for enough to join and make up a reasonably sized squad.

Although the tenor of his military duties at this period was undemanding, he put the free time at his disposal to good, professional use. Leo's *National Review* was now flourishing and during 1895 and 1896 Ivor wrote three articles for it, which were in due course published by J M Dent in a booklet entitled *Our Military Problem: For Civilian Readers*, price 1/- (5p). It is an extremely clear and well-written account of the army's roles, its history, its current organisation, and its many problems. Although these problems differed in nature and origin from those faced by the army 100 years later, in that they were mainly concerned with Imperial responsibilities, the result was much the same: just as today 'overstretch' is threatening to destroy the morale and efficiency of many units, in the 1890s both Liberal and Conservative governments consistently refused to provide proper backing for the many tasks they required the army to perform. Ivor quoted a German officer's comments, made after making a world tour:

> I cannot understand these English: they plant out adventures with nothing but a few spare Union Jacks: after a lapse of many years they land three red soldiers, order them to 'form fours', and leave them to shift for themselves![7]

Although the modern army no longer 'forms fours', the concept of doing so with only three men is still well understood.

During 1896 Ivor was twice on leave, both times crossing the Atlantic. During the first visit to America in February and March he wrote enthusiastic letters home about his experiences. On 12 February, he reported on his luck to be taken to 'a full parade inspection of the crackest of the US Militia Regiments, that is, the 7th NY'. Having told how the parade took place at night in a magnificent drill hall, lit by electric light, in which 1,000 men were able to manoeuvre, he went on to say:

> There is respect and plenty of it for Great Britain: and whatever may appear in the press to the contrary, the stronger we show ourselves the higher is the respect. Recollect that they are a competing people and are apt to judge a man entirely by his success.

Due to letters of introduction to various important public figures, he was able to write from Washington on 22 March 1896 that 'I had a very interesting half hour alone with Cleveland and Senator Gray on the President's private day: and he talked to me in a very friendly manner . . .'. No better example of the respect for Great Britain could be shown than allotting a half hour of the President's time for a talk to a young army captain, even though his family's political connections in England must have been known.

A second spell of leave in the autumn was also spent in the United States from which he returned to the Guards Depot. Here he was notified on 23 December that he had been personally selected by Colonel Kitchener to do active service as a Bimbashi, or Major, in the Egyptian Army, in the campaign which had just started in the Sudan. In joining Kitchener's field force he was to find himself serving among the cream of the young officers considered to be the most promising in the army, many of whom were to become well known to students of the Boer War and the First World War.

Notes

Letters from Maxse to his father can be found in WSRO, file 219.

1 *Guards Magazine*, Spring 1993, p. 5.
2 Sitwell, Osbert, *Great Morning* (Reprint Society, 1949), p. 195.
3 Sitwell, p. 199.
4 *Guards Magazine*, May 1892, p. 219.
5 Gore, John, *Mary Maxse, 1870 to 1944*, p. 35.
6 Milner, Viscountess, *My Picture Gallery, 1886–1901* (Murray, 1951), p. 61.
7 Maxse, Captain F I, *Our Military Problem* (Dent, 1896), p. 91.

On Active Service

5

Campaigning in
the Sudan,
1897–98

———•◆•———

Ivor arrived in Cairo at the end of January 1897. He was soon on his way
south in a Nile steamer to join Kitchener's army, of which the leading element, or field force, was by this time established in the recently captured
town of Dongola, some 250 miles into the Sudan beyond the border with
Egypt. On the border lay the town of Wadi Halfa, itself roughly 800 miles
from Cairo, from which a railway line was already being driven south on
the east bank of the Nile, and had by this time covered most of its eventual 200-mile route. Before following Ivor's adventures, a brief description
is necessary of how the campaign had got under way in 1896, and of the
first engagements with the Dervish enemy. It is fortunate that his own
writings, both in letter and book form, can be used as the basis for recording most of the events in this chapter. Although it did not come out until
1905, several years after the events of which it tells, this is the moment to
introduce the second book which Ivor wrote, called *Seymour Vandeleur:
The Story of a British Officer*. It was published for him by Leo's *National
Review*, and beneath the title on the first page are the words: 'Being a
memoir of Brevet Lieutenant-Colonel Vandeleur, DSO, Scots Guards
and Irish Guards, with a general description of his campaigns.' Vandeleur
was eventually killed in South Africa towards the end of the Boer War in
August 1901. By this stage he had become a 'legend in his own lifetime'
through his African exploits, as witness the words of John Buchan's hero
Richard Hannay, in *The Island of Sheep*, when telling of a friend in East
Africa who . . . 'was full of the heroes of the past, like Roddy Owen and
Vandeleur and the Portals'.[1] Using the story of Vandeleur's life as his
theme, Ivor wove around it a multi-patterned web of his own theories and

prejudices, combined with extensive studies of the history, geography and populations of the parts of Africa to which Vandeleur's campaigns took him. In this remarkable and often entertaining book, the five chapters concerned with operations in Egypt and the Sudan occupy 132 of the book's 288 pages, most of them concerned with events in which Ivor was himself involved.

The first of the five chapters gives the background to the campaign of 1896–99 in considerable detail, but must here be briefly summarised. Following the fall of Khartoum and the death of General Gordon on 26 January 1885, as a result of the failure of the relief column to arrive until two days too late, the Egyptian and British forces withdrew from the Sudan, leaving the country to the mercy, if that is the right word, of the Dervishes, fanatical Moslems under the leadership of the man known as the Mahdi, or restorer of the faith. The same year the Mahdi died in June and his place was taken by the Khalifa, a title meaning successor to Mahommed, named Abdullah Abdullahi.

While the Khalifa concentrated on imposing his authority on his huge empire stretching 1,400 miles from north to south, and up to 1,000 from east to west, his northern border with Egypt remained relatively stable. There were Egyptian garrisons at Wadi Halfa on the Nile and at Suakin on the Red Sea coast. In 1889 the troops at Wadi Halfa repulsed a tentative advance into Egypt by the Dervishes at the battle of Toski, but otherwise the 11 years from 1885 to 1896 were peaceful. During this period, however, great improvements were made in the Egyptian army. The man who made the biggest contribution was Herbert Kitchener. He had arrived in Egypt in 1882 on secondment to the Egyptian Cavalry with the substantive rank of Lieutenant in the Royal Engineers, and by 1892 had risen to be Sirdar, or commander, of the whole army as a full Colonel. In his book Ivor elaborates on the way in which the transformation of the army from little more than a cowardly rabble to a first-class fighting force was achieved.

At the heart of the improvements was the posting-in as 'bimbashis', or majors, of young British officers to replace many of those described by Ivor as follows:

> The officers, drawn from the class which supplies Egypt with a bureaucracy and boasts a leaven of Turkish blood, were, in no sense, leaders of men. . . . They were consumed with the spirit of intrigue, through which alone lay the avenue to promotion and lucrative posts. It did not occur to them either to share or alleviate the privations of their men.[2]

When the young British officers took over command of the squadrons, batteries and battalions of the reorganised army, the change was, as Ivor put it, 'so bewildering to the native officers and men, that at first the task seemed hopeless'. However, with regular pay, decent barracks and food, proper leave, and a discipline not enforced by arbitrary floggings, the soldiers began to take pride in themselves. Promotion went by merit, and intrigue no longer served to win it. Gradually a completely different army grew out of the shell of the original one.

Ivor goes to some pains when writing about the infantry to give credit to the Egyptian battalions as well as the Sudanese, refugees from their own country who made up a third of the strength. While admitting that the natural fighting qualities of the Sudanese men made them outstanding soldiers, he stressed the courage and steadiness in action of the Egyptians when commanded by good officers. Sudanese recruits came largely from tribes driven away from their own homelands by the Baggara, the tribe from which the Khalifa's main strength was drawn.

Throughout the years following withdrawal from the Sudan, the government in London had no interest in its repossession, but most of the British population shared, with the increasingly efficient Egyptian army, a different response to the still vividly remembered shame of Gordon's death and the Mahdi's victory at Khartoum. To the many both in Britain and in Egypt who still hankered after another expedition up the Nile, an event on 1 March 1896 provided an opportunity to see their hopes fulfilled. A battle on the border between Italian Somaliland and Abyssinia at Adowa resulted in the Italians suffering a serious defeat at the hands of the Ethiopian army of King Menelek. The possibility then arose that the Khalifa might take advantage of this weakening in the Italian forces by attacking their garrison at Kassala, which he had already threatened. To divert the Khalifa's attention, and lessen the threat to Kassala, the British government authorised a sortie to be made south from Wadi Halfa towards the Dervish garrison at Firkeh. Ivor enjoys poking fun in his book at the way in which the Cabinet eventually came to give this authorisation, and how it was inadvertently extended from permission to make a small sortie into authority to recapture the whole province of Dongola:

> A few of England's councillors left the room with a vague recollection of some unfamiliar African names which had been referred to on the map, and one aged politician in particular was so bewildered that when, in the street, a reporter of his acquaintance hurriedly asked him what the meeting had been concerned with, he could remember nothing but the word 'Dongola', which he murmured unconsciously . . .
>
> In the evening to all parts of the British Empire the various press associations telegraphed the welcome news that the long delayed Nile expedition was to start, and that Dongola would be its objective – nor was this the first time a hesitating administration has had its hand forced by a smart reporter possessing the gift of intelligent anticipation.[3]

Having obtained assurance from Lord Cromer, the British resident minister in, and virtual ruler of, Egypt, and from Kitchener, that the

operation would be undertaken immediately, the government confirmed
the press reports.

By 20 March, less than three weeks after the Italian defeat at Adowa, a
column composed of the 13th Sudanese infantry battalion, with supporting cavalry, camels, artillery and maxim guns, had covered 85 miles to
Akasha, lying on the east bank of the Nile only a few days' march from a
3,000-strong Dervish army at Firkeh. After explaining the numerous
administrative problems which faced Kitchener as he launched the army
into a desert campaign, Ivor describes the course of the Nile, and the
importance of using it as a waterway during the months of the annual
flood from August to September, when there is water enough to pass
boats over the many rocky cataracts that lie along much of its length. Next
he records the build-up of the force at Akasha to a 9,000-strong division
of three infantry brigades with supporting arms, and the rebuilding of the
old torn-up railway from Wadi Halfa to within one day's camel march of
this new base. Then on 6 June 1896, Kitchener suddenly issued orders to
all units to make a night march and assault Firkeh at dawn. Achieving
almost complete surprise, his troops began their attack at 5.30am on 7
June and by 7.30 had driven out the Dervishes with heavy losses while suffering relatively few themselves: a complete victory which brought with it
several important results. It reinforced Kitchener in his position as Sirdar,
and brought him the approval of the government at home as well as promotion to acting major general; this ensured that he and his young team
of officers would not be superseded by older men and inexperienced
troops from home stations; it showed that the Egyptian army could now
win decisive battles without the support of British troops; and it dealt the
Dervish empire a blow which paralysed its military enterprise for a year,
while giving Kitchener time to gather strength for further advances.

Moving south, with the railway being constructed behind it as it moved,
the Egyptian army arrived by early September at Kerma, a village on the
bank of the Nile. Pushing on another 35 miles during the following three
weeks, Kitchener's men caught up with the enemy at Dongola. On 23
September, 1896 at 4.30am the two armies faced each other on a sandy
plain outside the town. As the Egyptian force advanced, the numerically
inferior Dervishes decided to withdraw, and Dongola was entered without
a shot being fired. The Dervish foot soldiers then marched 350 miles
along the course of the Nile to Abu Hamed, while the horsemen made
across the desert to Metemma and Omdurman.

News of the surrender of Dongola caused great alarm in Omdurman as
the defeated Dervish generals exaggerated the strength of the Egyptian
army, and the speed of its pursuit, to explain their own flight. The Khalifa
reacted quickly, steadying the nerves of the population of Omdurman by
promising to lure the infidel army to destruction in front of the city, and
regrouping his own forces. He recalled his cousin, and best general,

EGYPTIAN SUDAN

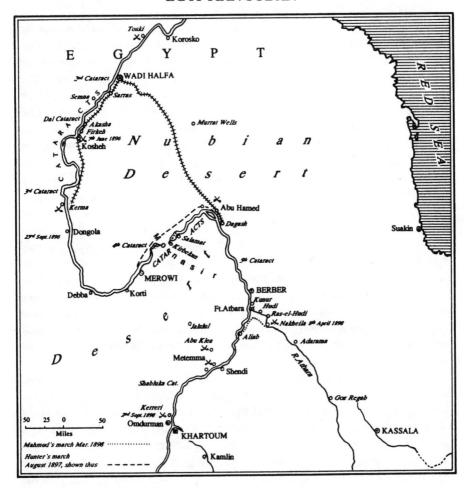

Mahmud from Darfur to Metemma with 14,000 men; withdrew some elements from Suakin to Adarama; put detachments into Abu Hamed and Berber; and slowly assembled over 60,000 fighting men from all over his empire into the area of Omdurman itself. While the Khalifa reorganised his army, Kitchener was hard at work building up a supply and transport system to support his advance into territory where every item would have to be brought up from hundreds of miles to the rear.

It was during this lull in the fighting, while both armies were preparing themselves for the next stage of hostilities that Ivor arrived in Egypt in late January 1897. The first of a remarkable series of letters was soon on its way home. These provide many vivid glimpses of daily life during the campaign as well as recording the main events, and must have been invaluable to Ivor when he came later to write *Seymour Vandeleur*. The first, dated 5 February 1897 was written from Wadi Halfa, followed four days later by one headed 'On stern wheel steamer taking in wood fuel at Hafir, Sudan'. The letter soon turns to the subject of building railways, which was to be Kitchener's main preoccupation for much of 1897. Ivor describes the Sirdar as 'a marvel at getting things done cheaply and in getting solid, hard, self-sacrificing work out of both officers and men'. He goes on to mention Percy Girouard, the remarkable young French Canadian Sapper subaltern who was the driving force in getting the railway built under the most difficult conditions. Ivor's letter ends by recording how Kitchener dealt with a War Office effort to send out a senior Royal Engineer major to supervise the railway construction by recommending that Girouard should instead be promoted to major, and also that whether the War Office accepted this suggestion or not, 'he had no need of any other engineer as Girouard satisfied his requirements very well'.

A hundred miles upstream beyond Hafir, Ivor soon arrived at Debbeh, or Debba, where he joined the 13th Sudanese Battalion as a bimbashi. He was quickly at work 'learning to drill with *Turkish* words of command and *Arabic* explanations to the men', since none of the native officers or men spoke more than a few words of English. To master Arabic, whenever possible he put in up to four hours a day working on the language. He was full of enthusiasm for his new battalion, about which he wrote at length in his letter from Debbeh on 9 April 1897.

> . . . For instance, one of these Sudanese Regiments, my own, the 13th, are all blacks derived from the tribes of the central Sudan between the Nile Valley and the Nyer Valley. Some were once slaves, others wandered away to escape slavery; every sort of reason may be imagined by those who care to speculate on the subject. Personally, I believe that regular and 'generous' pay, uniform, fair treatment, boots, putties, a blanket or two, regular food twice daily are the chief inducements. Imagine the effect of all these luxuries on a man who has never had

anything but what he could carry and that only in daily fear of having it taken from him by one or two stronger men. Boots and putties are what they mostly rejoice in.

We British officers serve 70 to 80 in an army of 18,000, controlling a large body of native officers. About half the officers of the six Sudanese Regiments are Sudanese blacks risen from the ranks. They can neither read nor write and their only home is the battalion. They are perhaps despised by the Egyptian 'Effendi' officer and they certainly never could have become officers but for us. But there they are, and a more reliable, stout-hearted, cheery set of old boys you could not wish to have; hard as nails and commanding their men most efficiently. Fortunately in my battalion, five of the six companies are commanded by 'black' captains.

By the end of May the army had established a base 120 miles further up the Nile from Debbeh at Merawi. On 4 June 1897 Ivor's letter reported that:

I am sitting on a blanket under a small tree perched upon the precipitous bank of the Nile overlooking the island of Auli – north-east of Merawi.

I have just finished what will perhaps be the hardest week's work it will ever be my fortune to do and I am in the best of rude health. I received orders to proceed as staff officer to a strong patrol to reconnoitre Essalamet and ten miles beyond – to a distance by route march of 100 miles from Merawi.

The letter goes on to give the composition of the patrol: three squadrons of cavalry; three companies of the Camel Corps; 100 men of the 9th Sudanese Battalion mounted on camels; and 60 transport animals, making a total of 600 men. In three marches of 25, 34 and 24 miles a day they reached Essalamet, passing through country 'where we found the villages absolutely deserted, the fields everywhere gone out of cultivation and the whole land in that indescribable state of desolation and despair which follows recent Dervish occupation'. The patrol found Essalamet to be extensively fortified, but there were no enemy to defend it. Having taken a look at the ground beyond the village, the troops prepared to return downstream to the temporary camp which had been set up at the south-west end of the long Shukuk Pass which lay at the other side of the village. Ivor had watched the main body retire through the pass,

. . . when a cavalry orderly galloped up with the astounding news that a large force of Dervish Cavalry had suddenly attacked our rear guard, killed several men and wounded Paton who was in command of the rear squadron.

On receipt of this news at 2.45 p.m. the CO and I had already done a full day in the saddle. We had hardly been off our horses since 4.30 a.m. and had had nothing solid to eat all day. In fact the cook was at the time engaged in unpacking his camel load and I was giving orders to have a bucket of water brought for me to dip my head in. The doctor was in the same plight, but off we started with only our orderlies carrying the first necessaries for wounded men.

They met up with the rearguard in due course and rescued Paton, who was found to have a nasty spear wound in the back. In view of Paton's 'splendid constitution' Ivor had 'no doubt now that he will recover and be as well as ever he was'.

While the field force with which Ivor was serving followed the course of the Nile as it made a huge 500-mile bend from the railhead at Kerma to Abu Hamed, a second railway was advancing steadily south-east across the desert from Wadi Halfa in order to cut off this bend. In *Seymour Vandeleur* Ivor tells how Kitchener backed his own judgment against that of many doubters when he ordered the construction of this line.

> Between Wadi Halfa and Abu Hamed the Nile makes an enormous bend and struggles through two long series of cataracts. Sir Herbert Kitchener therefore decided on a line of advance which would cut across this bend and would permit the main portion of his railway being completed at a safe distance from the enemy's raiding parties. The opponents of this scheme declared that only a madman could propose to supply water to 2,000 plate layers in mid desert, and that the further the railway advanced, the more impossible would the task become. But the problem depended on just the kind of calculation in which Kitchener excelled. He worked out the figures to his own satisfaction, and in spite of remonstrance, had started construction at Wadi Halfa in January 1897, so as to be ready to move at the rise of the Nile. It was a daring resolve, daringly carried out and amply justified by results.[4]

By July 1897 this desert railway was over half-way to Abu Hamed, and it was clearly unsafe to go further until the Dervish force there had been driven out of the town from which, if left undisturbed, they could so easily harass further construction work. The task of clearing the enemy out of Abu Hamed was given to Major General Hunter and the field force based on Merawi. Hunter set off on 27 July with a flying column 3,400-strong to cover the 140 miles along the north bank of the Nile to Abu Hamed. With him he took cavalry, artillery and four battalions of infantry: the 3rd Egyptian, and 9th, 10th, and 11th Sudanese. Ivor was put in charge of the transport train of the cavalry, gunners and two battalions of infantry, while Bimbashi Walsh, from the Rifle Brigade, was in charge of the rest. He recorded that: 'Our duties were no sinecures; for indeed you may say that the transport on this occasion, more than on most, was the life blood and vitals of the whole expedition.'

On 6 August Ivor found time to write a brief note from Camp Ginnifab, 12 miles from Abu Hamed, reporting that

The spirits of the men are first class and they have marched in the hottest month of the year at the rate of 15 miles every day for nine days. They are cheery and have absolute confidence in their handful of British Officers. I have my transport duties and am on Hunter's staff for the engagement.

A week later, on the 13th, he was on his way back to base, and able to write at length from Camp Shebabeet, 26 miles north-east of Merawi and 114 from Abu Hamed. His first paragraph summarises his adventures

Since I wrote to you a hurried line, I have seen a good deal of active service and have been so occupied day and night that sleep has claimed every unemployed moment – often for a stretch of about ten minutes on the line of march. To put it in a sentence: I left Merawi with General Hunter on 27th July, made a forced march with his column (carrying 18 days food and forage for the whole force on 1,314 camels), fought the battle of Abu Hamed on 7th August, left Abu Hamed on 8th in command of a convoy of camels and 167 prisoners of war (including Baggara women and the Baggara Emir Mahomed El Zain) and, marching at an average rate of 24 miles a day, I hope to reach our advanced depot with my convoy tomorrow morning.

After describing the long march from Merawi, during which he fed with Hunter and learned much from hearing the general talk over his plans each day, Ivor's letter began with a night march of some 16 miles throughout all the hours of darkness between 6 and 7 August. When the column reached a point one and a half miles from Abu Hamed, a 'zariba', or breastwork, was formed around all the camels and transport animals, using the camel saddles, forage, and boxes of supplies to make a parapet. This left the rest of the force, less part of the 3rd Egyptian Battalion who were guarding the 'zariba', free to move forward at daylight to attack Abu Hamed. Ivor was one of the small party sent forward to reconnoitre the enemy positions in the town. Looking down on it from a ridge, which lay between it and Hunter's 'zariba' by the Nile, the observers could see no sign of Dervish movement. Ivor reported back to Hunter, who deployed his infantry in close order and ordered them to advance to the crest of the ridge, halting behind it with fixed bayonets. Supported by the six guns of the mountain artillery battery accompanying the column, the infantry were then ordered to attack the town. For a while the well-controlled Dervishes held their fire, but as the attacking infantry drew close a heavy fusillade greeted them. Two senior officers were killed, one of them the commanding officer of the 10th Sudanese, at a spot where Hunter had been unconcernedly sitting on his horse a few moments previously.

As the assaulting troops entered the town, the men became scattered in the streets and small alleyways, engaging in street and house-to-house fighting which Ivor considered 'would have tried any troops'. It took some time to clear the town, but by 7.30am the cease-fire could be sounded. The Baggara horsemen rode off towards Berber, and many Dervishes without horses tried to swim to Mograt Island, lying in the Nile opposite the town. Most of these were shot in the water as they swam. Losses in Hunter's force amounted to 26 killed and 64 wounded, while the enemy losses were estimated at over 300 killed, as well as the 167 prisoners which Ivor was instructed to escort back to Merawi the next day, 8 August 1897.

As Ivor was making his way back downstream to Merawi, a party of friendly Arabs were scouting south from Abu Hamed towards Berber in the wake of the retreating Baggara horsemen. What happened next was reported by Ivor in a letter to his father from Merawi dated 10 September 1897

> You who have been following events here more carefully than most people will perhaps realise the importance of the news which has come in – Berber on being reconnoitred by a body of our friendly Arabs after the battle of Abu Hamed was found to have been evacuated on 25th August and the town (formerly of 8,000 inhabitants) was at once occupied in the name of the Egyptian Government. Since then General Hunter has arrived there with four or five gun boats.

In giving the go-ahead to Hunter to occupy Berber, Kitchener was taking something of a gamble, since it was possible that his troops were being lured forward to overextend their supply lines, and to give the Dervishes the opportunity to cut off the garrisons both there and at Abu Hamed. However, his own extensive knowledge of the African mind suggested 'that the enemy would be unlikely to give up such a prestigious town unless it was essential'.[5] He agreed to the occupation of Berber in spite of the risks, and the gamble paid off.

Throughout the campaign in the Sudan Ivor was in his element, discovering his own full potential as a soldier, and enjoying release from the stultifying influence of peacetime service in England. In *Seymour Vandeleur*, he wrote of the Egyptian army: 'To join it after some years of garrison duty at home was like walking into fresh air after a journey on the old underground railway.' Later in the same chapter he elaborates on this theme:

> Whether it be hauling steamers up cataracts, furnishing escorts to gunboat patrols, acting as a station master, postmaster, or supply officer, commanding a squadron, battery, camelry, or a fort, as brigade-major or as staff officer – wherever British supervision is required there the bimbashi is to be seen, directing native officers and men and discharging duties which in European armies are often entrusted to generals. With such varied and continuous employments during the intervals between important actions, is it surprising that, compared with his brother in England, he becomes a handy-man and a distinct personage – useful in peace and invaluable in war?[6]

At another point, when explaining the popularity of Egyptian service due to quick promotion and ample financial rewards, he also stressed that: 'The work is hard, the sun hot, fevers are weakening, relaxations are few . . .'.[7] One relaxation was reading, and on 4 April 1897 he wrote to ask his father to 'send round and tell Leo that he could not send all the various magazines to a place where they are more appreciated than Debbeh'. He mentioned that the British officers and the native officers who read English – there were three in the 13th Sudanese – liked magazines such as *Harpers*, *The Strand*, *Temple Bar*, and anything American. Not popular was the *National Review*, with which he alone struggled, though he found the March 1897 number 'deadly dull from start to finish!'.

Requests for various comforts included a variety of items, among them two very thin nightcaps from Thresher & Glenny in the Strand to help keep dust and flies out of his eyes; a big khaki-coloured umbrella from the same shop with an extra stick to put in the ground and bivouac under during the hot hours of the day; and in a letter on 10 June, a 28/- rubber and canvas bath from Cordings in Piccadilly, and a water bottle. Directions for this last item were detailed:

> Also please go to Silver & Co and get me a large vulcanite water bottle to hang on a camel saddle. Mind it is a good big one – if not actually the biggest he makes. If there is any simple arrangement for filling it through a cloth gauze – so as to keep out a large proportion of the brown Nile mud – all the better. Please don't reply that water ought to be 'filtered' or 'boiled' because you might just as well suggest that my champagne should be frappé!

Following Hunter's occupation of Berber on 4 September, the last months of 1897 were fraught with problems for Kitchener, even though his gamble in seizing the town had not been challenged in the short term. This did not mean, however, that there was not a constant threat that the Dervishes might come out in force from Metemma, or even Omdurman, to attack Hunter's advance field force before it was firmly established in the Berber area. To add to his troubles, the urgently required extension of the railway south from Abu Hamed was now delayed for lack of steel rails, due to strikes and disputes at home. As the level of the Nile dropped at the end of the flood period in November, the delays on the railway became more frustrating.

Apart from these worries on the ground, Kitchener faced difficulties in another direction. His Egyptian army had proved itself in the battles fought up to this point in the campaign, but it was clear that a stiffening of at least a British regular brigade would be required before a major action against the full might of the Dervish armies could be contemplated. This, Ivor commented in *Seymour Vandeleur*, was 'obvious to all concerned', but the vital 'question which engaged our thoughts was, would the British troops be placed under the Sirdar's command? or would he and his army fight under a senior general from Pall Mall?'.[8] Largely through the influence of Lord Cromer, and to the immense relief of all officers and men on the ground, it was eventually agreed to leave Kitchener in full command of all troops in the Sudan, including the British battalions when they arrived.

By the end of December 1897 much had been done to consolidate the army's bases along the Nile, in spite of the fact that the railway had only reached a point 18 miles south of Abu Hamed. The most advanced base was at Dakhilla, at the confluence of the Nile and the Atbara river, which was in the process of being turned into a defended encampment soon to be known as Fort Atbara. Ivor visited it for two days at Christmas, as described in his letter from Berber on 31 December 1897, which included two other important pieces of information:

> Since I last wrote, I have been up for a couple of days to our most advanced post Dakhilla on the Nile and Atbara. I believe too I am the first Englishman who has crossed the Atbara river for many a long year. It was very easily done for that 400 yards wide stream is already so reduced that I rode across on a polo pony without seriously wetting my feet – at a point about half a mile from the junction with the Nile. This was on Xmas eve . . .
>
> There is something in the wind but I cannot make up my mind what it may turn out to be. All I know is that many reports have reached us from the south to the effect that the Khalifa boasts that 'he will march north with all his forces and smite the unbeliever and the Turk and drive all Egyptians into the sea'. He has been saying this for many years: but on this occasion the Sirdar seems to attach more probability to the words than heretofore. For he is concentrating all the available strength of the Egyptian Army at or within reach of Berber and the various posts are being moderately fortified. . . .
>
> Meanwhile it has been whispered to me that in case of field service I am to be Brigade Major of the Second Infantry Brigade, commanded by Colonel Maxwell and consisting of the 4th, 12th, 13th and 14th Battalions which are all Sudanese with the exception of the 4th.

During January 1898 the rumours about the Khalifa's advance north became fact when he set out from Omdurman with a large force. Fortunately for the Egyptian army the difficulties in supplying this vast Dervish horde before long forced the Khalifa to halt, with results described in *Seymour Vandeleur*: 'He therefore hesitated, called together a council of war, mistrusted its advice but yet feared to delegate to any of the fighting Emirs the command of his precious troops. Finally he moved the army back to Omdurman and ordered Mahmud's division to attack Berber from Metemma'[9]. Had the Khalifa instructed Mahmud to attack Berber on the earlier occasions in the later months of 1897 when he had implored to be allowed to do so, a Dervish victory would have been the likely outcome. However, by the time he was finally given his orders in February 1898, Mahmud faced a much more difficult task. Not only had Kitchener been given time to reinforce Berber, but the British brigade commanded by Major General Gatacre was now nearing the end of its long journey from Cairo to join him.

Having crossed the Nile from Metemma to Shendi, where he took under command Osman Digna's contingent, Mahmud set out with the aim of attacking what he assumed would be the fortified town of Berber, protected by the usual trenches and strongpoints. If these proved impregnable, he anticipated being at least able to cut the lines of communication north of the town. On reaching Aliab, 80 miles from Shendi, he learnt that instead of making preparations for the static defence of Berber, Kitchener had moved his troops out of the town and was established 18 miles south of it in the area of Kunur, a village lying five miles from the confluence of the Atbara river with the Nile. On 19 March (1898), Mahmud set out from Aliab with the intention of taking up a position at Hudi, some seven miles from Kunur. Forestalled by Kitchener, who moved there before him, Mahmud was obliged to turn away south-east. At Nakheila, on the north bank of the Atbara, as shown on the map at page 45 he prepared a strong fortified base while waiting to decide what to do next. It was at this point that, due to Kitchener's forestalling moves, the initiative passed from the Dervishes to the Egyptian army, soon to be joined by its British contingent.

It took some time for reconnaissance parties of the Egyptian cavalry to discover the location of Mahmud's cleverly concealed camp at Nakheila. Since small patrols were constantly checked by the screen of Baggara horsemen protecting the site of the camp, it was eventually decided to send out virtually all the Egyptian cavalry, supported by horse artillery and maxim guns, to make a reconnaissance in force on 30 March. At last they were successful, and in Ivor's words, 'suddenly came to a point where they looked down on "zaribas" (made of thorns), palisades and trenches at least a mile in length, one behind the other, enclosing an immense area, swarming with Dervishes'.[10]

Preoccupied with administrative problems, including finding boots for the newly arrived British brigade, whose home-issued footwear had not stood up to desert marching, Kitchener was not ready for another week to launch an attack on Mahmud's camp. By 7 April he had moved his force to within 12 miles of the enemy, and that evening at dusk his four infantry brigades set out on a night march towards the Dervish stronghold. There followed the successful Battle of the Atbara, which Ivor described in a letter written on 20 April, 12 days after it had taken place. He was full of praise for his Sudanese soldiers.

In the same letter, as well as giving his description of the battle, he commented on several other matters. There was some resentment at the fact

that most of the war correspondents attached to the force concentrated to
such an extent on the actions of Gatacre's British brigade, particularly the
Seaforth and Cameron Highlanders, that, as Ivor put it, 'you probably all
feel that the battle of the Atbara was won by white men alone'. He also
listed three aspects of the battle which had particularly struck him:
Kitchener's administrative preparations; the excellent dressing kept by
the whole advancing line as it approached the enemy zariba; and the great
bravery of the Dervish soldiers. His letter ended by stating that: 'I am
more full of work personally than ever as I have just been appointed staff
officer of the whole garrison of Berber consisting of cavalry, artillery and
six Sudanese battalions.'

Following the victory at the Atbara, a long pause was necessary for
several reasons before the campaign could continue: to complete the construction of the railway from north of Berber down to Fort Atbara; to
build up the necessary stock of supplies to make a further advance possible; and to wait for the Nile floods to start in August. 'So the army retired
into summer quarters,' wrote Ivor in *Seymour Vandeleur*, 'under the substantial roofs of Berber and neighbouring villages, whilst Kitchener and all
the departmental services made adequate preparation for future events.
During four long, weary months they toiled without rest beneath a pitiless
sun.'[11] Ivor himself took advantage of the pause to go back to England in
July for some leave, returning in time to rejoin his brigade on 20 August
1898. It had by this time been moved upstream to a camp at Wadi Hamid
at the foot of the Shabluka cataract, only 53 miles from Omdurman.

Notes

Letters quoted from Maxse to his father can be found at the WSRO, file
367.

 1 Buchan, John, *The Island of Sheep* (Penguin, 1981), p. 14.
 2 Maxse, Colonel F I, *Seymour Vandeleur* (National Review, 1905), p. 134.
 3 Maxse, p. 148.
 4 Maxse, p. 173.
 5 Warner, Philip, *Kitchener: The Man Behind the Legend* (Hamish Hamilton), p.
    78.
 6 Maxse, pp. 138 and 140.
 7 Maxse, p. 140.
 8 Maxse, p. 184.
 9 Maxse, p. 188.
10 Maxse, p. 199.
11 Maxse, p. 212.

6

The Battle of Omdurman

———·◆·———

At Wadi Hamid, Ivor started a letter on 22 August which he continued the next day, and completed on 1 September. In this last section he told how the army had left Wadi Hamid on 24 August and was now eight miles from Omdurman. After a tedious march through heavily wooded country intersected by numerous valleys, they had arrived near some small hills known as the Kerreri Ridges. He finished the letter by recording that news of the Dervish Army's advance from Omdurman had been received. He commented: 'Thank goodness we are in a camp at last which is free of trees, and which affords an almost perfect field of fire, with our backs to the river. Of course now we must either be attacked or attack today or tomorrow.' Twelve days later, on 13 September, he sat down to describe in a voluminous letter of over 5,000 words the events that followed, starting by apologising that he had 'been so hard at work at odd jobs from morning till night that the time has slipped by, and in spite of my daily desire – I have not written you of our doings'.[1]

Reports from the cavalry outposts during the evening of 1 September were passed back from a section of cavalry signallers on Jebel Surgham – also referred to as Signal Hill – to the effect that the Dervish army had halted to the south-west of its position. Ivor's letter tells how battle was joined after a night when every precaution had been taken against a possible attack in the dark. During it his brigade slept ready to fight at a moment's notice, everyone in his assigned place along the entrenchment dug to cover the 600-yard front allotted to the brigade.

At 4.30 a.m. on 2 September we all stood to arms ready for anything. At 5.30 a.m. we were about to advance in the direction of Omdurman – viz

55

south – when definite news reached us from our cavalry which had gone out early to reconnoitre, that the whole Dervish army was advancing to attack; our cavalry retiring slowly and deliberately in front of the vast horde.

Soon we could hear in the distance a loud murmur – the enthusiastic shouting of many thousand voices – a curious weird sound. Cavalry officers have told me that they (the Dervishes) were letting off their rifles in the air in jubilation, but this we could not hear at the time from our lines, though the shouting was quite audible. We had to wait for some time in expectation, watching our squadrons of cavalry as they retired at a walk across our front towards Kerreri Ridges and over the very ground on which 10,000 Dervishes were soon to die. Then we saw the tops of numerous flags, then the heads of swarms of men marching in regular formations and without hesitation. Not a sign of any confusion in their ranks. Our artillery opened fire – one British 15 pounder battery on the left and our four batteries of Egyptian Army mule artillery from various points in the line. At first the Dervishes seemed to be bent on marching across our front to the Kerreri Ridges, but the shrapnel fire from our guns determined them to face us. The shrapnel only was at work on them at this period – range about 2,000 yards from us – some say 2,500.

No amount of fire seemed to affect the steady advance, though many were killed. Later at about 900 to 1,000 yards our maxims opened on them: some say at 1,500 yards. It was now that, to us sitting on our horses or cantering along the rear of the line of our men in a shallow trench, waiting, ready for the order to fire, the appearance of this first part of the Dervish attack was of supremest interest. Looking at them advancing straight on our two Sudanese (Maxwell's and Macdonald's) brigades and on Wauchope's brigade through field glasses, at a distance of 800 yards, with all our field guns belching shrapnel and our maxims pumping lead into that vast mass of men, the question arose in our minds shall we or shall we not kill sufficient numbers of them to render the attack of the survivors, at close quarters, ineffectual? You see we were in a thin line to enable every possible rifle to bear. If this line were pierced at any one point – it would be more than uncomfortable for us all! Personally I felt no doubt at any time that as soon as our infantry fire was opened at 500 to 600 yards we should break up the attack. But what if the Khalifa had timed his attack in the night before the moon rose, when we could distinguish little or nothing 300 yards beyond our bivouac?

However, here we had everything in our favour as the sun rose behind our backs and the country to our front was open, fairly level, and above all unwooded and unhoused.

The Dervishes began firing upon us long before our infantry opened fire, and we had one Egyptian officer killed and 15 men wounded in my brigade alone, by bullets fired at us at a considerable range; perhaps as much as 1,200 to 2,000 yards – the shots being aimed promiscuously at

our camp. They continued firing at us all the way, and several staff officers' horses were wounded. It was indeed a grand sight and a wonderful
exhibition of fanatical valour on the part of our assailants who were all
the time suffering terrible losses.

Then at about 800 yards range we gave it them with infantry fire: and
yet still they continued to advance steadily, many lying down to die en
route, some lying down to shoot from the bed of a little watercourse,
and one man, carrying a defiant banner, actually got within 200 yards of
the brigade before he was shot dead. That banner was picked up by a
man of the 12th Sudanese who paced the distance, after 'cease fire' had
sounded, and was shot at for his pains.

In fact there was still a good deal of promiscuous shooting from
wounded Dervishes lying in small depressions – one lot of 50 men
being so persistent that the maxims had to be kept on them till they
desisted.

Thus the attack of these thousands of misguided, brave men died
away from sheer loss in killed and wounded: and there they lay before us
in thousands – mostly directly in front of my brigade, though many of
those had been killed by the splendid volleys, fired half right, by
Wauchope's (1st) British Brigade: I cannot speak too highly of the excellent fire discipline of this brigade and the wonderful power of their Lee
Metford rifles at 1,000 yards and less: the other British Brigade,
Lyttleton's, being away on the left rear towards the river bank was barely
engaged: Macdonald's Sudanese did not open any infantry fire at all,
nor did Lewis or Collinson, as they were not attacked, at this period.

Thus was closed the first event of the day, and our bugles rang out
the 'cease fire': and I went round and collected the brigade casualty
return. Meanwhile artillery fire was continued from Macdonald's and
Lewis' forces at long range upon a large body – rather several bodies –
of the enemy still moving northwards behind Kerreri Ridges. My own
personal impression is – as regards the action I have tried to describe –
that the Khalifa's plans were not carried out as he had intended. I don't
believe it was part of his scheme to attack us where he did in broad
daylight.

The letter goes on to give Ivor's explanation of why he thought the
Khalifa's plans had gone wrong in the first phase of the battle. It then
turns to the second phase, telling how the half of the Dervish army not yet
involved nearly brought disaster to the Egyptian and British force.

To return to my own brigade (Maxwell's) and the rest of the infantry and
21st Lancers, after repulse of first Dervish attack. Everything had up till
now gone well with us: the Dervishes had entirely played our game by
attacking us, in our chosen position, across the open: we had inflicted
enormous losses with the least possible loss to ourselves: we had thus
smashed up an army five miles outside Omdurman instead of dealing
with a desperate foe in the intricate streets of a city of some 400,000

inhabitants: we had the whole day before us: but we did not know that a large portion of the Khalifa's force remained in two blocks still unbeaten and undemoralized. This fact gives you a measure of their pluck! One of these blocks was halted in the Dervish rear, with the Khalifa himself behind Signal Hill: the other under the next chief of the Army, Ali Wad Helu, was returning round the west end of Kerreri Ridges bent on a further attack – but we did not know all this at the moment.

We did not know, and I don't know how the Sirdar could know, that these two blocks still had fight in them. Accordingly with a beaten army on its right flank and a very mobile army under his command, he gave the order to march straight on Omdurman in echelon of brigades, the left directing, with its left flank close to the Nile. I fancy his idea was to interpose his army between Omdurman and the beaten foe.

We therefore issued from our bivouac, formed up deliberately and started on our march without attempting to explore the field of the recent battle where thousands were dead, dying and wounded.

The intention was to march the whole army in between Signal Hill and the river. Off we started for Omdurman – the Sirdar himself marching with the British on the left and well in front of everyone.

At this point in his letter, Ivor told of the charge of the 21st Lancers, the story of which had been related to him by Hubert Howard, *The Times* correspondent with the army. While far from complimentary about the action in his letter, Ivor was even less so when he later described it in *Seymour Vandeleur*:

Thus at the commencement of the second phase of the battle we find Kitchener's army marching southwards by brigades, separated from one another by very wide gaps, with the 21st Lancers acting as advanced guard. . . .
It was at this interesting climax that there occurred an episode which, owing to the praise bestowed upon it by public opinion at home, proves beyond doubt that England is the paradise of amateurs.

Having described how the inexperienced regiment had galloped into an ambush in a hidden *khor*, or gully, and suffered heavy losses which forced their withdrawal from further action, Ivor finished with this condemnation:

The Lancers charge was not only unnecessary, but had the greater disadvantage of incapacitating the regiment from the performance of the particular duty it was brought into the Sudan to accomplish – namely the capture of the Khalifa – and the fact that both officers and men behaved with great gallantry in a nasty place is no excuse for a blunder.[2]

Ivor's letter of 13 September continues:

So we were marching off gaily to Omdurman at 10 a.m. when we became aware that we still had a large unbeaten force on our flank: a force bent on as determined an attack as the early morning. Each brigade faced round to the right at the double to meet their enemy and another action commenced.

Fortunately Macdonald's Sudanese brigade had been kept back by General Hunter and placed on our extreme right flank otherwise a disaster might very easily have occurred. 'Mac' as he is called is a real fine soldier and was up to the occasion and manoeuvred his brigade splendidly: and indeed there was occasion for a good man and steady troops, for his brigade was more or less unsupported and isolated when it was first attacked by the Khalifa's force from behind Signal Hill, then by Ali Wad Helu's force from west of Kerreri Ridges. Lewis' brigade faced to the right, Maxwell's did likewise at the double, and we both fell upon the lot with heavy rifle fire, whilst Mac withstood all alone the onslaught of Ali Wad Helu's 10,000 men headed by cavalry. I was unfortunately too far off to see what occurred and can give but a rough idea of the manner in which Mac beat off the attack. Lyttleton's British Brigade was ordered to march direct from the river to his support and it started: but it would have been too late to save Mac if the latter had failed to save himself.

I don't quite know the position of our batteries of mobile field artillery but believe three of our four mule batteries were with Hunter and I saw the British 15 pounders in action with Wauchope's brigade on our left.

My brigade had all its four battalions deployed for attack with no reserve: this was necessary in order to try and fill the wide interval – a mile I should say between Lewis and Lyttleton. In front of us was Signal Hill up which the 13th Sudanese toiled slowly and wearily, firing away like fun into the Khalifa's force from the top of the hill. I personally was told off to look after the general advance of the 8th battalion (an Egyptian commanded battalion without an Englishman in it) and when we reached the spot just between where the 5th and the 12th came out from the rocky hill slopes, I found a big Krupp gun with limber and a number of mules still attached to it: boxes of ammunition and shell. Under the gun were some wounded men who surrendered, and these told me that the Khalifa had been standing near the Krupp gun when we topped the hill and opened our volleys on the Dervishes. The Khalifa then mounted his horse and galloped away towards Omdurman. Thus we were within a few minutes of killing or capturing him. From other sources I have every reason to believe that this was where the Khalifa stood during most of the action.

Hubert Howard was with me most of this time: he was indeed the most on the spot of any correspondent I came across all day. But whilst I have been telling you all about what I saw at this period I should state that Macdonald was very seriously and very hotly engaged by the whole of Ali Wad Helu's force, and by some of the Khalifa's. I cannot go into details, but I know that some of the Baggara saddles were emptied so near to Mac's lines that riderless horses actually galloped through one of our mule batteries: that the brigade had 130 casualties (killed and wounded): and that had not Mac been the good man that he is, and had he not steady troops under him, his whole brigade would undoubtedly have been wiped out. They were attacked from three sides. Having thus beaten off all opposition the four brigades advanced westwards for a mile or two driving thousands of fugitives into the desert and killing a considerable number at long ranges. At last when all opposition had ceased, tired by the hot sun, and having had but little beyond a biscuit and a tin of sardines all day, we went 'fours left' and marched south to Khor Shambat, on the Nile and about 2½ miles from Omdurman. My brigade reached the spot at about 1 p.m. and found one British brigade already watering and resting. The other three brigades were still a long way behind us.

Here the Sirdar had a bit of lunch, and I managed to get a delicious bottle of beer and a captain's biscuit from Nigs and Watson. The heat was intense; the interest was intenser; especially when the Sirdar decided that Maxwell's brigade was to march again at 2 p.m. with the British 15 pounder battery attached to it, and that this small force was to have the honour of capturing Omdurman all alone. The Sirdar and his staff accompanied us and we moved from Khor Shambat at 2.10 p.m.

You will have gathered thus far that our brigade had already played a conspicuous part in the morning attack on our camp. I have since been carefully over the ground, where 10,800 Dervishes have been counted dead, and from the lie of the bodies and in view of our brigade being the only one that directly faced the Dervish attack, I am positive that no other brigade could have been half as hotly engaged as we were.

Again when we advanced from our first position it fell to our lot to attack the flank of the Khalifa's main force just as it was itself attacking Macdonald, Lewis being somewhat in the rear, tho' he came up afterwards. The brigade having now been selected to take the city itself, I think it may very fairly be claimed that we played a conspicuous part in the operations of the day and its ultimate success – in fact that we had more to do from start to finish than anyone else.

I don't think you will find in the newspapers any adequate description of the occupation of the town because we paraded Maxwell's Brigade with only ten minutes notice. It was arranged whilst Maxwell was lunching with the Sirdar and the troops were drinking water and munching their biscuits along Khor Shambat, into which the Nile had flooded. Thus no one knew we were off, not even General Hunter who caught us up (without his staff) when we were in the city; and no newspaper correspondent was present except Hubert Howard. He was killed, poor fellow, by one of the last shots in the evening.

When we marched off from Khor Shambat at 2.10 p.m. we none of us, not even the Sirdar, knew how much or how little resistance we were to expect; a spy had reported that the Khalifa (and some 2,000 riflemen) was praying in the Mosque square and that he was exhorting his men to make a last stand.

We entered the outskirts of the place immediately on leaving Khor Shambat and the difficulties of keeping communication up between the different units of the brigade in the intricate alleys and when crossing various Khors full of water was a most difficult task, which fell chiefly on my shoulders and those of Maxwell's ADC.

As the brigade advanced, Kitchener moved with the centre column, following the leading company of the 14th Sudanese battalion. The Khalifa's great black flag had been captured on the battlefield after being defended by 40 fanatically brave Dervishes, who had died in turn as they kept it held high until the last one stuck it in the ground. To show the inhabitants of Omdurman that he was the undoubted victor, Kitchener had the flag carried behind him as the brigade entered the town. Being on a very long pole it could be seen moving through the streets by other members of the force, since it flew well above the tops of the majority of the one-storey houses. Ivor found the flag an invaluable reference point as he galloped up and down the narrow streets controlling the movement of the units of the brigade.

In due course, they came to the twenty-foot high masonry wall of the *Sur*, the enclosed area containing the Mahdi's tomb, the houses of the Khalifa and the other great Baggara emirs, and the great open square, partly roofed with matting held up by long poles which constituted the mosque. A messenger was sent in to tell the Khalifa to surrender, but returned with his refusal. In spite of the risks, Kitchener then ordered Maxwell to sound the advance.

Having found a gate into the *Sur* with some difficulty, Ivor entered it with Lieutenant Colonel Horace Smith-Dorrien commanding the 13th Sudanese Battalion. They found that the Mahdi's tomb had been largely destroyed by shells from a howitzer firing on the town from a position 3,400 yards away on the right bank of the Nile. Ivor considered that this bombardment, coupled with shells from gunboats in the river, knocked out any stuffing there might have been left in the Dervishes. Near the tomb, one of the Khalifa's servants showed them the door to his master's house. Having broken it down, Ivor and Smith-Dorrien found the building empty. The servant then suggested that the Khalifa must have left by the southern gate leading out of the mosque square, which lay on the other side of the house. They ran out into the square, which they found full of hundreds of wounded men, some of them being nursed by their wives. It was soon apparent that the Khalifa had made a successful escape.

Shortly afterwards, a group of officers with men of the 13th Sudanese gathered by this gate from which the Khalifa had escaped. The group included General Hunter and Maxwell as well as Smith-Dorrien and

Ivor. Also with them was Hubert Howard, *The Times* correspondent. Suddenly two Baggara appeared from nowhere, one mounted and one on foot, and charged the party. They were shot down, but not before the mounted man had hurled a spear which went straight through the skull of an unfortunate corporal standing nearby and killed him instantly, with his head transfixed to the wall.

As it was now just about sunset, and there was a long way to go back to the brigade camping area outside the town, the order was given to retire. Ivor's letter ended on a tragic note. Although there was still shooting going on all over the town, and an occasional shell landing, he took little notice of the various explosions as he moved off with the last section of the 13th Sudanese through the Khalifa's courtyard. Then, he wrote, 'to my amazement I saw a terrible sight – Hubert Howard lying gasping on his back, his horse standing over him and his head in a pool of blood! . . . The wound was right through his brain and he never recovered consciousness. We buried him next day out in the open and a cross is being erected over his grave.' A later letter reported that it was almost certain that Howard had been killed by shrapnel fired from one of the British guns which had continued to pour shells into the city without realising how far the infantry had penetrated into it.

Maxwell's brigade eventually reached their camp at 9pm on 2 September. In Ivor's words they 'slept the sleep of the tired out'. It had been a long day.

Notes

1 This long letter was later typed out by the Hon. Mrs Maxse, and there are several copies of it. The one used for this chapter is in the possession of the family.

2 Maxse, Colonel F I, *Seymour Vandeleur* (National Review, 1905), pp. 227–8.

7

Fashoda, and Exploration of the Sobat River, 1898–99

———•◆•———

Two days after the battle, Colonel Maxwell was appointed Military Governor of Omdurman, with a garrison of three battalions and powers of life and death over the whole population. With Ivor as his chief staff officer, he moved into the comfortable new house recently built for Yacub, the Khalifa's brother. The two of them faced a massive task in cleaning up the city and restoring life to normal. In spite of the difficulties, Ivor was able to mention in a further letter that . . . 'we have done a lot already to cleanse and discipline the city and we have any amount of labour: but no currency until Egyptian money comes up!'

While appreciating the importance of the work he was doing he had one regret: 'I have thus missed my great object – i.e. going up to Fashoda where Marchand is in a fort with 120 black soldiers, practically our prisoners.' He was referring to the immediate dispatch on 3 September, the day after the battle, of the first part of a convoy of gunboats with infantry and artillery support, followed a week later by the rest of the force under Kitchener's personal command, on a 469-mile journey up the White Nile. The destination was the hitherto unknown, half derelict fort at Fashoda, which for a time was to assume a remarkable importance in the conduct of politics in Europe as well as North Africa. To understand why, the background to what became known as the 'Fashoda Incident' must be briefly touched upon. In what is sometimes called the 'Scramble' for Africa in the nineteenth century the major prize in the north-eastern quarter of the continent was seen as control of the Nile. In particular, the eyes of three nations were fixed on the course of the White Nile as it flowed through relatively unknown territory where no European power yet held sway. From colonies already established in the west the French and Belgians hoped to open up lateral trading routes across Africa, while Britain envisaged extending its position in Egypt to create a system of communications running from north to south. For all three the long-deserted post at Fashoda could be seen as an advantageous base to hold on the river. The fort had been originally built in 1855 by the Egyptians as a base for anti-slavery operations – rather half-hearted efforts, it must be added, made more to impress European governments than effectively to stamp out lucrative slave trading. French and Belgian expeditions set out in 1896 to cross the heart of the continent, but disaster struck the latter in 1897 when already within striking distance of its destination, leaving the way open to its rivals. The French party was commanded by Captain Jean-Baptiste Marchand, of the marine artillery, and consisted of 10 French officers and NCOs with 150 Senegalese *tirailleurs*, or sharpshooters. Having struggled through every type of difficult terrain, during a journey of nearly 4,000 miles lasting for two years, 'la mission Marchand', as it became known, arrived at Fashoda on 10 July 1898. Inspired by Marchand's determination, they had not only surmounted endless difficulties and discomforts, but had also brought with them their own 50-ft river steamer called *Faidherbe*, which had been broken down into sections and carried overland by porters for hundreds of miles.

The last stage of Marchand's route was along the mosquito-ridden Bahr-el-Ghazal, or 'river of the gazelles', which brought his party to the Nile at Lake No, roughly 150 miles upstream of Fashoda. On arrival at his long-sought destination, in a state of great excitement he hoisted the French tricolor above the fort, claiming for his country not only the province taking its name from the Bahr-el-Ghazal, but the whole vast belt of territory above the equator stretching across Africa from the Atlantic to the Red Sea. Before providing an account of Kitchener's action at Fashoda, and Ivor's involvement in the last stage of the 'incident', a question must be raised about which there are conflicting points of view: how much was Kitchener's whole campaign influenced from the beginning by French ambitions in central Africa. One theory, supported by D L Lewis in his important book *The Race to Fashoda*, suggests that countering the French advance was a major factor from the start. Against this, Ivor's humorous tale in *Seymour Vandeleur* of how authority was given by the Cabinet for the advance to Dongola in 1896 would suggest that the initial impetus was the Italian defeat at Adowa, as officially claimed. Whichever version is correct, there is no doubt that during 1897, when knowledge of the various expeditions setting out for the Upper Nile had become widespread, the speeding up of Kitchener's progress, along with further financial support for his advance towards Omdurman, sprang from a British determination to prevent the French, or any other nationality, seizing the Bahr-el-Ghazal and Fashoda. It was this resolve which caused the Sirdar's departure from Khartoum to confront Marchand so soon after the battle of Omdurman was over.

A polite but inconclusive meeting between Kitchener and Marchand on 19 September 1898 ended with the two of them agreeing that the rights and wrongs of the situation were outside their competence and had to be decided between London and Paris. It was agreed that a small Egyptian garrison under Bimbashi H W Jackson of the 11th Sudanese Battalion would remain at Fashoda in a camp next to the French base. The next day, 20 September, Kitchener's flotilla sailed on towards Port Sobat, 80 miles further upstream where the Sobat river, a major tributary, flowed into the Nile from the east. Here another garrison was left, with instructions to create a fort and to watch over all traffic passing up and down the two rivers. Having gone as far as his instructions allowed in re-establishing Egyptian influence over the upper Nile, Kitchener returned to Khartoum.

In the diplomatic exchanges between London and Paris, the balance swung steadily in favour of London. Threats of war between France and Britain were soon seen to be no more than half-hearted sabre rattling, and by 3 October the French Council of Ministers had decided that Fashoda would have to be evacuated. Use was made of a British boat to deliver a letter to Marchand, which reached him on 9 October. In it he was promoted to Commandant, or Major, and Baratier to Captain. Less cheering was an order to send an officer to Paris to see the foreign minister, Theophile Déclassé. Baratier was chosen and arrived at the Quai d'Orsay on 27 October. He was instructed to return to Fashoda to warn Marchand that the expedition must be withdrawn from Africa. In the meantime, unable to wait for a decision, Marchand had applied for a passage to Cairo on a British steamer and had sailed from Fashoda on 24 October. It was at this stage that Ivor first became involved in the story, as is explained in his own letter of 28 October 1898: 'Marchand had just arrived here from Fashoda, I have not seen him, but he dines with Maxwell and me tonight and goes to Cairo tomorrow.' During this short visit Ivor was able to show him the Omdurman battlefield and to explain the course of the fighting.

Marchand's intention was to telegraph a comprehensive report to Paris from Cairo, which he hoped would encourage his government to support him. However on 4 November, the morning after his arrival and before he had a chance to send his report, the French minister in Cairo showed him a wire from Déclassé ordering the surrender of Fashoda and the withdrawal of 'La mission Marchand'. Protestations were to no avail. The only concession made by Paris was that Marchand could leave Africa via Abyssinia under his own arrangements rather than face the humiliation of being brought down the Nile in the readily offered British steamers. He and Baratier, who had now joined him on return from France, left Cairo on 13 November. On the same day Ivor wrote home to report having just heard that the two were on their way back, and that: 'On their arrival at Omdurman, I am to accompany them to Fashoda in the gun-boat, so I shall see the ceremony of evacuation!' On 29 November a hurried note told that he was . . . 'just starting in an hour with three gun-boats, half the 13th Sudanese, Major Marchand and Captain Baratier for Fashoda'.

The three steam-driven gunboats *Nasr, Abu Klea,* and *Sultan* made three to four miles an hour against the current of the Nile, so that the journey took six days to complete. Roughly half way, as they chugged south between Abba Island and their destination, Ivor wrote on 2 December in glowing terms to his father about Marchand and Baratier, with whom his relations were 'of the very best'. About the former he commented:

> He is quite the most superior young Frenchman I have ever come across – intelligent, well read, *pas trop emporté*, and especially modest. He knows his subject, i.e. Northern and Central Africa, well: both as an explorer and leader of fighting men, and from the study of books and official documents. . . . He is a good talker, with a charming frank expression: and he looks you straight in the face, and gives me the impression of being endowed with a singularly honest mind. My only regret is that he is not an Englishman!

The letter went on to give a description of the *Sudd,* the great floating marsh bordering the main channel of the Nile for much of its length, which he claimed had 'its roots three to five yards below the surface of the water, and its head two to three yards above the surface'. A sketch by Marchand was enclosed giving a view 'd'une "tranche" de marais' as envisaged through a 'coupe verticale'. Turning back to politics, Ivor suggested that the French were prepared to accept Anglo-Egyptian rule on the Nile, but would like to have access to it for trading purposes. An opening for commercial traffic from the Ubangi province of the French Congo would be welcome, since that colony was at present dependent on use of the Belgian Railway to the Atlantic port at Stanley Pool for the carriage of its products to outside markets.

Ivor felt that the granting of such access to the Nile for purely commercial purposes would be reasonable, and deplored the idea of constant friction over boundaries with the French. Both he and Marchand abhorred the thought of officers of their two nations leading black troops against each other over frontier squabbles. The letter ended by saying how freely Marchand had been talking about all these matters, and ended with a suggestion:

> I need not tell you that what I have set forth, with Marchand's express permission, is only put down privately. None of it should ever appear in any British newspaper.

But if you care to show my letter to Lord Salisbury or to Mr

EGYPTIAN SUDAN

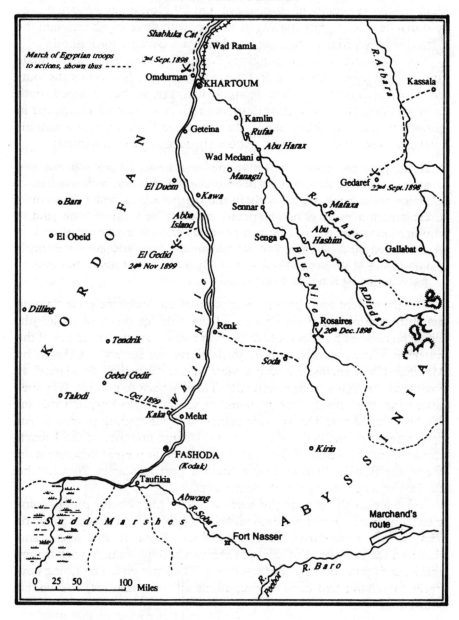

Chamberlain, privately, there would be no harm – indeed it might be advisable to do so.

The suggestion was taken up by the Admiral, and was to bear fruit later.

On 3 December, a halt was made to cut wood to fuel the boilers of the gunboats, during which Ivor took Marchand and Baratier ashore for a shooting expedition, lending the former one of his guns. The five guinea-fowl shot by Ivor proved very good eating. Baratier, armed with a carbine, found it impossible to get a shot at the gazelle and antelope which they glimpsed occasionally through the head-high grass.

On 4 December the convoy arrived at Fashoda, and Ivor reported to Jackson, now promoted to 'Kaimakam', or colonel, and appointed 'commander of Fashoda and the South'. During the two and a half months that Jackson's force had been stationed alongside the French, the two detachments had established a satisfactory *modus vivendi*. As Darrell Bates explains in his book *The Fashoda Incident of 1898*, . . . 'while their countries' governments and newspapers seemed to be locked in the grip of conflict and mutual abuse, even at times to be on the brink of war, at Fashoda itself the soldiers of both sides were drawn together by their common need to survive the heat and the rain and the mosquitos . . .'.[1]

Ivor's hopes of being present to observe the final surrender of the fort, as expressed in his letter of 13 November, were quickly dashed by Jackson. He was given orders to leave the following day to move south to assume the post of 'Commandant of the Sobat Sub-District'. In a letter recording all these events, he said of his new command: 'Well, the "Sobat Sub-District" sounds alright, and may mean a great deal or very little according to how you like to look at it.' There were two reasons for sending him to take control of the Sobat river and its environs. The short-term reason, which was the cause of his immediate despatch to his new area of activity, was to establish a system for monitoring Marchand's progress once he had left Fashoda and was on his way towards Abyssinia. It was essential that he should follow the correct tributary of the Sobat, which would take him east in the desired direction, and not slip south down a different one leading back towards the Nile. The second, longer-term task facing Ivor was to explore and to survey the course of the Sobat and its main branches.

While pleased about his new independent command, Ivor's letters at this period were of his worries about promotion. His award of the DSO, notified in November, did not make up for the fact that some others who had acted as brigade majors in the recent battles had been given brevets as lieutenant colonels while so far he had not. In one letter he commented:

> It is no use risking one's whole life in these climates unless one has a real good chance of getting near the top of one's profession, and without a brevet I don't see that I can do much more good, professionally out

here. With a brevet and the consequent command of a Sudanese battalion, and the prospect of commanding that battalion on active service,
I foresee a possible career. Without a brevet I see none at all.

These concerns did not prevent him throwing himself into his new
duties with zest, and sending home long descriptions of his activities,
with detailed maps of his route and observations on all he saw as he travelled. After a 'champagne déjeuner' with Marchand and his officers he left
Fashoda during the afternoon of 5 December with his convoy, the composition of which he set out as follows:

'Gunboat *Sultan* – Lieut Cowan, DSO, RN
Gunboat *Abu Klea* – with two troop barges to hold 350 men.
Half 13th Sudanese battalion – Bimbashis Gamble and Capper.
2 field guns and 2 Maxims'

Apart from allotting him the task of investigating the course of the
Sobat and its tributaries, Ivor's instructions gave him a free hand to act as
he thought best, as long as he kept on friendly terms with the natives he
met, and avoided clashes with Abyssinians unless deliberately attacked. As
he put it . . . 'it is not possible to lay down minute instructions in Cairo or
Omdurman, or even in Fashoda, for an officer in charge of a frontier
which is as yet unexplored'. On arrival at Fort Sobat early on 6 December,
work started immediately on stocking up with supplies and ammunition.
Leaving Bimbashi Gamble in the fort with two companies and all the sick,
Ivor set out with the well-provisioned convoy the same evening, and travelled 10 miles up the Sobat before mooring for the night. As the first 182
miles of the river's course up to the town of Nassar (now spelt Nasir) had
already been reconnoitred, and roughly mapped, the only requirement
was to push along as quickly as possible over this first stage. The bar to
speedy progress was the gunboat *Sultan*, ostensibly the finest and best
armed of the Nile fleet, but in reality, as Ivor put it, 'a terrible white elephant'. Specially designed by the Admiralty with a very small draft, and
successfully tested on the Thames, the *Sultan* had two insurmountable
faults. First, her voracious boilers required large quantities of unobtain-
able coal, or so much wood that it took half a battalion all day to cut
enough to keep her moving for quite a short time. Second, her boilers
needed clear, clean water, while one of the most valuable attributes of the
Nile is the mud it carries down from its many sources, when the water is
high, to fertilise the land along its lower reaches, When the *Sultan* eventually arrived at Nassar on 11 December, Ivor moored her there as a
floating fort, taking the stern-wheel *Abu Klea*, which had arrived a day earlier, to carry him on up the unexplored waters ahead. Roughly 30 miles
upstream from Nassar the Sobat splits into two branches. To the north the
Baro, also referred to in Ivor's days as the Adura, flows down from the
Abyssinian mountains. Coming into the junction from the south is the

Pibar, known in his day as the Peebor, or sometimes Juba. It was up the Peebor that Ivor began his exploration. Since this was the route that Marchand was to be kept from using, he left a small garrison to build a fort at the mouth of the river.

After a moving ceremony, with an Egyptian guard of honour drawn up on the river bank, and Jackson and his officers saluting with their swords, Marchand and his party sailed from Fashoda in the *Faidherbe* on 13 December. Some six days later they passed through Nassar, and continued on without incident to enter the Baro as intended. Eventually, they were forced to abandon the *Faidherbe* in the headwaters of the Baro. They moved on through Abyssinia on foot, and reached Addis Ababa, the capital, on 9 March 1899. On 3 April they were received in friendly fashion by the Emperor Menilek, and 10 days later set off on the last stage of their journey to the coast at Djibouti, where a French ship waited to take them back to a rapturous welcome in France. Ivor made good progress up the Peebor after leaving Nassar, and by 14 December was able to write to his father, at length as usual, from a point he calculated to be 292 miles from the mouth of the Sobat, and therefore roughly 80 up the Peebor. He described the various native tribes he had met, the most important of which were the Shilluk, Dinka and Nuer, and his efforts to get on friendly terms with them. The weather he found to be 'most pleasant: no rain: no mist or fog: not too hot: and not relaxing. But the insects, especially the *battalions* of mosquitos are a veritable plague'.

By 5 January 1899 he was back at Nassar. The unexpected arrival of a steamer with rations and official mail sent up from Fort Sobat prevented him from writing another long letter as he had intended, but in the short note he had time to scribble before it began its return journey, he gave one piece of important news:

> I have been promoted a 'Kaimakam' (Turkish lieutenant-colonel) which carries the title of 'Bey', so I am now known as 'Maxse Bey'! I have also been appointed to command the 13th Sudanese, one of the best, if not the best battalion in this army. But at present it is much cut up in detachments. Out of 1,000 men, I have 230 here, 300 at Fort Sobat, and over 400, chiefly recruits, at Omdurman under Vandeleur.

This appointment to command a battalion was what he had particularly wanted, but his promotion to temporary lieutenant colonel did not at this stage bring the brevet rank, with its permanent status, that he was so anxious to achieve. In a letter to General Sir Arthur Fremantle written the next day, 6 January, thanking him for congratulations on the award of the DSO, Ivor came back to the subject: 'I am very proud of having a DSO, but of course from a professional point of view a brevet is the only thing to get one on, and to get one in a responsible position in the British army before one is too old.' Since he was now a battalion commander at 36, albeit temporarily, his fears about his professional future were perhaps a little groundless.

During the seven weeks that he was away on his expedition, Ivor surveyed and mapped 210 miles of the hitherto unexplored courses of the major rivers: 30 miles of the Sobat above Nassar: 110 miles of the Peebor; and 70 miles of the Baro. He also followed various minor tributaries, discovering, for example, that the Gilo, which flowed into the Peebor from the east, was blocked by 'sudd' 20 miles upstream from its confluence with the main river. For his work he was later elected a Fellow of the Royal Geographical Society.

Some extracts from the letter he wrote to his mother on 7 January, to acknowledge her congratulations on his DSO, give a vivid impression of his journeyings and the things he observed:

> I don't quite know what would most interest you on the Sobat River? The stark naked men and women? Or the very numerous crocodiles, 20 lying together on one small sandbank? The noses of the frequent hippopotami which are constantly visible looking at our steamer as we approach. The mile upon mile of green grassy alluvial plain which the Sobat traverses for 400 miles without even a small hillock in the dim distance? All green grass, or green reeds and large green woods with occasional baboons and monkeys in them, and a large population of 'new' birds which may have lived here for many hundreds of generations? or the waterfowl which abound all along the river, and flocks of grey pelican? These big birds swim as fast as they can in front of the steamer, and then, when we are about to catch them up, extend their great wings and skim through the air for a couple of hundred yards and then slide along the water and settle again, and swim with dignity till we again approach with our unaccustomed steamer noises?
>
> Thus the pelicans and other smaller white waterfowl are spread out in front of us like a huge moving sheet as we ascend some narrow river which no steamer has ever been up before. Does that interest you? Or would you rather land in a bit of marsh and wade to your knees along a path leading to a large native village 300 yards from the water? The houses have door holes, two feet high, through which you might perhaps crawl with difficulty. Having got inside you would find very little or nothing but a thick layer of very fine, soft wood ashes, in which the naked gents and ladies sleep; and from which they emerge the colour of light slate.
>
> The dwelling with the door tightly blocked with matting at sunset, and when all the family is lying down in the soft ashes, is said to be mosquito proof; it usually holds from 10 to 15 persons, from grandmothers to last borns, all in one bed of ashes.

The primitive tribes encountered along the banks of the rivers were wary and nervous, often disappearing completely into the marsh or high grass on the approach of strangers. Once powerful and numerous in their own areas, they had been raided so often in recent years by slave hunters, descending on them from both east and west, that their numbers had been greatly reduced. The Nuer was by now the most numerous tribe, by virtue of its territory being the least accessible, and its members the swiftest to avoid outsiders. Regrettably they were not themselves above carrying off members of neighbouring tribes to sell to the slave traders. Though none of these primitive people could have realised it at the time, the arrival in the area of the Anglo-Egyptian troops would prove the best possible protection against further depredations by slave hunters.

Towards the end of January, Ivor was back at Fashoda, from where he wrote on the 26th to say that his battalion had been ordered to return to Omdurman. The reason for his recall was to prepare for a royal review of Kitchener's army by the Duke of Connaught, to be held on 19 February 1899. By the time he had gathered all the detachments together on 13 February he had only five days to drill them as a battalion before the parade. Fortunately the 400 new recruits waiting at Omdurman, mostly ex-soldiers of the Dervish army who had previously fought for the Khalifa, had been well drilled by Vandeleur since joining. On 24 February Ivor was able to tell his father: 'The change from the sort of duties we have been at for the last seven months into "ceremonial parade" form was a bit of a jump, as you can easily see. However I am glad to say we just managed to do it, and the result was not altogether bad.' After the parade, he and four others were presented with their DSOs by the Duke. About this time a strong reconnaisance party managed to locate the Khalifa and the estimated force of 8,000 fighting men who were still loyal to him. They had taken up a strongly fortified position in the province of Southern Kordofan, about 100 miles west of the Nile and 400 from Khartoum, where they were sitting on the only supply of water for many miles around. Since they posed no immediate threat, and would clearly have to devote most of their energies to finding food in a very barren area, no efforts were made at this stage to mount an operation against them.

Following Marchand's withdrawal from Fashoda, and the surrender of his claims to the Bahr-el-Ghazal, the British and French governments negotiated an agreement on the boundaries of their respective spheres of influence in northern Africa. During April and May, Ivor's letters to his father were largely taken up with comments on the arrangements being made by the two governments. Some of these letters were also passed on to Lord Salisbury by the Admiral. At the end of May, on hearing that Ivor would shortly be arriving in London on leave, the Prime Minister, who also carried out the duties of Foreign Secretary, wrote to the Admiral on the 31st:

> I am much obliged to you for letting me know that Colonel Maxse is to arrive in London this week. If he would call on me at the Foreign Office

on Saturday afternoon, say at three, I shall be very much obliged to him.
His friend Monsieur Marchand has had a great reception.[2]

This last comment referred to Marchand's recent arrival back in France.

Ivor's interview with Lord Salisbury lasted an hour and at the end he was asked to see Lord Balfour of Burleigh, a junior minister who was due to set off shortly to Balmoral, where he would presumably pass on some of Ivor's information to the Queen.

During his three months' leave, of which one was spent entirely in travelling to and from England, Ivor became engaged to the lady he had first met in 1894, on the day they had both careered round Olympia in Buffalo Bill's 'wild west' coach, the Honourable Mary Wyndham. They had seen each other quite often at social functions and staying in country houses in the intervening five years, but there were no serious signs of affection between them until this late stage. Known always by the nickname from her nursery days of 'Tiny', she was by now 28, and by the standards of her class at the time relatively old to get married. The privately printed biography *Mary Maxse, 1870 to 1944* records that: 'Mary grew up with a pretty figure, though she was never remarkably good-looking . . .'.[3] Although her intelligence, wit, and energy meant that she had many friends among the members of aristocratic 'Society', as described in Chapter 1, she was not one of the beauties who were quickly snapped up in marriage soon after 'coming out'. At the same time, her strong character and shrewdness would not allow her to accept any suitor without similar qualities, though it can be guessed that as the elder daughter of one of the largest and richest landowners in Britain she would have had attractions for many men in search of wives.

Lord Leconfield approved of the match, as did the Admiral, and a letter from Ivor from Petworth on 4 August, a few days before he set out on his return to the Sudan, dealt with the financial arrangements made by the two fathers. The Admiral promised £10,000 to the marriage settlement, while Lord Leconfield proposed to hand over £32,000 immediately with a further £8,000 payable to Mary when both he and his wife had died, Ivor ended his letter by reporting his father-in-law-to-be's insistence that '. . . nothing less than a joint income amounting to £2,000 a year (apart from military pay) would satisfy him for his daughter's sake'. All these amounts can be multiplied by 40 to give their values 100 years later.

Because of the rule in the Egyptian Army that no married officers could serve in it, the engagement was not officially announced at first. Ivor was anxious to be in the Sudan to command his battalion in the final operations to kill or capture the Khalifa and his few thousand remaining supporters. He therefore decided that for the time being his engagement should remain a secret, to avoid any possibility of being sent home before the last phase of Kitchener's campaign. On his return journey to

Omdurman, Ivor travelled up the Nile in the stern-wheel steamer *Zafir*, passing Metemma on 28 August, where the burnt-out, ruined remains of the town were still littered with the bones of the inhabitants massacred by Mahmud two years before. On the other hand, he was impressed by the work done to recultivate the surrounding rural areas, and noted the railway line now running up the east bank of the river. Soon after reaching Omdurman in early September, he was busy with preparations for an advance into Kordofan in pursuit of the Khalifa, and on the 22nd he wrote to his father to tell him that the expedition was about to set off. To his intense disappointment the operation was a failure, leading him to write a thoroughly dejected letter home on 1 November 1899, soon after return to base. Having explained the abortive attempt to catch the Khalifa, he went on to give his doubts about any further chance of active service in the Sudan for some time to come. Another setback to his hopes of furthering his career in a fighting zone reached him at the same time from the Regimental Headquarters of the Coldstream Guards, to whom he had sent a telegram asking for a chance to join the battalions recently sent to Cape Colony on the outbreak of the war in South Africa. He was told that there was no vacancy for him, and so he ended his letter with a gloomy forecast of his future:

> This means that I shall have to join the battalion now at home, and all chance of active service and a possible brevet seems to have gone. It's real bad luck. The battalion I commanded was in the forefront of the expedition [against the Khalifa]! However, such is soldiering! Can you be surprised if I look forward to at least the only consolation I know of – viz my marriage to Mary?

This proved to be the dark hour before a much brighter dawn. A few days after this letter had been sent off, rumours began to circulate in the bazaars of Omdurman that the Khalifa was advancing to attack the city – rumours which were confirmed by a report on November that his advance guard had reached Abba Island, roughly 200 miles south, and had fired at an Egyptian gunboat on the river. The next day a field force of roughly 2,400 men, with 900 local irregulars, was despatched down the Nile towards Abba Island. Ivor's 13th Sudanese Battalion and the 9th Sudanese were the infantry element, supported by a troop of cavalry, a camel corps detachment, a battery of artillery and six Maxims. Kitchener was in Cairo at the time but wired a message for Colonel Wingate, now Sir Reginald, to command the force. Disembarking well above the Island on 21 November, the Egyptian troops made a forced march of 60 miles to a watering place called El Gedid, just getting there ahead of the Dervish army on 24 November. Cut off from the water, the Khalifa decided to attack immediately. The ensuing battle was described by Ivor in an article written for Leo's *National Review*:

From the Dervish camp a mile and a half distant could be heard the war drums and at odd intervals the weird boom of the Khalifa's 'Ombeya' (a huge war horn made from an elephant's tusk) calling the faithful to arms. All accounts agree he was confident of victory, and the Arab and Sudanese prisoners I afterwards examined declare that when the Khalifa put himself at the head of his troops, all were convinced that they were on the winning side. The action took place about a mile and a half from the Dervish camp which thus escaped our bullets and my own belief is that the men decided to come out and attack us instead of awaiting our attack in order to safeguard their women and children.

After the fight, seeing that no further resistance was being offered, we advanced with every precaution towards the camp. We were met by a deputation of the enemy who throwing down their rifles asked for quarter for the whole force. One of the wounded Emirs told me that early in the engagement the Khalifa was grazed by a bullet in the hand, and so determined was he to carry out the attack that he concealed the wound by drawing his sleeve over it to prevent his followers being discouraged. He went forward into the thick of the fight where he fell struck by a splinter of shrapnel in the mouth and by a rifle bullet in the chest.[4]

Wingate's victorious force arrived back in Omdurman on 1 December with 3,000 prisoners. For Ivor it was the start of a hectic month, because on 3 December he received orders from the War Office to start for South Africa, where he was required for special duties in the recently declared war against the Boers, which at this stage was going disastrously wrong.

Notes

Letters from Maxse to his parents can be found at the WSRO, files 367, 368.

1 Bates, Darrell, *The Fashoda Incident of 1898* (OUP, 1984), p. 167.
2 The letter from Lord Salisbury is in the Maxse Papers, WSRO, File 368.
3 Gore, John, *Mary Maxse, 1870 to 1944*, p. 14.
4 *National Review*, (Jan., 1900).

8

The Boer War, 1899–1902

———————•◆•———————

In order to understand why the Boer War broke out in 1899 it is necessary to know something of the previous history of South Africa. There was a long saga of friction between the two dominant groups of white settlers: the Boers, meaning farmers who had been there since the Dutch East India Company took possession of the Cape of Good Hope in 1652, and the British, who had later annexed the territory in 1806 during the Napoleonic wars, as a result of French claims to it following the conquest of Holland by the armies of the Revolution. The first major event caused by this friction was the northward exodus in 1836 of many of the Boers, called *Voortrekkers*, into the territories later to be known as the Transvaal and the Orange Free State. Among various grounds for disagreement, the treatment of natives was high on the list, the slave-owning Boers being infuriated by the abolition of slavery in the Cape in 1833.

The sovereignty of the new territories was always in dispute. Both were recognized as Boer Republics in 1852, but in 1877 the British Government annexed the Transvaal. The ensuing first Boer War gave victory to the Afrikaners, following a crushing defeat of the British at Majuba Hill on 27 February 1881. Peace was patched up, and under the leadership of Paul Kruger the Transvaal gained its independence. Five years later, the discovery of gold in the Witwatersrand area in 1886 was to lead to yet another cause of friction. By 1896, in the 10 years that had passed since the first gold diggings, the Transvaal had progressed from near bankruptcy to being the richest state in South Africa. The people who had created this wealth were known by Kruger and the Boers who held the political power as *Uitlanders* or foreigners. They were of several

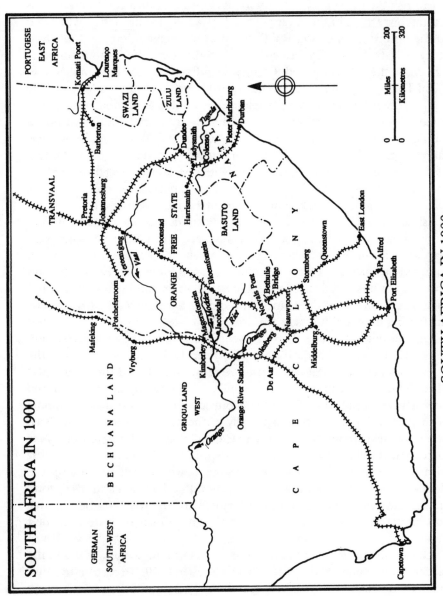

SOUTH AFRICA IN 1900

races, but the majority were British. Heavily taxed, and with no political rights, the *Uitlanders* grew restive under the relentlessly unsympathetic rule of Kruger's archaic Afrikanerdom. But they were not restive enough yet to risk their financial security in an uprising against the Boers. It was a total misreading of the extent of the *Uitlanders'* dissatisfaction which led to the notorious 'Jameson Raid' in 1896. Reducing a long and involved story to a few lines, Dr Jameson was at this time the administrator of Rhodesia, the colony created through the influence of the gold millionaire, Cecil Rhodes, at the time prime Minister of the Cape Colony, in the country then known as Matabeleland, and today as Zimbabwe. With a force of some 600 horsemen drawn mainly from the Rhodesian police with a few adventurers attached, such as Colonel Rhodes, Cecil's brother, Jameson crossed the Transvaal border north of Mafeking in the last hours of 31 December 1895. Undertaken with the aim of overthrowing the Boer government, after joining up with an expected force of rebellious *Uitlanders* in Johannesburg, the whole enterprise was amateurish and ill-considered, and soon ended in abject failure. Jameson and his men were stopped half way to their destination at a place called Doornkop and were arrested without firing a shot. The few rebels in Johannesburg were also rounded up speedily, and by 7 January 1896, all was over. Evidence soon appeared to link Cecil Rhodes' name to the affair, forcing his resignation as Prime Minister of the Cape, and ending his chance of bringing any further imperial ambitions to fruition.

On the political front the only beneficiaries of Jameson's expedition were the people against whom it had been launched, Kruger and the Boers. Kruger was indebted to it in three ways. It united the Boer 'volk' of the Transvaal behind him, ending all previous wrangling between various factions; it rallied all Boers living outside the Transvaal to the support of their traditional loyalties, especially in the neighbouring Orange Free State, but also among those living in Cape Colony; and it gave him cause to reorganise his citizen army and expend large sums on equipping it with new weapons. It was the sorry state in which so many among the Boer citizen soldiers had turned up to round up Jameson and his followers that gave the impetus to these reforms. Far from reducing Boer power and influence as intended, Jameson's abortive efforts only strengthened them.

During the three years that followed the Raid, the scene was gradually set for the opening of hostilities on 11 October 1899. To restore to some extent badly dented British prestige, the government in London sent out a new man in 1897 to be High Commissioner of South Africa and Governor of Cape Colony. This was Sir Alfred Milner, regarded as having one of the most brilliant intellects of his day, and known as a firm believer in the civilising mission of British imperialism. To Milner, the situation in South Africa was a mess: the result of 'a century of struggle for supremacy between Britain and Boer – and of abysmal blunders from the imperial standpoint.'[1] In his view, the only satisfactory remedy was to bring the whole country under strong, enlightened British rule, to which the Boers should be made to acquiesce either voluntarily or as a result of defeat in war. This concept of the whole country being united under one ruling authority was not on his side alone. Among the Afrikaners in all states, including those under direct British control in Cape Colony and Natal, there was a yearning for the day when the Boers would be supreme throughout the land. Although such aspirations had lain quiescent for many years in most areas apart from the Transvaal, the Raid inspired them with new life. And there was a movement already in existence to give further impetus to them. Founded in 1881 in Bloemfontein after the battle of Majuba Hill, the *Afrikaner Bond* was a political movement openly proclaiming its aims in the Transvaal and Orange Free State while keeping them 'under wraps' in Cape Colony and Natal. These aims were the elimination of British influence and the creation of a Boer republic over the whole of South Africa. The cause which eventually brought the two sides into open conflict was the continuing resentment of the *Uitlanders* on the Rand around Johannesburg. This came to a head in early 1899. Negotiations between Milner and Kruger at Bloemfontein from 31 May to 5 June failed to reach agreement on improved rights and conditions for the *Uitlanders*. Following the breakdown of the talks the possibility of war became of increasing concern to both sides. The Boers were already rearming as described earlier: Milner was anxious for British troops to be sent out to reinforce the small garrison of regular troops then stationed in South Africa. Throughout the summer of 1899 continuous pressure was maintained on the government at home to send out a powerful military force either to overawe the Boers, or be ready to conquer them if war became unavoidable. The first result of Milner's pleas was a small concession, while arguments still raged over the despatch of a large body of troops.

Through this small concession there was Maxse family involvement in the war from the very beginning. In July, the plan was hatched to send out a British officer with a small staff to raise a force of irregulars for the defence of Mafeking, the town on the railway line close to the Transvaal border, 180 miles due west of Pretoria, and not far from where Jameson had launched the Raid. The chosen commander was Colonel Robert Baden-Powell of the 5th Dragoons, and the two officers with him were Major (later General Sir) Alexander Godley and Lord Edward Cecil, 'Nigs', accompanied by Violet. His sister's presence at the Cape was to be useful to Ivor when he and Tiny came out later, while the friendship Violet herself created there with Milner was to lead in 22 years' time, after Lord Edward's death, to their marriage.

Two months passed before, on 8 September, the Cabinet authorised the first major reinforcement of the troops in South Africa by an addition of some 10,000 men drawn from India and various imperial outposts. By 18 September most of these were well on their way towards Durban to strengthen the defences of Natal. Four days later, on 22 September, the Cabinet took an even graver decision by ordering the despatch of the army's strategic reserve, I Corps, commanded by General Sir Redvers Buller, to Cape Colony. By 9 October the first men of this corps began arriving at Cape Town, followed by Buller himself, who arrived to a tumultuous welcome on 31 October.

The date 9 October was significant on another score. It was the day on which Kruger made war inevitable by handing to the British Agent in Pretoria an ultimatum which he must have known would never be accepted. It demanded the withdrawal of all troops from the Transvaal borders; the withdrawal from the whole of South Africa of any reinforcements who had arrived since June; and the turning back of those at the time sailing out from Britain. If not agreed to within 48 hours the Republic of the Transvaal would 'with great regret be compelled to regard the action as a formal declaration of war'.[2]

On 11 October 1899, as soon as the 48 hours had expired without British acceptance of the ultimatum, hostilities opened with Boer columns crossing into Cape Colony from both the Transvaal and the Orange Free State. By 14 October Mafeking and Kimberley were under siege. In Natal, the brigade at Glencoe was under threat. The events of the next two months, up to the time when Ivor was handing over command of his battalion in Omdurman before setting off for home, provided the British nation and its army with a series of nasty shocks. Although the soldiers from British ports, and their fellow countrymen welcoming them in Durban or Cape Town, might shout 'Remember Majuba', the commanders in the field failed to do so, and carelessly underestimated their enemies time and time again. An early victory at Elandslaagte, north-west of Ladysmith, on 21 October was followed by a series of humiliating defeats. The worst were at Ladysmith on 30 October, on the Modder River on 28 November, and then, in quick succession in one infamous 'Black Week', at Stormberg on 10 December, at Magersfontein the next day, and at Colenso on 15 December.

Ivor arrived in London on 14 December. While no doubt sharing the dismay of its citizens at the appalling news from South Africa, the preoccupation of organising his own private life must have absorbed most of his thoughts. He had sent a message to Tiny by telegraph from Alexandria during his journey home, asking her to arrange for the wedding to be held as soon as possible after his return. This she had done, and the ceremony took place at St George's, Hanover Square, on 18 December. After a short honeymoon the newly married couple sailed from Southampton in a gale on the 30th. At this point, it should be mentioned that Ivor had in fact told Kitchener about his plans to get married not long after his return to the Sudan in September 1899 in spite of the original intention to keep the engagement secret. No doubt he thought it unlikely that the secret could be kept for long, and that it was more sensible to break the news himself rather than have the Sirdar hear it at second hand. It proved a sound decision. His posting to South Africa was not affected, since he was one of the officers from the Sudan nominated by Kitchener for special duties with Buller's corps. Another was Seymour Vandeleur, who was home in time to be best man at the wedding. It was not until Ivor met up with Kitchener in South Africa during 1900 that he learnt the full story of how his posting came about. Kitchener's own arrival in the war zone was as Chief of Staff to Field Marshal Lord Roberts, famous for his victory at Kandahar in Afghanistan in 1879, and known throughout the army as 'Bobs'. The decision to send him out as Commander-in-Chief was made by the Cabinet on 18 December, following the news of Buller's defeat at Colenso. Salisbury made the recommendation that Kitchener should go with him. The two of them sailed on 23 December, and arrived in Cape Town on 10 January 1900. On their arrival Buller reverted to being commander only in Natal, as Roberts' subordinate. Violet was on the quayside when the steamer with the two famous generals on board docked in Cape Town harbour, and she recorded her impressions in a letter to her mother two days later:

It was wildly exciting, as the ships came nearer and nearer, trying to make out where Roberts and Kitchener were. The passenger decks were all under an awning so that they were difficult to see. At last Kitchener saw me and raised his hand and I waved mine and a sort of rustle of excitement went through the crowd which was some way off, kept back by police and soldiers; and then Roberts, very white haired, stepped out where we could see him and I wanted to cry, remembering all there is to remember about Roberts and Table Bay and his terrible private sorrow. After that everything was confused and the next thing I remember is Kitchener holding my hand tight and asking again and again after Nigs, and everyone saying 'How's Ladysmith?' and one's heart being very big with long pent up feeling. I believe the band played, but I never heard it.[3]

Roberts' terrible private sorrow was the death of his son Frederick, a subaltern in the 60th Rifles, at Colenso, the news of which had come to him almost simultaneously with his appointment as Commander-in-Chief.

Violet was now living in the mansion called Groote Schuur which Cecil Rhodes had built outside Cape Town, while he himself was besieged in Kimberley. She and Lady Charles Cavendish-Bentinck had been specially asked to stay on in the house as guardians when he had set off to

Kimberley in October. Their presence there was a blessing to Ivor and Tiny when they reached South Africa in mid-January 1900. Although there was not room for Tiny to move into Groote Schuur when Ivor went up-country to the battle zone, lodgings were found for her nearby, and she came to the big house for all her meals. Not long afterwards, Admiral Maxse came out. The hordes of well-to-do civilians who sailed out to see their friends and relations eventually became so great that Queen Victoria ordered Chamberlain to take steps to curb their numbers, especially the women. Such restrictions would never affect any of Violet's relations. As the Prime Minister's daughter-in-law, and a powerful personality in her own right, she was already influential with Kitchener and Milner, and from earlier acquaintance in Ireland had the ear of Roberts as well.

The special duty to which Ivor was soon appointed was with a transport column. Seymour Vandeleur was employed in the same way. The reason why ambitious officers from the Brigade of Guards with DSOs were used in this apparently unusual role are explained by Ivor in his biography of his friend. He begins by giving an outline of the plans made by Roberts as soon as he arrived in Cape Town:

> The Commander-in-Chief's plan was to strike at Bloemfontein in the heart of the Free State from the western railway between Orange River and Modder River, with 30,000 men – his object being to interpose this force between Cronje's 9,000 Boers at Magersfontein and Kimberley and their base. The march to Bloemfontein, 100 miles, would also place him in rear of 7,000 Boers near Colesberg and give him possession of the railway through the Free State. To be successful, this flank march within striking distance of Cronje must be sprung upon the Boers as a complete surprise and then be carried out with the utmost rapidity. To move slowly to a flank and give the enemy time to concentrate upon it at leisure was the very thing which Lord Roberts meant to avoid: and contrary to other experiences in the campaign, he did avoid it.[4]

He goes on to suggest that the successes achieved by Roberts, especially the first major one at the Battle of Paardeberg, on 18 February, which led to the surrender of Cronje and over 4,000 Boers, could not have been achieved without fundamental reorganisation of the army, in particular of the transport system. Since there are two conflicting views on the merit of this reorganisation of the transport both will be given, starting with Ivor's. He begins with a brief explanation of the method in use before Kitchener, the active instigator of the new scheme, made his changes:

> Each battalion, brigade and division was allotted a separate set of vehicles for its own exclusive use. The waggons when handed over to a battalion became practically its property during the campaign, and were looked after by one of its officers. Hence the system came to be called the regimental system, and was much favoured by regimental officers.

The waggons accompanied the battalion wherever it went but, as they only carried food for two days, required constant replenishing. This was provided for by *supply columns*, which accompanied the brigade or division, carrying rations to the regimental waggons from the real carriers of the army's food and forage – namely the *supply park*. The latter moved in rear and drew from the railways.

While admitting the advantages of the regimental system, Ivor's support for the changes is based on the fact that 'it wasted the waggons of the numerous battalions and brigades which have to remain stationary during long periods in any campaign'. The numerous units employed guarding railways, bridges and static installations needed only a few carts, while those on trek in pursuit of the Boers needed far more than their regulation scale of transport. His exposition of the case finishes with a description of the new methods, and of their efficacy:

> It was therefore decided to impound the regimental waggons, except the first line transport – viz.: water-carts, ammunition-carts, ambulances and the technical vehicles of engineer and other units, all of which are part of their indispensable equipment. The supply columns were likewise impounded from brigades and divisions, and the whole of the mule-waggons thus withdrawn were reformed into companies of forty-nine each, under a major or captain specially detailed to command them. Thus the mobile transport was amalgamated into one service under the Director of Transport, who also controlled the supply park, consisting of ox-waggons. Such a serious change on the eve of a campaign could only be justified by considerations of paramount weight, which were not at the time understood by the regimental officers whose waggons were taken from them, or by those departmental officers who were wedded to the system which they knew. . . .
>
> The ownership of the waggon is of minor importance provided the soldier is fed, and fed he was throughout the war with remarkable regularity, in spite of numerous difficulties, by the new companies which combined the duties of regimental transport and supply column under one officer. The latter's business was to maintain touch with the men he had to feed, however scattered they might be; to be posted with the latest information regarding probable moves and the position of the supply park; to replenish empty waggons wherever possible; to feed and care for his mules (ten to each waggon); to pay his non-commissioned officers and Cape-boys; and to know exactly where all his waggons were when detached on odd jobs. It meant plenty of work for an active man during such a campaign as we were engaged in, and necessitated an intelligent appreciation of coming events.[5]

In direct opposition is the case put forward by Thomas Pakenham in his masterly book *The Boer War* where he draws on evidence given to the *Royal Commission on the War in South Africa*, and other sources recorded in his notes. He begins with some criticism of Roberts' generalship, before coming to the matter of transport:

> His sweeping changes in the system of transport and supply were to prove one of the great blunders of the war.
>
> Strange to say, for the two most famous British soldiers of the period, neither he nor Kitchener knew much about the working of the British army. They were both, in a way, outsiders. Bobs, the 'sepoy general', had lived all his army life in India. Kitchener, the Sirdar, had served too long, in both senses, in the wilderness. As a result, they did not understand the War Office system of transport and supply adopted in South Africa: the so-called 'regimental', or decentralized, system. The key to this system was that each battalion CO was made responsible for their day-to-day food supplies, each battalion had a transport officer, and the system was integrated into the normal army organisation. Roberts and Kitchener shared two crucial misconceptions about the system. They believed that to allow each battalion its own carts must be extremely wasteful in transport, not realizing that the system had proved quite flexible enough for battalion transport to be recalled at any time by the superior officer who had overall charge of transport. Nor had they grasped the existence of the non-regimental transport, the brigade's supply columns. Apart from the 'first-line' regimental transport (with ammunition and fighting material), they decided to sweep away the system completely. Instead they created a 'general transport' system, an extraordinary makeshift in which largely untrained transport officers, hustled into mule-cart and ox-waggon companies, were to supply all the different needs of the army.
>
> When a highly technical part of the army system, evolved and refined over a long period, is suddenly replaced in the middle of a war, there is bound to be trouble. And trouble there was. Kitchener, K of K, became known as 'K of chaos'. The professional transport officers prophesied disaster. They did not have to wait long.[6]

Pakenham's criticisms fail to appreciate the enormous experience already gained in other parts of the world by both Roberts and Kitchener in the moving of armies across desolate, inhospitable terrain. Both had infinitely more practical knowledge of such work than those who had developed 'the War Office system of transport and supply'. Indeed Kitchener's campaign in the Sudan owed its success far more to his understanding and mastery of systems of transport and supply than any tactical ability. Those who had served there with him had devoted most of their energies to matters of administration and troop movement, so that to describe men of the calibre of Maxse and Vandeleur as 'largely untrained transport officers', while possibly correct from an official War Office standpoint, was in practice far from the truth. The fairest summing up of this conflict of opinion about the reorganisation of the transport system is to say that it was necessary, but that the need to carry it out in a hurry while operations were already under way led inevitably to some confusion. Kitchener might become 'K of Chaos', but the changes had to be made, especially for the support of Roberts' advance on Bloemfontein.

Ivor's posting was to F Transport company at Orange River Station, which he took over on 25 January while it was still in the process of formation. Writing to Tiny on 6 February he thanked her for all her letters which he described as his 'one consolation in a sea of endless matters of detail' that had occupied him since his arrival. He went on to say:

> This transport service is quite interesting as long as one has lots to do and can see oneself progressing towards an ultimate success, in a matter vital to the big move forwards. That is one's only satisfaction. The thing is being run on good sound lines: but of course when it is running, the part played by an individual in command of a company will be small and narrow and somewhat uninteresting.

Four days later, and before either anyone expected or the army was really ready, the 'big move forwards' began. It was not until 18 February that Ivor was able to write again. He told how he had received sudden orders at Orange River on the 10th to accompany Colonel Hannay and his Mounted Infantry brigade. Put in charge of the three transport companies covering the brigade's food, forage and baggage for five days, he had plenty to keep him occupied:

> The first night's march was a trying one and there was no sleep for the O. C. Transport, for each wagon (and there were some 150 of them) had to be brought across a drift with double the number of mules – viz 20 instead of 10. Starting at 9 p.m. on the 10th we thus reached Rondeval on the Orange River at 10 a.m. on the 11th and next day our force was the first to cross over into the Orange Free State where we have been ever since.

On 23 February Ivor wrote to his new father-in-law, Lord Leconfield, from Paardeberg Drift on the Modder River, where the action was in progress which shortly afterwards led to the surrender of the Boer General Cronje and over 4,000 of his followers. In this letter he described how the transport companies operated:

> . . . each company comprised 54 wagons. A buck wagon is drawn by 10 mules and driven by a Cape boy on the box called 'driver' and another Cape boy called 'leader' runs alongside and helps in various way – either by using a very long whip with scientific agility, or by running to the head of the leading pair of mules and keeping them straight at difficult places, or by running to the back of the four wheeled buck wagon and putting on the brake and loosening it quickly in going over 'drifts'.

Where possible, he moved his own company across the veldt in four or six parallel columns 'so as to shorten the length of column on the line of march and make it easier for the military escort to defend'. In respect of the matter of length of columns he pointed out that, if all the ox and mule wagons with the army were ordered to march the 100 miles from Kimberley to Bloemfontein, the first would reach its destination before the last had begun the journey.

During the following four months, Roberts' army advanced over 400 miles north-west, with the railway line as its axis, finally entering Pretoria on 5 June 1900. Ivor remained with the mounted infantry all the time, at one stage coming under General John French's command on attachment to his cavalry force, and later as part of the mounted infantry division of two brigades set up in April under Ian Hamilton.

Ivor's letters during the four months of the advance throw interesting light on several aspects of the campaign. The over-hasty beginning is mentioned in one from Bloemfontein on 10 March. He writes about a report in which Kitchener considered that another two weeks should have been spent in making proper preparation in February for the commencement of operations. He lays the blame on famous shoulders:

> I myself believe that Cecil Rhodes was responsible for the too early start. One of his own particular friends, straight from dining with him at Kimberley came to breakfast with me at Paardeberg before Cronje's surrender and volunteered it was Rhodes who had the articles written in the Kimberley papers which gave the impression that the civil population there meant to give up the place. This 'friend' of Rhodes thought it was a clever trick to get such articles written, so as to 'hurry up the military'.

Given that Violet was living in Rhodes' house and that she was eating her meals there, Tiny no doubt kept this information to herself at the time of receiving it, although it must have reached her only a few days before she sailed for home. Her decision to leave Cape Town was applauded by Ivor in a letter of 23 March, in which he also expressed hopes that Mafeking would soon be relieved, allowing Nigs to rejoin Violet for a short holiday, after which his sister 'should go home for good'.

By this time the Admiral had arrived in Bloemfontein and was staying at a hotel. While pleased to have obtained permission from Roberts for his father's visit, Ivor was not so amused when the old man then arranged for Violet and Lady Charles Bentinck to be invited to visit Bloemfontein as well. They did not stay long, and Ivor was soon able to report that his sister and her friend had been sent off south again. He considered 'that ladies are out of place in a military camp' and was glad to see them go.

From a camp two miles north of Bloemfontein, he wrote on 6 April to explain why the army was so inactive after the first stage of the campaign had been completed successfully. The reason why 40,000 men were sitting in the Orange Free State doing so little was simply 'that we do not have the horses nor the mules to move against the enemy with'. Putting most blame on the statesmen at home for the failure to supply animals to replace those lost in action and on the line of march, Ivor ended by stating that 'we are now an immobile mass – the worst state an army can be in'.

The Commander-in-Chief's entourage was becoming something of a laughing stock throughout the army, as explained in a letter of 20 April:

> Roberts seems daily to increase the number of his staff without in the least augmenting their efficiency. I fancy he cannot say 'no' to anyone who wants to join him. The last addition is the Duke of Marlborough who was not wanted anywhere else by anyone. R's staff is now a source of merriment to the army, especially since Lady R and the two girls have joined it: the 'banjo players' and the men who are conspicuous for 'parlour tricks' and extra obsequious manners, are now all agog for commands of divisions and brigades. Fortunately K is there and still has influence.

Reference to the Duke of Marlborough is followed in a letter of 2 May by mention of his cousin Winston Churchill, of whose obsession with self-publicity an example is given:

> . . . so keen is he to obtain advertisement that he actually went up to Julian Ralph of the *Daily Mail* and begged him to write in the D. M. a disparaging article on himself – in order that W. Churchill might write a rejoinder!! Ralph was quite disgusted with him, both in manner and tone, & refused to have anything to do with it.

The next day, 3 May, the advance towards Pretoria was resumed. On 4 May a flying column under Colonel Bryan Mahon was sent off to the north-west and 11 days later raised the siege of Mafeking on the 15th. News of the relief of this relatively insignificant outpost caused an outburst of rejoicing at home quite out of proportion to its importance, with crowds dancing in the streets of London. Accompanying Hamilton's force, travelling to the east of the railway line, Ivor's work was of a less glamorous nature. His first chance to write a letter came on 13 May, when a rest was ordered on the tenth day since setting out. The column was now between Kroonstad and Lindley on the Valsch River, having covered 150 miles since leaving Bloemfontein. He described the crossing of the Zand River on 9 May, which provides another picture of the extent of his responsibilities:

> Hamilton ordered me to start the transport from camp. I got its head into the drift just as the last guns of the horse artillery crossed, and from that moment, [viz noon] until 11 a.m. next morning one continuous stream of transport was crossing by that drift, wagon by wagon for 23 solid hours. I remained there in charge till most of it was across and a pretty rough time it was and precious cold.

A further 170 miles north, the army entered Johannesburg on 31 May 1900. As they neared the city, Ivor had a fall from his horse and broke his arm. He stayed with his transport for a further week until Pretoria was captured on 5 June, but the next day wrote to say that he had been made 'a fixture for 10 days to rest and cure my arm'. In the event he was to remain a fixture in the area for the rest of his time in South Africa. Shortly after the city was taken over, Ivor's recent commander in the Sudan, now Major General J G Maxwell, was appointed Military Governor of Pretoria and district. He immediately asked for the brigade major who had lately helped him in the cleaning up of Omdurman to be made his Commissioner of Police. At the same time Ivor heard that he had at last been given his brevet as a lieutenant colonel, the accolade he had been so anxious to receive for over two years. On 26 June he sent a jubilant telegram to Tiny to announce his new appointment.

In his telegram, he gave brief news of Tiny's brother Charles having a slight fever, and also asked for news of the Admiral's health. The answer reached him next day in a telegram, which must have crossed with his, telling him that his father had died. During his stay in Africa the Admiral had been in good health, but somewhere had picked up a fatal typhoid infection. This struck him soon after his arrival home at the end of April, though at first his illness did not seem too serious. In June, his condition worsened rapidly, and he died at Dunley on the 26th. In spite of their long estrangement his widow was deeply upset by his death, while his daughter Olive took it so hard that Violet was forced to leave her exciting life at the centre of activity in Cape Town to go home to console her sister. A letter from Clemenceau was needed to remind her of this duty: he wrote: 'Why are you not in England where Olive greatly needs you?'[7] Up in Pretoria, Ivor wrote on the evening he received the news that it was a 'knock down blow' which made him feel 'that for the time being I don't quite seem to know where I am'. He was fortunate to be starting an interesting and demanding job which left little time for thinking too much about his father's death.

In setting up the new police force all Ivor's fierce energy and considerable organising ability were given an outlet which he found thoroughly satisfying. Not only did the demands of his work cause him to forget his father's death, but they also helped him to ignore continuing pain in his arm and a general deterioration in his health after four years of hard living in unfriendly climates at either end of Africa. The extent of his new responsibilities he explained in a letter to Tiny dated 5 July 1900, which started by saying that: 'I now have 26 officers and 740 men under me – mostly colonials and yeomanry.' He went on to provide more details:

The work is most diversified as I have the following entirely under my personal control – (1) Constabulary, foot and mounted, which polices this town and neighbourhood and is responsible for all law and order: (2) The Gaol and lock-up: (3) The Detective and Secret Service departments: (4) The enrolment of all officers and men for the future Transvaal Constabulary, which in my opinion should number 3,000 to 5,000 officers, N. C. Officers and men.

Towards the end of July, Maxwell received a letter about police organisation from the Military Governor of Johannesburg, which he passed on to Ivor for his comments. The long, detailed paper dated 30 July which he received in reply provided a clear picture of how Ivor had arranged the selection, discipline and administration of the Pretoria constabulary, and ended with the submission 'that the police for the whole Transvaal should be organised under one authority'. On 8 August, a letter to Tiny told of a successful operation to forestall an attempt to kidnap Lord Roberts and hand him over to a party of Boers waiting on the veldt outside Pretoria. The leading figures in the plot were officers of the Boer Transvaal Artillery who were left behind 'on parole' to hand over guns and forts when Botha pulled out of the town in June. Because they had stayed on voluntarily the conditions of their parole were not arduous. All the plotters were rounded up before any damage was done, and in due course the leader, a German called Hans Cordua, was court-martialled and shot. The case attracted a great deal of publicity at the time.

Early in September, Mary's brother Charles Wyndham, who had returned to England, sent a telegram asking Ivor to obtain leave to come home and sort out his father's will and problems with the estate at Dunley Hill. At first his application for leave was refused by Roberts, and he was told that he would have to wait. It was not long, however, before the reason for delaying his departure became clear. Baden-Powell, the hero of Mafeking and now a major general, had been appointed commander of all the police forces in South Africa. He was touring all the states and provinces under his newly created authority and everywhere, as Ivor put it in a letter on 23 September. 'B-P is being fêted, and it's a thing he loves and cannot resist indulging in'. The great man arrived in Pretoria on 29 September, and a letter written a week later told how the result of his visit was to put Ivor on the horns of a dilemma:

I have just spent three days with Baden-Powell, during which I have been taking him round and showing him everything which I have been working at during the past four months. He was I think extremely pleased with all he saw, especially with the results – namely that I have got a regularly organised force fit to be expanded into anything which may be required.

B-P expected to find nothing – and this would have meant that he would have had to begin at the beginning, just as I did when I was appointed on 7th June . . .

He had written to Lord Roberts and asked him that I may be allowed to accept service in the new 'South African Constabulary' in spite of my probable appointment as a 2nd in command of a Coldm Battn: and he has asked Lord R that this may be arranged in such a manner as not to preclude me from commanding my battalion when the time comes. He has also offered me the post of being 2nd in command of the whole S. A. Constabulary – consisting of some 8,000 mounted men and some artillery under himself – and at the same time its Chief Staff Officer.

Having heard in the meantime that his leave had now been approved, he ended the letter by saying that he had asked B-P to keep the post open for him until he arrived home, when he promised to send a telegram with a definite 'Yes' or 'No'. Although he had finished with a sentence saying that nothing needed to be decided until he had seen Tiny and had been to the War Office, in the event he had made up his mind before he left South Africa. No doubt as a result of time for reflection during the long train journey from Pretoria to the coast, and prompted by the poor state of his health, he was ready to send a telegram to Tiny, on arrival on 12 October at Cape Town, saying: 'Decided accept second-in-command Coldstream. Will wire date sailing from Cape Town on leave. Ivor.' What some of his contemporaries might have referred to as his 'bush-whacking days' were over for good.

Notes

The letters quoted in this chapter can be found in the Maxse papers at the WSRO in file 53.

1 Pakenham, Thomas, *The Boer War* (Weidenfeld & Nicolson, 1979), p. 14.
2 Pakenham, p. 103.
3 Milner, Viscountess, *My Portrait Gallery, 1886–1901* (John Murray, 1951), p. 161.
4 Maxse, Colonel F I, *Seymour Vandeleur* (National Review, 1905), p. 258.
5 Maxse, pp. 261–2.
6 Pakenham, p. 318.
7 Milner, p. 215.

Peacetime Soldiering

9

Mainly Regimental
Duty, 1901–10

———•◆•———

On arrival home in England in November 1900, Ivor did not take up the expected appointment as second-in-command of a Coldstream battalion, but instead was posted to the War Office in the mobilisation department. During the following two and a half years there was time to enjoy his private life with Tiny to the full. Soon after his return they bought a house in London at No 2, Gloucester Place, Portman Square. There on 17 October 1901, their son John, first of three children, was born. One of his godfathers was Lord Kitchener, though a letter from Tiny to her mother suggests that the great man failed to keep at least one appointment to see his new godson.

In January 1901 Queen Victoria died in the 64th year of her reign, believing that victory had been achieved in South Africa. She was fortunately spared the need to witness the further 16 months of bitter struggle before the Boer War finally came to an end. Of less national importance, but of more significance to Ivor and Tiny was the death of her father in the same month. Her brother Charles now succeeded as the third Lord Leconfield. The friendship between Ivor and Charles is mentioned in the book *Mary Maxse, 1870–1944*, with a comment on their shared interests. The author also records that

> . . . right up to the First World War, a regular and welcome fixture of the Maxse's year was a two month visit by all the family to Petworth, a visit which embraced Christmas and all January and, coinciding with Ivor's winter leave, was devoted to hunting and children's parties.

The leisurely pace of life compared to the demands of his military duties during the previous five years gave Ivor the opportunity to start work on his book *Seymour Vandeleur*, soon after hearing the news of his great friend's death on 31 August 1901 in a train ambush near Pretoria. The early chapters covering Vandeleur's travels in Uganda and Nigeria comprise about a third of the book, and required considerable research and reading before they could be written. In this he was greatly helped by Tiny, who also wrote some sections of the book for him. The two-thirds covering the Sudan campaign and the Boer War were, as already shown, as much Ivor's own story as that of his friend. The book was completed in 1904, and published by Leo's *National Review* in 1905.

During 1902, Ivor was approached by Sir Reginald Wingate in connection with the 'finale' of the Sudan campaign at the battle of El Gedid on 24 November 1899, during which the Khalifa was killed. The reason was that Wingate, who had commanded that operation, had received a request from Winston Churchill for help in connection with a revised edition of his book *The River War*. The first edition had been published in 1899, too early to tell the story of the 'finale'. Churchill wished to bring it into the second edition. A slightly strange series of letters followed, starting with one from Wingate's house at 31, Great Cumberland Place on 26 June 1902 to 'My dear Maxse':

> Perhaps we could combine business with pleasure if you could look in here at about 10.15 a.m. Sunday next – Winston Churchill has asked me to give him some detail for his revision of *The River War* about the 'finale' of the Khalifa and I have suggested he looks in for a half hour chat before church, and I would much like to have you beside me to jog my memory over points connected with our little expedition.

Next comes a letter dated 28 June to Ivor thanking him for a copy of that article in the *National Review* from which there is a section quoted in Chapter 5. Finally Wingate wrote on 2 July 1902:

> W. Churchill was particularly reticent about meeting you and under the circumstances I did not like to press it. He carried off your article on the 'finale' but I hope he will return it. I wish you could have guided him – but I take it he prefers going his own way.

One can only speculate on why Churchill should have been unwilling to meet the man who had commanded the 13th Sudanese Battalion which had played such an important part in the defeat of the Khalifa. Possibly he knew of Ivor's disapproval of the charge of the 21st Lancers at Omdurman, in which Churchill had taken part, and also of his notoriously self-advertising conduct as a war correspondent in South Africa. Although reluctant to meet Ivor, he made good use of the *National Review* article, on which he clearly relied heavily for details in recounting his own story of the last stages of the Sudan campaign in his usual, fluent style. In the spring of 1903, Ivor was posted to the 3rd Battalion Coldstream Guards as second-in-command. Formed in 1898, this battalion had acted in a holding and training cap⌐city during the Boer War, as well as carrying out public duties in London, while the 1st and 2nd battalions were on active service. Ivor did not stay long with the 3rd Battalion for on 29 November he took command of the 2nd Battalion now based at Ramillies Barracks, Aldershot, having moved there on return from South Africa the previous October.

Ivor's arrival was not greeted at first with great enthusiasm. He had only spent four and a half years serving with the regiment before taking command, and until the short period just completed with the 3rd Battalion had been on extra-regimental employment for some seven years. Not only that, but the first formative period of his commissioned service, during which young officers usually make their mark in their regiments, had been spent with the Royal Fusiliers. It was not long, however, before his officers and men learnt to appreciate his qualities. Along with his sharp tongue and intolerance of inefficiency they discovered that he had a genuine interest in the welfare of all ranks, and a warmer nature than appeared on the surface. He soon set about enthusing his battalion with his ideas on training, and demonstrated an original approach to some aspects. A good example is the way in which he improved the rifle shooting in the battalion, which was of a very low standard when he took over.

Knowing that a move from Aldershot to Windsor would soon take place and that there, as in London, there were no proper ranges within reasonable distance, he decided that a miniature range should be provided, although the official military view at the time was that such ranges were of no practical value. On a visit to Windsor before the move, his first step was to persuade the garrison engineer to build a wall to stop the bullets at the end of the range. Since this would be what was known as an 'encroachment' he had to agree to have it taken down at his own expense on leaving the barracks, if the next commanding officer to arrive did not wish to keep it. Money was then needed to construct the range itself and purchase small-bore rifles and other equipment, but there were no official funds available. Sir John Hall's book *The Coldstream Guards 1885–1914* explains how Ivor overcame the problem:

> The initial difficulties being thus overcome, he assembled his battalion and put the case before them. Would they consent, he asked, to a small stoppage amounting to about two days pay during the course of the year, in furtherance of his scheme? No further payments, he assured them, would be demanded, and ammunition on the miniature range would be provided free of charge and on so liberal a scale that the whole battalion could, if it were desired, fire continuously from breakfast to 'lights out'. No question of parading would arise; any man wishing to practise could stroll down to the range, attired as he saw fit, and there

find rifle and ammunition awaiting him. For the next quarter of an hour they could regard themselves as a republic and talk the matter over and at the end of that time he should ask them to vote 'yes' or 'no'. During the prescribed fifteen minutes the subject was eagerly discussed by the men and when in due course, Col Maxse called for silence and a show of hands he learnt to his intense satisfaction that they were unanimously in favour of his experiment. Henceforward shooting on the miniature range became a favourite pastime of the whole battalion. So popular was it as a sport that competitions, the expenses of which could lawfully be defrayed by the canteen funds, were organized and evoked the keenest speculation.[2]

The dramatic improvement in the battalion's marksmanship became evident when it won the McCalmont Cup at the London District Rifle Meeting in 1905, and was classified as the best shooting battalion in the whole of the home-based army in 1906. On each move of station during his tour of command Ivor had miniature ranges constructed, and it was due to his initiative that small-bore shooting was eventually given official approval throughout the whole army.

After taking part in various field exercises during the summer of 1904, the 2nd Coldstream joined I Corps in Aldershot for the main army manoeuvres that year. The corps marched through Alton and Winchester to Southampton where it was embarked on 10 transport vessels. Accompanied by a cruiser squadron the force sailed up the Channel and round the coasts of Kent, before striking north-west to land at Clacton-on-Sea on the Essex coast. Unfortunately, this invasion force was deemed to have failed in the attacks made against the defending troops, and in due course was obliged to withdraw and sail back to Southampton. Soon after returning to Windsor at the end of these manoeuvres, Ivor's battalion once more changed its home on moving to Wellington Barracks in London.

1904 was an important year for Tiny. Her second son, Fred was born in January in London. The family had moved back to the house at 2, Gloucester Place when Ivor's battalion went to Windsor, which was also convenient for the next posting to Wellington Barracks.

The other big event in Tiny's life was a visit to Joe Chamberlain's family home at Highbury, Birmingham in July 1904. As described earlier, the Maxses and the Chamberlains had been close friends for two generations. During the visit there was much discussion of Joe's campaign for tariff reform, designed to give preference to goods imported from countries in the Empire, so strengthening both their own economies and the bonds which bound them to Britain. Tiny showed such enthusiasm for the idea during the discussions that a few days after the visit she was invited by Viscount Ridley, then the chairman of the Tariff Reform League, to join the council of the women's branch. She accepted this invitation readily, and for many years this movement was a major interest in her life.[3]

After a successful period of musketry training at Pirbright in the summer of 1905, culminating in the success at the London District Rifle Meeting already mentioned, the 2nd Coldstream returned to Windsor in October.

Soon after settling in, a detachment of the battalion took part in a river crossing on the Thames arranged in the form of a competition against 'C' Squadron of the Life Guards. A large crowd turned out to watch the 60 troopers undress and swim their horses across from the racecourse in 17 minutes. Meanwhile 50 Coldstreamers, who had constructed a raft, crossed in two relays in 15 minutes to win. The *Guards Magazine* commented that the passage of rivers and canals by swimming was then very fashionable.[4]

In 1905, the birth of a daughter, Violet, named after her aunt, completed the family. Tiny was by this time 35, which was considered on the elderly side for child-bearing in those days. Ivor was now 43, which was then young for a lieutenant colonel already two years into a four-year tour of command of a battalion. Writing from Windsor on 24 January 1906 to Tiny at Petworth, Ivor told of royal invitations to the Castle:

> The King has been more than civil to me. When I dined there on Sunday he sent for me after dinner, sat me down and talked alone for more than half an hour, asking my opinion especially about the men, the affairs, and the general situation in the Brigade of Guards. Also my views about Aldershot. Luckily I possess pretty definite opinions on these points so was able to give them clearly.

On another occasion shortly afterward, he was asked to shoot in Windsor Park. He finished his account of the day by saying that he had been asked if Tiny would be with him, and that he wished she could have been. He then gave his verdict on the duties of those in full-time royal service: 'I like that sort of thing occasionally, but what a life an equerry leads all the year round! It is appalling to contemplate!'

For the summer of 1906, the Maxses took a large rambling house near Windsor called Down Place with grounds running down to the Thames. Tiny's mother joined them and they entertained on what Tiny's biographer calls 'rather a large scale'. No doubt Lady Leconfield's contribution to the household expenses was appreciated, as well as the work of the servants she brought with her. Given the importance attached to entertaining in style during the Edwardian era, Ivor's reputation must have been considerably enhanced by these activities in the eyes of people able to advance his career – which cannot have been entirely fortuitous!

On the military side, rifle shooting was again Ivor's main preoccupation during 1906. During the year the battalion was issued with the short Lee Enfield rifle and the long sword bayonet that went with it. The rifle, with slight modifications was to be the British Army's main personal weapon for the next 50 years, though a shorter bayonet came into use during the Second World War.

After recording their successes at the London District and National Rifle Association meetings at Bisley in the summer, the 2nd Coldstream moved back again to Ramillies Barracks, Aldershot in October 1906. The miniature range Ivor promptly had built on arrival was opened in November by General Sir John French, the Commander-in-Chief, Southern Command.

Ivor's tour of command came to an end in March 1907. Its successful completion was marked by his promotion, and appointment to be Regimental Lieutenant Colonel Coldstream Guards, a post requiring some explanation, starting with the fact that the incumbent was a 'full' rather than 'lieutenant' colonel! Ivor took up his duties in a building in Wellington Barracks where, alongside the Grenadiers and Scots Guards, in Osbert Sitwell's words . . . 'he possessed as his headquarters an appropriate shrine, a kind of small Greek temple in stucco, with fluted pillars and capitals of the Doric order, placed, as if for the sake of inviolability, behind the stout, spear-like iron railings of Birdcage Walk.'[5]

From Regimental Headquarters Ivor commanded the three Coldstream battalions in respect of all matters concerned with their manning, daily running, discipline, recruiting, and postings, both inter-battalion and extra-regimental employment. In London, this authority was extended further to include direct command of the battalions stationed there in respect of all duties and training, under the direction of the Major General commanding London District. Outside London, those aspects were the concern of the commanders of the Guards Brigades to which the battalions might be posted. In 1907 the final steps were being taken to create, from the volunteers and militia who had to date composed the army's part-time, home-based reserves, a new organisation called the Territorial Army. This body, coming into existence in 1908, was made up of brigades and divisions, based on the military districts into which the country was then divided. As an additional appointment, Ivor was put in command of the new 3rd London Territorial Brigade, composed of the 9th, 10th, 11th, and 12th London Battalions of the Royal Fusiliers. In August 1908 he went to annual camp with the brigade at Larkhill on Salisbury plain, and lodged with one of the battalions. In a letter to Tiny, staying at Alcombe Hall near Minehead on the north Somerset coast, he mentioned that the food 'at my Territorial Army is the worst I ever saw', but ended by saying: 'The first week went off very well in camp here and yesterday I was very well satisfied with the Field Day and with the way my men worked.'

Earlier that summer the ceremonial responsibility of his position as Regimental Lieutenant Colonel had led to his selection to command the King's Birthday parade in June when it was the turn of a Coldstream battalion to provide the Escort to the Colour. Edward VII took a great interest in all aspects of ceremonial duties, especially details of uniform, and on these matters Ivor might be called upon occasionally to report to the King direct, in his capacity as Colonel-in-Chief of all regiments in the Brigade, although normally General Sir Frederick Stephenson, the Colonel of the Coldstream, would be the link with the monarch.

In spite of being on good terms with Edward VII, Ivor became involved with a cause in 1909 which did not meet with the approval of his son, the Prince of Wales. It was an odd matter to bring forward, and either Ivor's good judgment was lacking on this occasion, or perhaps his sense of humour got the better of him! In May 1909, a special War Office committee was considering the granting of additional Battle Honours to any regiments which could produce good evidence for being accorded them. At the head of a conventional list Ivor submitted the battle of *Dunbar, 1650*, when General Monk's regiment, the forerunner of the Coldstream Guards, had helped Oliver Cromwell to defeat a Scottish army fighting for the future Charles II. Aware, as he wrote in a circular to all officers of the regiment, that this claim 'may perhaps meet with some slight opposition', he composed a length document in support of this submission. However, on 21 June 1909 a letter from the private secretary to the Prince of Wales, who was dealing with many matters on behalf of his already ailing father, knocked the application firmly on the head:

> His Royal Highness . . . cannot help thinking it would have been a pity to place amongst all the glorious distinctions which the Coldstreams [sic] have earned, the name of a battle which was fought by a Republican Army against one which was fighting for their lawful King, who was afterwards to occupy the Throne.

The private secretary, a Grenadier named Frederick Ponsonby, followed his regiment's usual custom in putting an 's' at the end of Coldstream, which must have made the letter mildly annoying to Ivor, as no doubt intended!

For his 3rd London TA brigade, Ivor produced a directive headed *Company Training 1909*. In it he gave expression to the ideas which he had developed in the Sudan about the importance of the junior leader at the company and section level keeping the same men with him at all times and being personally responsible, under proper supervision, for training them himself. Two extracts from the directive sum up what might be called his training philosophy at the unit level:

> As the time available and the outdoor opportunities in London are limited, it is essential that every captain should think out before the hour of parade exactly how he means to employ his men. He should realise that training their intelligence and practising his NCOs in field work is more important than drill and more difficult to acquire. He should also recollect that there is only one method of learning how to command men, namely, to constantly take command of them.

He then went on to give instructions as to how section commanders were to keep records of their men, and if possible to recruit them themselves, before moving on to state that:

> The efficiency of a battalion will be judged by the progress made by its independent companies at the annual camp, and I propose during the first week of camp to test the handiness of every company in outposts, defensive positions and attack formation. The quality of section commanders in these important duties will be carefully noted.

These were themes to which he constantly returned in directives, lectures, and training manuals throughout his service.

As 1909 came to a close, Ivor's eyes were lifted towards a further goal to be achieved in his professional advancement. He knew that command of 1st Guards Brigade in Aldershot would become vacant in the late summer of 1910, and he set about ensuring that when that occurred he would be the next incumbent of this prestigious post. In his determination to satisfy this ambition he pulled every possible string, and lobbied every individual who might help his cause. Also anxious to be given the appointment was Colonel F Romilly, Regimental Lieutenant-Colonel Scots Guards, who was hard at work along similar lines. In the end Ivor was successful, and was ordered to take over the brigade in August 1910. One of his last duties as the Lieutenant Colonel, took place on 19 July 1910 shortly after the death of Edward VII, when he was called to see the new King, George V, at Marlborough House, where he was still living. The King handed over to Ivor a magnificent silver-gilt cup, which had originally been presented in 1807 to the Duke of York to mark his retirement from the Colonelcy of the Coldstream Guards after 21 years in the post in 1805. The cup had passed on his death in 1827 to his nephew, the Duke of Cambridge, who in turn died in 1904. It was sold at Christies shortly afterwards by the Duke's family and purchased by a Bond Street dealer. From the dealer it came into the hands of a private person who approached the King through the Keeper of the Privy Purse with a view to returning the cup to the Royal Family, as long as his name remained a secret. It was then agreed that the cup should return to the regiment whose officers had originally subscribed to have it made. Ivor wrote two memoranda on the subject: one secret one with the whole story for the benefit of future Lieutenant Colonels. and a second one for general information to the rest of the regiment. This second memorandum ended with his account of receiving the cup from the new monarch with the hope that '. . . this, the King's first act as their Colonel-in-Chief, marks the commencement of a long period of devoted service to His Majesty's person and Throne by the Coldstream Regiment of Foot Guards.' It was a nice note on which to end his three years as the Regimental Lieutenant Colonel before moving onto his next more active and demanding tour of duty.

Notes

Letters and documents quoted, other than those shown above, are in the possession of the family or can be found at the WSRO, file 339.

1 Gore, John, Mary *Maxse 1870–1944* (Rolls House, 1946), p. 43.
2 Hall, Colonel Sir John, *The Coldstream Guards, 1885–1914* (Clarendon Press, 1929), p. 314.
3 Gore, p. 50.
4 *Guards Magazine*, Oct. 1906, p. 537.
5 Sitwell, Osbert, *Great Morning* (Reprint Society, 1949), p. 182.

10

Command of 1st Guards Brigade at Aldershot, 1910–14

———— •◆• ————

One of Ivor's first requirements on taking over his brigade at the beginning of August 1910, was to find a suitable house in the Aldershot area for the family to occupy during the four years of his tour of command. He was fortunate to find Farnborough Park, which Tiny described in a letter to her mother as 'most charming', the only drawback being that 'it will want acres of carpets and curtains as the rooms are very large and high'. She ended the letter by asking her mother to urge everyone she knew to help find a buyer for the house in Gloucester Place in London.[1]

Although designated a Guards Brigade, there were only two Guards battalions in Ivor's new command, the 2nd Grenadiers and the 2nd Coldstream. The other two battalions were from the infantry of the line, the 1st Norfolks and the 1st Queen's Own Cameron Highlanders. That the Camerons should be part of a Guards Brigade was interesting in view of the fierce fight the regiment had fought in the 1890s to avoid being made the 3rd Battalion Scots Guards, a battle in the end only won by the personal decision of the Queen herself. Under the conditions then prevailing, Ivor was now a Brigadier General, with the status of a general officer. Based in Aldershot were two commanders superior to him, the GOC 1st Division, Major General S H Lomax, and the GOC-in-C, Aldershot Command, Lieutenant General Sir Horace Smith-Dorrien, an old friend from Sudan days. Eighteen months later Smith-Dorrien was to be succeeded by Sir Douglas Haig, whom Ivor had also known in the Sudan and South Africa. The Aldershot area was also base for the formations and units which comprised the main striking force of what, it is sometimes claimed, the Kaiser was to refer to as 'a contemptible little army', and which would in the event of war make up I Corps in the British Expeditionary Force (BEF).

Soon after assuming command, Ivor was able to see his brigade operating in the army's annual manoeuvres. A letter to Tiny dated 11 September 1910 gave a full description of the exercise which took the form of a battle between 1st Division and 2nd Division. He reported that '. . . my brigade came straight onto 4th Guards Brigade marching towards one another on the same road'. 4 Brigade attacked, which the umpires deemed unsuccessful, so they prepared a new attack while Ivor obtained the assistance of one and a half battalions from a neighbouring brigade. This enabled him to 'launch such a strong counter attack against his flank that he was driven off the field and ordered back five miles by the umpires'.

For all the family, the years spent living at Farnborough Park were among the happiest and most interesting of their lives. Endless entertainment and hospitality was provided for everyone from important political and military figures to members of the Army Mothers' Union and children from the garrison, who played games in a field beside the house or came to dancing classes in the hall. Among the well-known military names in the visitors' book could be found Lord Roberts, Douglas Haig, Henry Wilson and 'Wullie' Robertson. From France, in connection with the pioneer flight of a French airship to Aldershot, came the old family friend Clemenceau. Tiny's biographer mentions that 'the children vividly recall their mother's fluent and vigorous exchanges with "the Tiger" on a variety of topics, small and important'.[2]

It was at this time that Bertram Potter came to join the family as a soldier servant. He was to stay for a further 46 years, moving on from his military position to that of civilian butler, and only leaving the family when Ivor moved into a nursing home following a stroke near the end of his life.

In June 1911, King George V was crowned, and the whole of 1st Guards Brigade was involved in the procession. Six weeks later the battalions found themselves back in London on the less glamorous duty of keeping order during a dock strike. On 19 August 1911 Ivor wrote to Tiny from Southwark Park, Rotherhithe, east of Tower Bridge on the south side of the Thames:

Here we are in a very good camp ground, pitching our tents under shaded trees, and being gaped at by men, women and children who have never before seen soldiers and their habits of life. My Brigade Headquarters is with the Cameron Highlanders and the Norfolks here, and my area of command extends over a very wide area with detachments of 100–150 men guarding railway stations, goods yards and river bridges, both north and south of the Thames.

The 2nd Battalion Grenadiers are at the General Post Office with numerous detachments in that vicinity. The 2nd Coldstream are at the Tower with other detachments north of the river.

The letter went on to explain how the soldiers on detachment were given 1/6d daily to feed themselves locally, which Ivor considered a very good arrangement.

He also mentioned the poverty in his district, but noted that, apart from 'elements of hooliganism' which his troops could easily deal with there were no general signs of excitement or discontent in the area. He ended by saying that the prevailing opinion was that the strike would be a short one since most of the dockers 'are a law-abiding lot as a rule, and only came out because ordered and will return as soon as they see they have not won'.

A much more attractive duty brought Ivor back to London yet again towards the end of the year. For some time, there had been much discussion within infantry circles about changing the number of fighting or rifle companies in battalions from eight of approximately 100 men each to four companies of 200. The remaining 200 men in a battalion of 1,000 were made up of corps of drums, specialists, and administrators. As a firm protagonist of this change, Ivor was invited to address an important audience on its merits. A large body of officers gathered at the Royal United Services Institute building in Whitehall to hear him on 19 December 1911. The chairman conducting the meeting was General Sir John French, the CIGS designate, due to take over the following spring. Sir John Hall in his Coldstream history tells how:

> General Maxse explained the advantages of the four-company system so clearly and so convincingly that its adoption at an early date was to all intents and purposes assured. Experimental companies were formed at Aldershot, and after the manoeuvres of 1913 the Army Council issued the necessary orders for the reorganization of the whole of the infantry upon the new lines.[3]

Information reached Ivor and Tiny during 1912 which was to have a major effect on the rest of their lives, A letter arrived from the gardener working at a house called Little Bognor, lying some three miles east of Petworth, to say that the owner, a Mr Dobede, had just died. The significance of this news is made clear in notes written for Tiny's biographer by her daughter Violet, which start by telling of a day's hunting while the family were staying at Petworth in 1909:

> While following hounds at great speed my father beheld for the first time a gloomy house on a hill concealed in trees and shrubberies. He has never been able to explain the conviction that suddenly came over him that he was looking at his own house. When riding home from the hunt

in the evening he went to look at the house more closely and enquired at a gardener's cottage who lived there. The owner was an elderly recluse called Mr Dobede. My father returned to Petworth and said to my mother: 'I have found the place we are going to live in when I leave the army.' He was in part at least a true prophet.[4]

Since Mr Dobede guarded his privacy fiercely, the Maxses could only make clandestine visits to Little Bognor during the three years after first catching sight of it, but during this time they were able to make friends with the gardener, who promised to let them know as soon as his employer died. Immediately they heard the news, Ivor and Tiny set about buying the house from the executors, and took possession of it in early 1913. Throughout that year Tiny spent as much time as she could spare in supervising the many alterations and additions they wished to make to the house, which was finally ready to be occupied in January 1914. Although busy with the work at Little Bognor, the Maxses did not let up in their entertaining at Farnborough Park. The composition of the brigade had changed since 1910, with the 1st Black Watch replacing the Camerons, the 2nd Royal Munster Fusiliers the Norfolks, and the 1st Coldstream, commanded at first by Lieutenant Colonel H C Sutton and then John Ponsonby, taking over from the 2nd Battalion. Ponsonby later recorded that life at Aldershot could be dull and monotonous, especially for the unmarried officers, but that: 'Mary Maxse, who inherited that strong sense of humour from her family, went out of her way to ask us all, and very often, to her house, where we could always look forward to a happy and amusing evening and a break in the monotony.'[5]

1st Guards Brigade was by 1913 regarded as the best trained in the Aldershot Command. Though training remained Ivor's primary interest, his insistence on sound administration, based on his own active service experiences, was never relaxed. He took a keen, and in those days not always common, interest in the feeding of his troops. His attitude is demonstrated by the story of his reaction in meeting the Master Cook during an inspection, illustrated by a cartoon still to be seen in an old 1st Coldstream scrapbook: 'The most important man in the battalion is the Master Cook. I always take my hat off to the Master Cook.'

Giving added impetus to Ivor's determination to train his brigade well was the threat of war with Germany, which many military and political figures had been fearing for several years. In 1911 the Agadir crisis, following the unlawful arrival of the German gunboat *Panther* in the North African port, had brought Europe to the brink of hostilities. Peace had been restored, but the possibility of war still overshadowed a continent apparently more secure and prosperous in 1913 than it had ever been, where few even noticed the shadows.

The army manoeuvres of 1913 took place in the second half of

September. The aim was to simulate the initial operations of the BEF in
a continental war, so in fact they became the dress rehearsal for the actual
operations that were to unfold in France and Belgium 11 months later. As
part of I Corps, commanded by Haig, Ivor's brigade acted as advance
guard for the whole of the two corps-strong First Army. He was supported
by the 26th Brigade Royal Field Artillery, and a detachment of the Royal
Flying Corps. More aircraft were employed in the manoeuvres than had
been seen previously in any exercise. Marching from Aldershot in stages
of 20 to 30 miles the brigade arrived near Tring in Hertfordshire on 19
September, where Ivor wrote to Tiny the following day:

> Here we are in Alfred Rothschild's park . . . It looks as though we are
> going to have the best of the show as far as I can guess. Rothschild is
> doing us bang up. He is feeding 130 officers and 3,400 men every day.
> Each night 70 officers dine at his house, the remainder in a tent. I have
> never seen soldiers so well done in my life. He seats in one tent 3,400 at
> a time. I believe Rosebery [Tiny's uncle] and others dine to-night and I
> hope I shall not have to make a speech.

Other letters described the progress of the manoeuvres, and in one he
made the comment that soldiers seemed fitter than when he joined 31
years before. Certainly the long marches were valuable training for the
distances which they would, before long, find themselves covering in
1914.

Writing from Farnborough Park at the end of manoeuvres on 28
September, Ivor described his meeting during the previous week with a
French army mission whose members had been in England as observers
during the operations. His fluent French enabled him to have several
interesting conversations with them, and he was determined to follow
these contacts up for . . . 'a spell of duty with the French Army and perhaps will do a staff tour with them. I have been asked to do this by no less
a person than the Chief of Staff of their whole army [Général de
Castlenau], with whom I lunched yesterday.' In spite of the doubts he
expressed at the end of the letter, as to whether the War Office would
agree to let him go, he was in due course given approval to attend a staff
tour with the French Army in May 1914, to which Henry Wilson, also a
Brigadier General at the time, was invited as well.

In January 1914 the family moved into Little Bognor. The house had
been thoroughly modernised and fitted with electric light, still something
of a rarity in those days, and fed from banks of batteries charged by their
own engine. A great deal of work was still needed on the garden, and
Violet later recalled that for years 'the tools most used in the garden were
axes, billhooks and saws'. She also told of Tiny's delight in gardening, and
her appreciation of the tameness of all the birds around the house.
Feeding them had been a special interest of Mr Dobede, and it was partly

his love of birds as well as his desire for privacy that had caused him to allow the garden to become so overgrown.

Ivor was due to hand over command of his brigade on 31 July 1914, not long after returning from the staff tour in France, which had started in Paris and then moved to study the ground opposite the German frontier with Lorraine. However, due to the series of moves and counter-moves of European armies that followed the assassination of Archduke Francis Ferdinand in Sarajevo on 28 June, war became increasingly likely. Just before Colonel Scott Kerr of the Grenadier Guards was due to take over, Ivor received a telegram to say that he was to remain in command for the time being. On Tuesday 4 August, war was declared with Germany, and the following day mobilisation began. Scott Kerr moved to command 4th Guards Brigade.

The progress of events during the days following the declaration of war were fully described in a memoir written by Tiny for her children later in 1914, while everything was still clear in her mind.[6] She told how, since there is 'nothing for a brigadier to do on the first day of mobilization', the family spent Wednesday quietly at Little Bognor, where the reluctant children were made to come out to help their parents hoe weeds out of a young holly hedge. The next day the children were taken to stay at Petworth, and Ivor and Tiny loaded their motorcar and drove to Aldershot. On arrival they found the whole area teeming with troops, and reservists pouring in from all directions. Ivor was soon busy visiting all the units in his command with the object of speaking to as many officers and men as possible. On Tuesday, 11 August the brigade was sufficiently organised to carry out a short route march, and the battalions were met as they neared the end of it by the King and Queen, who had come down from London to go round the troops in the garrison that day. Tiny wrote that she 'had never seen them pass at war strength before, they took twenty minutes to pass a given point'. The BEF had started its move to France on Sunday 9 August. Ivor's brigade left during the night of Wednesday and the morning of Thursday. When he and his staff set off at midnight Tiny was not present, experience having taught her 'never to go to the station on these occasions'. Arriving at the port of embarkation the following morning Ivor began a letter: 'In glorious weather, and full of spirits, the whole brigade expects shortly to start in two steamers. This one takes three battalions, and the other the transport wagons.'

Notes

Letters quoted in this chapter are either in possession of the Maxse family or in WSRO files 230, 234.

1 Gore, John, *Mary Maxse, 1870–1944* (Rolls House, 1946), p. 55.
2 Gore, John, p. 53.
3 Maxse, Brig Gen F I, 'Battalion Organisation', *Journal of the RUSI*, Vol 56, Jan 1912, No 407, pp. 53–86.
4 Gore, p. 52.
5 Gore, p. 57.
6 Gore, pp. 63–74.

The First World War

11

With 1st Guards Brigade
in Action,
1914

————•◆•————

On arriving at Le Havre, after an uneventful crossing from Southampton, the brigade marched to a transit camp where they could wait for the trains that would take them up to the front. They were given a tremendous reception by the people of the town, who lined the route they marched along and cheered them all the way. Before long they boarded the trains that were to convey them on the 200-mile journey to Le Cateau, the detraining station for all troops joining the BEF. Ivor and his brigade major, Charles Corkran of the Grenadier Guards, had a carriage to themselves and slept comfortably throughout the journey, but he considered that the accommodation provided on the trains for the men was too crowded, so they had little chance to sleep. The first volume of the *Official History of the War, Military Operations, France and Belgium, 1914* describes the concentration area of the BEF as being arranged so that the army 'was assembled in a pear-shaped area between Maubeuge and Le Cateau, about 25-miles long from north-east to south-west, and averaging 10 miles wide'.[1] Within it there were assembled, by 19 August 1914, I Corps, consisting of the 1st and 2nd Divisions; II Corps, with the 3rd and 5th Divisions; the Cavalry Division; and four squadrons of the Royal Flying Corps, mustering 63 aeroplanes. At the north-east point of the 'pear' was the Cavalry Division, ready to join hands with the French Fifth Army on the right. Behind it, I Corps was in the eastern sector of the concentration area, and II Corps in the western. Within I Corps area the 1st Division was on the right, and within the divisional area 1st Guards Brigade covered the right flank. Maubeuge lies only three miles from the Belgian frontier. The Germans had invaded Belgium on 4 August, and by the time

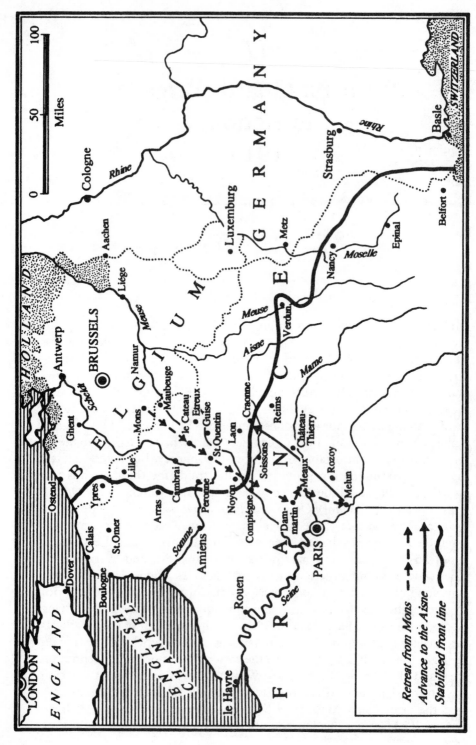

THE RETREAT FROM MONS

Retreat from Mons - - ➤
Advance to the Aisne ━━➤
Stabilised front line ∿∿

the BEF was assembling, in the locations explained above, the German First Army under General von Kluck, and their Second Army under General von Bulow, had already advanced over 30 miles into Belgian territory from their own frontier. The Belgian Army was still in being in the area to the west of the River Gette between Louvain and Wavre, providing the BEF's protection on its northern flank, albeit some 50 miles away to the north-east.

The Official History describes thus the events of 20 August: 'It was a fateful day in many respects, for during its course the main Belgian Army retired into Antwerp, the Germans approached within decisive range of Namur, and General Joffre gave his orders for the general advance.'[2] Following Joffre's instructions Field Marshal Sir John French, C-in-C, ordered the BEF to advance north-east into Belgium, moving north of the River Sambre while the French Fifth Army kept to the south of it. Ivor's hope of a few days to train his brigade, which he had mentioned in a letter to Tiny on 17 August, were not to be fulfilled. Setting off on 21 August, the BEF was by the 23rd established in the region of Mons, with II Corps to the west of the city and I Corps to the south-east. Still on the right flank of the 1st Division, the Guards Brigade was the nearest formation in I Corps to the River Sambre. The last stage of the long march which had brought the division to this final location had lasted for most of the day and night of 22 August, and as the Official History puts it, had 'tried the troops severely'. Throughout the BEF, reservists formed some 60% of the infantry, and being still out of condition for long marches they found them a great strain, though much worse was to come.

During the short battle of Mons on 23 August the weight of the German onslaught fell on II Corps, where some 1,600 casualties were sustained. I Corps was hardly affected, and suffered only 40. Although the enemy had been successfully checked by II Corps, and everywhere the BEF was preparing to fight the next day, the British could not operate without conforming to French plans. When informed just before midnight on 23 August that the Fifth Army's commander, General Lanrezac, had ordered a retreat to begin at 3am the next morning, Field Marshal French was forced to follow suit, since his army's position in advance of the general allied line would be untenable. Messages that followed soon afterwards from General Joffre confirmed that his action was in accordance with the overall C-in-C's wishes. So began the long retreat from Mons, which only ended when the German armies had almost reached Paris nearly a fortnight later. Ivor described in a letter his brigade's part in the retreat: . . . 'without remission almost day and night we have been marching a lot and fighting a little, and if it goes on much longer, we shall be very tired and war-worn, but extremely fit'. Visiting a hospital at home Tiny heard at first hand what conditions had been like:

A wounded sergeant in the Black Watch, in the Connaught Hospital in Aldershot, told me that the last time he had seen Ivor was during that retreat, when he, Ivor, had watched the brigade go by. It was late in the evening, they had been going all day, and as the Black Watch passed Ivor said, 'Stick it men, you've only two miles more'. But when they got to the village two miles on they found it was full, and they had to go seven miles further. That was only a tiny example of the strain that went on day after day. Ivor, himself, though he kept up his spirits and those of his men, thought they might have to go back to the boats.[3]

Although II Corps moving on an axis to the west of I Corps, was involved in a major battle at Le Cateau as well as other lesser actions, I Corp's progress was less troubled by the enemy. Only once did 1st Guards Brigade fight a serious battle, and this was not intentional. On 27 August, it had been given the task of acting as rearguard to the whole of I Corps. The battalions were positioned for this duty to the north of the small town of Etreux, which lies alongside the Sambre Canal, about 10 miles south-east of Le Cateau. The 2nd Division set off first at 4am on 27 August, and once they had passed through Etreux and were well on their way south the 1st Division began to follow. By midday the road through the town was reported clear of all transport. Then, in the words of the Official History: '. . . a little later Brigadier General Maxse despatched orders (time 1pm) to every unit of the rear guard, "Retire at once". This message, though sent by two routes, failed to reach the Munster Fusiliers.'[4] During the morning German pressure had been increasing on the Munsters, and as the day wore on they were subjected to attacks by six enemy battalions. Major Charrier, the acting commanding officer, carried out a fighting withdrawal in the afternoon to a village half-way back to Etreux. Here, in a fierce action, he was killed at about 7pm. By 9.15pm, the only officer left to command the remnants of the battalion, Lieutenant Gower, had taken up a position in an orchard where resistance continued until all ammunition was spent, and the group was overpowered by the Germans. Although half the company of the Munsters had escaped on a flank earlier in the day, the battalion virtually ceased to exist, and had to be replaced. To make up the loss the 1st Battalion Queen's Own Cameron Highlanders was posted into the brigade from GHQ reserve. Although a tragedy, the heroic stand of the Munsters was of great benefit to the retreating formations in I Corps, giving them an opportunity to make a clean six-hour break from the pursuing enemy, and so was not an entirely wasted sacrifice.

When the retreat came to an end on 5 September, the 1st Division found itself in the area of Rozoy, a small French town some 30 miles south-east of Paris. As the crow flies the distance from Mons was 136 miles: as the troops had marched it was nearer 200. Ivor admired his own corps commander's conduct, but was less complimentary about the C-in-C:

Haig keeps his head better than any other and remains unusually cool in his judgement. He stops to talk to me occasionally on the line of march and I must say he is the only superior officer who appears to me to grip hold of the essential points. Sir J.F. has not been seen by anyone in this army corps since we started! He lives in a head quarter camp containing 300 people and goodness only knows what they are all doing!

In some correspondence carried on many years later in 1920 Ivor gave his views on the staff work of 1914, starting with his experiences during the retreat. Although he marked it 'not for publication', sufficient time has perhaps elapsed for that instruction to be ignored!

In this retreat I was a Brigade Commander and can honestly say I detected no staff work either good, bad or indifferent. This is not a general criticism and may only apply to my brigade.

But the result was that, without much fighting, we 'did our men in' by our inability to put them on a road in fours for long marches. For instance – daily we were ordered to join the column from our billets at a *very* early hour, which meant reducing everybody's necessary sleep. This would not have mattered if we could have marched straight off and thus arrived at our destination at an early hour. But my brigade was never able to accomplish the mile march (approximately) to the starting point in less than 2 to 3 hours.

We were invariably blocked on the way to it, or, if we weren't blocked on the way we were stopped for a couple of hours at the starting point. This was so bad for everyone concerned that I took the risk on my own shoulders of ordering my brigade parade, daily, one hour after the time we were ordered to join the Divisional Column! Even then we were invariably one or two hours too early, and no complaint on my part to those above me ever made any difference during the whole retreat from MONS to PARIS . . .

The best part of the staff work on the MONS retreat was the astonishing success of the supply department under conditions which were certainly never foreseen. We never knew how far we were going, and some days we went very far backwards. My supply officer of the A.S.C. somehow or other never missed providing us with rations. This no doubt is easier in a retreat than in an advance. Except for two rearguard actions, in one of which I lost a whole battalion (Munster Fusiliers), we had practically no fighting, but we made up for it by wearying our men to death by means of bad General Staff work. This and the fact that 70% of the privates in the ranks were reservists with new boots on.[5]

Though Ivor's complaints did little good for his men, they may have done some harm to his own reputation, as will transpire shortly.

'If the war is going to last,' wrote Ivor some time after the retreat ended, 'we ought to be given a week of rest, reorganisation, replenishment, re-equipment, re-horsing, re-booting, re-clothing . . . the ranks should also be refilled with officers and men'. Of these requirements there was only time for some reinforcements to join on 4 and 5 September before the exhausted members of the BEF were called upon to turn and advance against the enemy. Most serious among the losses incurred during the retreat was one-third of the army's field artillery, which could not be made up before the advance began.

Early on the morning of 5 September, Joffre's orders for his armies to attack the Germans reached GHQ, with a request for the BEF to join them. After some hesitation, French agreed, and a visit from Joffre himself in the afternoon confirmed the decision. Orders were then issued for the following morning: 'The Army will advance eastward with a view to attacking.'[6] 1st Guards Brigade formed the advance guard of the 1st Division when I Corps moved off on the right of the BEF early on 6 September. The action fought on this day and the following three days constitutes what has become known as the Battle of the Marne, generally recognised as one of the decisive battles of European history, since it destroyed the German chances of a swift victory and the capture of Paris.

Ivor's brigade was checked not long after starting, but the opposition was found to be only a cavalry screen. The advance continued after a short skirmish and some 11 miles were covered that day. On 7 September, the Grand Morin, a tributary of the Marne, was crossed without meeting serious opposition. Setting off early on 8 September, the 1st Division was held up 10 miles further on by enemy rearguards holding the steep banks of the Petit Morin, where a sharp action took place. On 9 September, the Division pushed on and crossed the Marne unopposed. A further advance northward followed on 10 September, 10 miles being covered and German rearguards being steadily pushed back. Heavy rain fell on 11 and 12 September, preventing air reconnaissance of German movements. By the night of the 12th the BEF had reached the River Vesle, a tributary of the River Aisne, where strong enemy resistance was encountered. Having crossed the Vesle, I Corps was faced with a still more formidable obstacle ahead, the broad and deep River Aisne itself, with its steep banks on the north side. The night of the 12–13 September marked the end of the German retreat from the Marne, and brought Ivor to the eve of his first serious battle since arriving in France a month earlier.[7]

Although Ivor had recorded his good opinion of Haig during the retreat, this was not entirely reciprocated by the corps commander at the moment when the advance began on 6 September. Following the brush with the enemy cavalry in the morning, 1st Guards Brigade was advancing after midday when Haig came forward with General Lomax, GOC 1st Division, to instruct Ivor to send out patrols, supported by an advanced guard, towards a point where he believed the enemy were trying to check the British advance to cover their own retreat. For some reason Ivor demurred, possibly because he felt that his hands were full enough with (below) Ivor aged about six years.

(right) Admiral F A Maxse, 1886.

Near Alma, 25 September 1854. Lord Cardigan asleep, Lt F A Maxse RN (standing), his brother Fitz, ADC to Cardigan. (This was the day of Fred's ride with despatches from Raglan ordering the fleet round to Balaclava.)

Ivor in India, 1884-88.

M Clemenceau, Violet Maxse and Admiral Maxse riding in the Bois de Boulogne, 1888.

Troops of the 2nd Sudanese Brigade awaiting the Dervish assault, in a shallow trench, bayonets fixed.

As above. Ivor (Brigade Major) left, writing an order; Lt Colonel Maxwell commanding.

The Dervish gibbets found in Omdurman, which had been in frequent use by the Khalifa.

Dervish prisoners after Omdurman. Note the 'Djibbah' or patchwork uniform.

(above) Maxwell's instructions to Ivor to accompany Marchand back to Fashoda (Khartoum, October 1898).

(above) Baratier and Marchand in Cairo, inscribed to 'Commandant Maxse. . . . heureuse d'avoir fait connaisnace'.

(below) Loading wood to fuel the gunboats Abu Klea and Nasr.

(above) The British officers of the 13th, March 1899. From left: Capt. Elgood, Lt Whishaw, Capt. Gamble, Ivor, Sgt Russell – Scots Guard Drill Instructor, Major Capper.

(left) A native officer of the 13th Sudanese. One of those described by Ivor as 'reliable, stout-hearted, cheery old boys'.

(above) Ivor photographed as Kaimaka in the Sudan.

A native ferry boat on the Nile.

Ivor commanding the 13th Sudanese on a big parade for the Duke of Connaught who invested him with the DSO. The 1,000 in the battalion included 400 recruits from the Dervish Army.

'My wagon and staff', 5 June. From left: Pte Groom (Coldstream Guards, Ivor's servant), muledriver, Ivor, ASC groom, a Colonial trooper. The wagon had been captured from Cronje's Boers near Klip's Drift.

Ivor and his staff of the Transvaal Constabulary, October.

*(right) The
Honourable Mary
Maxse, always
known as Tiny.*

*(below) The officers
of the 2nd
Coldstream at
Windsor, 1905.*

G.O.C.

Major General F.I.Makse.
CVO.CB.DSO

A sketch of Ivor as GOC 18th Division.

Tiny, Ivor and Col Shoubridge (GI), Little Ashton, Codford, just before their division sailed for France in July 1915 after their training at Salisbury Plain.

The retreat from Mons, 1st Guards Brigade HQ at action at Voinsles. Ivor in the background on right of the left hand group. In front of him are Major Hewett, Sgts Gadsby and Malloius.

A portrait painted by Oswald Birley at Colchester in 1915 and exhibited at the Royal Academy that year. At the time Birley was serving in the 18th Division.

(above) In full dress as Lieutenant General, 1919–20.

(above) Corps Commander – decorating a sergeant of the Seaforth Highlanders, 51st Highland Division, Autumn 1917.

(below) At the opening of the Thiepval monument, 2 August. Also General Lee, General Anthoine and Comte Fleury.

Inspection of a Territorial Armoured Car Regiment commanded by Colonel Walker DSO at Hull, 23 September 1923.

Ivor, The Honourable P Leigh, Lt Colonel Miller, The Prince of Wales.

Little Bognor, April 1919. Mlle Guy (Governess), Ivor and daughter Violet.

Hunting was a favourite pastime during retirement. A meet at Petworth House, 20 March 1926.

Opening the Fittleworth Flower Show, August 1953, aged 90.

simply keeping his tired troops on the move without any extra commitments, the need for which he may have doubted. Haig gave vent to his
considerable annoyance over the matter in his diary: 'Maxse made difficulties and seemed to have lost his fighting spirit which used to be so
noticeable at Aldershot in peacetime!'[8] It is also likely that the constant
complaints Ivor made during the retreat, as recorded in his 1920 notes,
would have caused considerable annoyance at divisional and corps headquarters, although they had little effect. While other brigade commanders
no doubt shared the same views, few are likely to have been so vociferous
or outspoken in airing them. At this point, it is worth mentioning a problem of military command which has affected armies throughout history:
how much should the subordinate commander tell his superior about his
difficulties and his fears, and how much account should the superior take
of them?

There were many occasions during the First World War when commanders at the higher levels failed to take account of warnings passed to
them from their juniors with disastrous results, but there were other
moments when to have listened too attentively would have been wrong.
One of those moments came when the exhausted BEF was ordered to
turn on 6 September and advance to the Marne. The fact of starting to
pursue a retreating enemy acted as a tonic which overcame exhaustion.
Doubts as to the fitness of the troops to carry on effectively without time
to rest and refit were dispelled when they proved to have unsuspected
reserves of strength to draw on.

Writing about Haig in his later period as C-in-C, Churchill wrote in his
book *Great Contemporaries* of the 'high-tension current which flowed
ceaselessly from him' down the long chain of command from GHQ to
battalion and company level. Already when he was still a corps commander he was starting to apply what Churchill described as a 'ruthless and
often inevitably blind force':

> fight and kill and be killed, but obey orders, even when it was clear that
> the Higher Command had not foreseen the conditions; or go and go at
> once, to the rear, to England or to the devil.[9]

Commentators have argued about the rights and wrongs of applying
this 'blind force' throughout the long years since the war ended, but
whilst the conflict was in progress it was generally accepted as being a necessary part of the achievement of victory. Though Ivor might question
many directives reaching him from higher headquarters, he never doubted
that when converted to orders they had to be obeyed.

Most of 13 September was taken up with forcing a passage over the
River Aisne and the Aisne Canal which runs just south of it. During this
phase, 2 Brigade was in the lead in the 1st Division. The next day, 14
September, this brigade was given the task of seizing and holding an

advance position on the top of the long wooded hill above the Aisne, along which runs the road called the Chemin des Dames, a name to be wellknown throughout the rest of the war. Here its duty was to protect the left flank of the main body of the 1st Division, of which 1st Guards Brigade formed the advance guard. The Official History's summary of the day's action gives a good idea of the intensity of the fighting as the division struggled uphill from the Aisne, with mist and the rough wooded terrain combining with fierce enemy resistance to ensure that the 'fog of war' prevailed throughout the day. Casualties were heavy in what the history describes as 'the desperate character of the encounters on the Chemin des Dames ridge and on the spurs and in the valleys leading up to it'. The summary explains why the fight for the Chemin des Dames was so significant for the British:

> They found the enemy not only in position, entrenched and supported by 8-inch howitzers, but in such force that so far from manifesting any intention of continuing his retreat, he made every effort to drive the British back over the river. Thus the 14th September passed in alternate attack and counter-attack, and ended in no decisive result. It was the first day of that 'stabilization' of the battle line which was to last so many weary months – the beginning, for the British, of trench warfare.[10]

Ivor described the actions of his brigade during 14 September in a letter written a few days later. It starts by telling how the 1st Coldstream was the vanguard when the brigade set off very early in the dark from the site of its overnight bivouac. Enemy resistance was soon encountered:

> I put in the Cameron Highlanders on the Coldstream left, and pushed on to Cerny, taking the Germans in the flank. But they again on a wider front engaged the Camerons on their left, and I had to use part of the Black Watch merely to hold off the enemy. To cut the story short, this left me with only the Scots Guards in hand, of which half was kept under the 1st Division as escort to guns four miles away.
>
> We had a ding-dong battle under heavy German artillery fire to which our gunners could not then reply. The result was that we lost about 33% of my brigade in killed, wounded and missing in about a couple of hours or so. With the remainder we stuck to the ground we had gained, aided by two battalions of the 2 Brigade who also suffered as heavily as we did. It was absolutely essential to the whole Allied Army that we should not give way one inch of ground because we thus held an indispensable bridgehead over the River Aisne. If we had been driven off this bridgehead, the Allied line was cut in two and each wing would be dealt with separately, but probably with success. This I knew but most of the brigade did not at the time . . .
>
> Since the 14th we have continued to hold onto the same ground and the bridgehead over the Aisne is now secured, I think. . . . We are still at

this moment under the same well directed shell fire, but have had in the four or five days of it very few casualties because we hold the top of a high wooded bank and all our men are dug into trenches and all the reserves are protected in local quarries close up to the firing line. . . . The infantry look-out men would give notice if any German infantry attacked and the trenches would be manned in a moment as happened yesterday. I am in perfect safety most of the day in a cave which we have christened the 'funk hole' where my telephones and telegraph office is quite safe and undisturbed.

Our gunners are splendid at infantry targets but not equally successful at discerning hostile guns. The German artillery is beautifully served and *some* of their infantry is magnificent but that magnificent portion of their infantry has been put forward first into every fight and the result is that most of it has ceased to exist.

The heavy casualties incurred during this action were deeply distressing to Ivor and the divisional commander, Lomax. The fact that the men killed or wounded were friends with whom they had served for many years at Aldershot before the war made their loss especially felt. In his book *Douglas Haig* Major General E K G Sixsmith records that:

Lomax was distressed by the casualties. Three out of four commanding officers in one brigade had been lost, but Haig comforted him, taking the responsibility on himself and saying 'what a splendid action they had fought, after so many trying weeks retreating and marching'.[11]

The losses in I Corps amounted to 160 officers and 3,500 men, which in those early days of the war were shattering figures.

The Guards Brigade and 2 Brigade held onto their positions until the night of 19–20 September when they were relieved by 18 Brigade. During this period Tiny wrote to say that:

Gladdie [her sister-in-law] sends me a rumour that you are being sent home on promotion to train the new army here. It would be glorious to see you; nevertheless I hope it is not true for it would be desperately hard on you. I have written to find out her authority, it may be only gossip as you are known to be good at training troops. They must be very short of people who know anything about it – nevertheless it appeared to me that all the divisions were given away mostly to totally unknown people.

Three days after this, Tiny reported:

. . . then this morning arrived a letter from Coddy [General Sir Charles Codrington, Colonel of the Coldstream] to say he heard you were coming home because you 'wanted a rest' and that therefore he had been instructed to find out privately if you would be well enough to take up command of the 18th Division of the new army at Shorncliffe and

Purfleet – for which you had been selected. I wrote back that as far as my information went you were well and would be able to do it.

The rumours about Ivor's return to England proved to be true, and near the end of September he handed over command of his brigade to Brigadier General C FitzClarence, VC, of the Irish Guards. He was instructed to take command of the newly formed 18th Division of 'Kitchener's Army' on 1 October 1914, an appointment in accord with his promotion to acting Major General, which had taken place on 18 August. On hearing this news he must have remembered a sentence he had written near the end of the letter quoted two pages back about the fighting on 14 September: 'My conclusion is that we cannot afford to put inferior troops into the front line and "K's Army" makes me think furiously when I hear and see the German artillery fire.' He was about to have a chance to put 'furious thinking' into the training of his own new army division so that it could survive the heaviest German bombardment, and to discover that the men who composed it had the makings of far from 'inferior troops'. As he crossed the Channel to assume his new responsibilities he must have had mixed feelings about his return to England. Although he did so in an apparently creditable manner on promotion at the end of a long tour as Guards Brigade commander, which had only been extended temporarily in July, there were slight shadows over his departure from the BEF. There are pointers to these shadows in Tiny's two letters. First there was her suggestion that to come home 'would be desperately hard on you', indicating that anything other than service with the BEF was generally considered second-best; next there was her comment about the new army divisions being 'given away to totally unknown people', hardly implying that these commands were highly regarded; finally, reference to General Codrington's letter reporting that he might be coming home because he 'wanted a rest' could be taken as meaning not up to holding a front-line command. In fact, his handling of his brigade during the battle of the Aisne had probably wiped out the bad impression made on Haig on 6 September, but during the week from 6th to the 14th, before Ivor could put the record straight, rumours about his being tired may have drifted back to England. Throughout the whole war, with the nation's interest so focussed on the operations of the BEF, rumour and gossip circulated endlessly around Britain, especially about senior officers and their abilities or failings.

Notes

The private letters referred to can be found in the Maxse papers at WSRO in files 153, 440.

1 Edmonds, Brig Gen Sir J E, *The Official History of the Great War, Military Operations, France & Belgium, 1914*, Vol 1 (Macmillan, 1933), p. 49.
2 Edmonds, p. 50.
3 Gore, John, *Mary Maxse, 1870–1944*, p. 72.
4 Edmonds, p. 222.
5 Maxse papers, Imperial War Museum.
6 Edmonds, p. 545.
7 Marshall-Cornwall, Sir J, *Haig as a Military Commander* (Batsford, 1973), pp. 114–15.
8 Extract from the Haig Diaries in the National Library of Scotland.
9 Churchill, Winston, *Great Contemporaries* (Reprint Society, 1941), p. 189.
10 Edmonds, pp. 395–6.
11 Sixsmith, Maj Gen E K G, *Douglas Haig* (Weidenfeld, 1976), p. 78.

12

Raising and Training
the 18th Division

———•◆•———

Lord Kitchener, appointed Secretary of State for War the day after war had been declared on 4 August, was one of the few clear-sighted people in Britain who did not expect the war to be 'over by Christmas'. He believed that it would be necessary to raise a large number of extra divisions over and above those in the existing regular and territorial armies. Eventually, over a period of years, the whole army was to reach a grand total of 70 divisions. Almost immediately after assuming his new Government post he sent out his famous appeal for volunteers. The immediate result was the enlistment of the 'First Hundred Thousand', and by the end of August these recruits were formed into six divisions which became known as K1, or the First New Army. So overwhelming was the response that on 25 August Kitchener called for a further hundred thousand, a call answered by almost twice that number, 174,901 men joining up in one week alone. This second wave became known as K2, and it was from among these enthusiastic volunteers that the 18th Division was formed. The first units began to assemble on 10 September in Essex. At first most had only two or three officers and were lucky to have half a dozen regular NCOs. Commanding Officers were mostly elderly men recalled from the reserve and usually referred to as 'dug outs'.

Divisional Headquarters were established in Colchester, and in the immediate area were 53 and 54 Brigades. 55 Brigade was stationed 60 miles away at Purfleet, where there were some army ranges, in a dismal waterlogged area close to the Thames, just west of where the Dartford Tunnel now exists. 53 Brigade was composed of the 6th Royal Berkshires, 10th Essex, 8th Norfolks and 8th Suffolks; 54 Brigade of the 6th

Northamptonshires, 10th and 11th Royal Fusiliers, and 12th Middlesex; and 55 Brigade of the 8th East Surreys, 7th Queens, 7th Buffs and 7th Royal West Kents. Later the 7th Bedfords replaced the 10th Royal Fusiliers in 54 Brigade. The 8th Royal Sussex, the divisional pioneer battalion, was at Colchester, as were all elements of the divisional Royal Field Artillery. What are now known as regiments were then referred to as field artillery 'brigades'. In the 18th Division there were four of them, the 82, 83, 84 and 85 Brigades RFA, each with three batteries, eventually armed with four 18-pounder guns per battery divided between two troops. They were fortunate to be provided with 18-pounders. The Territorial divisions had inadequate 15-pounders, as was soon to be discovered when these divisions arrived in France. Gradually all the other component elements of a division were added. Field and Signal Companies, Royal Engineers; Field Ambulances, Royal Army Medical Corps; and Supply Companies, Army Service Corps were in due course joined by the heavy guns of the divisional artillery. Later still, well after arrival overseas, would arrive machine gun companies and trench mortar batteries.

The divisional history, entitled *The 18th Division in the Great War*, with the symbol (ATN) or 'a-tee-n' on the front cover, talks of: 'those eager, hearty, humorous, sometimes tedious early days' during which the volunteers experienced 'the difficulties and bewilderments of the swift switch from civilian to military life'.[1] One of the regular officers whose memories of the early days of Kitchener's army were typical of what was going on all over Britain was Lieutenant, later Lieutenant Colonel, A P B Irwin of the East Surreys. He was on home leave from service with the regular 2nd Battalion of the regiment in India when posted to be adjutant of the 8th Battalion in K2.

> I stood in the station yard at Purfleet and waited for the men to arrive. All I had for battalion headquarters was in my haversack. Three trains arrived during the day, bringing 1,000 men who had been wished upon us before any attempt had been made to provide accommodation.[2]

Once they had all arrived, Irwin led them off to what the divisional history describes as 'a desolate colony of tents in the marshes'. Here, it explains: 'There were not enough blankets to go round; the food was coarse; there were no recreation huts, no dining halls, no canteens such as the regular recruit found in barrack life. But the men's mood was to make the best of things.'[3]

By the time Ivor arrived in Colchester three weeks later on 1 October, living conditions had slightly improved, but the division was still barely recognisable as a military formation. He quickly found a house to rent in Colchester, called 'Kingswode' in Sussex Road, and was joined by Tiny and the family. With his own base firm, he threw himself into the task of creating what was to become one of the outstanding divisions in the BEF,

and was for more than two years to be the focus of virtually all his interest and energy. At the age of nearly 52 he was one of a group of senior
officers who were relatively young by the standards of 1914, and he still
possessed the drive and enthusiasm which made him the ideal leader to
teach and inspire the high-quality, if somewhat bemused, recruits he
found waiting to be turned into soldiers. His first priorities were administrative and organisational, especially the latter in respect of finding good
brigade and unit commanders. All possible strings were pulled, and letters
flew off in every direction. On 15 October he wrote to one old friend:

> Here I am promoted Major-General, brought back from the front (R.
> Aisne, September 30th) and just in command of a division – 18th.
>   We are training for war at a gallop. All bns are 1,100 strong of good
> men. Officers moderate. Will you come at once and command a brigade
> with rank and pay of Brig-General, if I can get you? Send me a telegram
> and tell me where you are, and whether 'yes' or 'no'. I will go to the War
> Office and arrange for your relief, privately, if you say 'yes'. Don't say
> anything about it.

Although Ivor was successful in many of his forays after high-grade
subordinates this was one that did not come off.

On 20 October he was in touch with General Sutton, a friend from
Aldershot, at the War Office, to ask for the removal of an officer posted in
from the Coldstream Guards to command the 10th Royal Fusiliers whom
he knew would 'ruin a magnificent battalion'. He wanted the second-in-
command, 'a first class man' to fill the vacancy left. Two of his brigade
majors were 'quite impossible' and he wanted them replaced as soon as
possible.

Lack of equipment was a serious problem throughout the winter and
well into 1915. Ivor reported that each battalion had only 100 service
rifles for its 1,100 men, and no bayonets, haversacks, water bottles or
entrenching tools. The first uniforms to arrive were blue serge suits dat-
ing from the previous century, dug out from reserve stocks long forgotten
about until the war began. Only gradually did khaki uniforms start to
arrive. The divisional history tells of the excitement this caused: 'Enough
to provide about one per platoon! Every man going on week-end leave
begged and bargained for the loan of that khaki from the individuals to
whom that uniform had been allotted.'[4] So few greatcoats were issued that
most men were wearing their civilian ones right through the winter.

It was long after the infantry companies got their rifles that the artillery
batteries received their own guns. At first the detachments were trained on
one wooden gun per battery, and only once a week were given the chance
to drill with a real 18-pounder. No battery had more than two dozen
horses to its 200 men, and any battery going out in drill order had to scout
round first to borrow animals from its neighbours.[5] However lacking in

weapons and equipment, the men of the division never lacked in keenness and enthusiasm. Given their living conditions, especially those of 55 Brigade on the 'marshes of Purfleet', they needed all their high spirits and sense of humour. In due course Ivor wrote some *Notes on the New Armies by a Divisional Commander, No 1*, a copy of which he sent to Kitchener. He was particularly impressed by 'the excellent physical and moral qualities of the subaltern officers'. He returned to one of his favourite themes, the importance of the leader training his own men:

> They spend eight hours a day with their platoons and identify them-selves with the men's interests both on and off parade. Their keenness to learn the work of training men makes some think that after six months service they will be as good platoon commanders as the average subaltern of the old Army. This is also the opinion of several commanding officers.[6]

Ivor's flair for training found an ideal outlet in shaping the 18th into a formation which reflected his own original ideas on warfare. One of his commanding officers recorded that: 'Attending his fortnightly conference was like a university course on how to make a fine fighting division out of 20,000 semi-trained, albeit enthusiastic soldiers.'[7] He became known throughout the division as 'the black man', with a reputation for suffering 'neither fools nor the inefficient gladly'. It was also discovered that a warm heart lay beneath the rather crusty exterior, and he liked men who were prepared to stand up to him when he barked at them roughly, a ploy often used to test them out. He swore frequently, and used his own orig-inal figures of speech to express his ideas, both habits helping to impress his personality on those who came in contact with him. Another feature which made a big impression is described in the divisional history:

> . . . the General's apparently uncanny memory for names threatened to become legendary. Maybe Captain F J O Montagu, General Maxse's ADC, one of whose tasks it was to learn the officers' names – and to prompt the General at the psychological moment – could supply an inner explanation of the General's gift. But, here again, this was one of General Maxse's properly thought-out methods of infusing his person-ality into the division. The young officer felt that the General was directly interested in him and his work, and went away persuaded that he was the finest fellow in the world – and the General a good second.[8]

All the time that the training and equipping of the division was in progress, Ivor went on searching for suitable people to fill key appoint-ments. In January 1915 he had an important meeting with a General Robb at the War Office, which he summarised in a note the next day. He recorded the limitations of the men then commanding 53 and 54 Brigades, both of whom lacked initiative, though they had learnt 'a lot about training troops during the past four months, and should therefore be quite useful in training freshly formed brigades in newer armies'. To replace one of these two brigade commanders he put forward the name of the commanding officer of one of the battalions in the division, and also suggested 'a successor for that battalion, but the successor is a Brigade Major in another command'. He finished by saying that he would avoid telling the two brigadiers about their replacement until the matter was 'definitely settled, because I should only diminish what little self-confidence they already possess'. Their lack of self-confidence may not have been entirely unrelated to his own treatment of them during the four months they had spent learning from him about training troops! His search for the best officers was not confined to the senior ranks. On 18 February 1915, he was writing to the War Office again, this time in what eventually proved to be an unsuccessful attempt to have a Royal Engineer subaltern posted into the 18th Division Signal Company as second-in-command. His eye for talent had noticed Lieutenant Wemyss, signal officer in 4th Guards Brigade, at some stage during operations in France. Knowing Wemyss to have been wounded, and unlikely to be fit for active service for some time, Ivor felt that while recuperating he could do useful work at Colchester. Unfortunately for the division his plan failed: Wemyss was sent out to the Middle East where he ended the war as Allenby's Chief Signal Officer. In the Second World War he held the important post of Military Secretary at the War Office as a full General, showing that Ivor's skill at spotting the right people had not failed, even though his plan had.

As spring came in, the training became more advanced, with exercises at brigade level. Ivor's instructions for '18th Division Brigade and Combined Training 1915' covered practical, and by the standards of the time highly original, schemes clearly based on his own experience of problems encountered in France. One was designed 'to bring out the value of a retired position, and the difficulty of issuing from a wood if the enemy's infantry and artillery are well placed'; another 'to bring out the difficulties of assembling a force scattered in billets at night, a night approach deployment and the assault of a "jumping off" position under cover of darkness'.[9] At the end of an exercise the director of it could expect full notes from Ivor highlighting all the good and bad points. One lengthy example of these has four paragraphs devoted entirely to explaining the numerous faults he had observed, but ends on a kinder note: 'I beg you will not make any reply to these notes, which are jotted down for your information, and such action as you wish to take. My only idea is to assist in the training of your brigade.'

In April, 55 Brigade moved from Purfleet to Colchester, arriving in time to take part in a gruelling, week-long exercise in Suffolk which tested the division's stamina to the limit. It started with what was regarded as an easy march of 18 miles from Colchester to Ipswich, though the hot sun and a hard road made it tiring enough. The brigades were then moved from place to place around the county, carrying out varied manoeuvres as they went. The final march back to Colchester involved covering 62 miles in the last 48 hours, with officers and men carrying full personal equipment and arms. As the divisional history puts it '. . . every man felt that he was being tested and he was proud of the fact'.[10] In May, the division moved to Salisbury plain, where it was based near Codford St Mary, seven miles from Warminster in the heart of the military training area. Ivor found a house to rent near Codford, and Tiny and the family soon came to join him. Although the division had now been in existence for eight months, and it was clear that it would be going into action across the Channel before long, many important items of equipment were still only trickling in. One of Ivor's major preoccupations was to ensure that the infantry soldiers were issued with the rifles which they would be using on active service in time to fire their range courses with them before leaving England. As ammunition supply was limited, maximum value had to be extracted from every round fired, not only by small arms but by artillery as well, as explained by young Lieutenant Billie Nevill of the 8th East Surreys in a letter written soon after arrival at Codford:

> We start another musketry course soon now. All our horses are to be at the firing point to get used to rows. We are all going to see our artillery fire soon. We are to stand and watch just between the guns and the target.[11]

Towards the end of June, King George V came down to inspect the Division near Stonehenge, which indicated that the time for embarkation was drawing near. As always when military moves are imminent, there were endless rumours about the destination. For some time everyone was convinced that it was to be the Dardanelles. Then in mid-July it changed, and on the 21st Billie Nevill was writing: 'But as a division we are due for France, though I hear some regiments may be drafted out to the Dardanelles.'[12] Even that last bit was wrong, as on 25 July the whole division started on its journey to France as a complete formation. The main body sailed from Folkestone to Boulogne, while the transport crossed from Southampton to Le Havre. Travelling with the leading elements, Ivor and his divisional headquarters spent the night of 25 July in the Louvre Hotel in Boulogne.

The 18th Division joined X Corps in the newly formed Third Army, commanded by General Sir Charles Monro. By 28 July it had mostly concentrated in the region of Fléselles, about 15 miles from Carnoy on the Somme front. It was to remain in this general area for more than another year. While his units were assembling, Ivor took the opportunity to accept an invitation to lunch with a French corps commander and visit a section of their trenches. His own fluency in French helped him in a way he was to explain later: 'As I speak French and always like seeing French officers, quite a number call in on me when passing anywhere near this locality. They know they will be more welcome than they seem to be in certain other British headquarters. The result is that I pick up a good deal which escapes some of my superiors.'

The first immediate advantage of his good relations with his French neighbours was described in a long letter written on 1 August 1915. Having told how each of his brigades was to go on attachment to a British division 'for ten days to get the atmosphere of trench life into their system', he went on to set out in detail how his artillerymen were being shown the way to handle their guns by gradual integration into French batteries:

> Today the gun position will be occupied by a battery of three French and one British guns, tomorrow by two British and two French, then three British and one French. All the time that battery will be commanded by the *French* Battery Commander who had never before seen a British gunner. Only when the battery has four British guns in it will the British Battery Commander take charge. But he will be there all the time, learning with his gunners all about the locality from the experience of the French gunners who have been there on and off since about November 1914.
>
> I need not tell you that the French are past masters at making such a situation pleasant for us, and our people will be truly sorry when the moment comes for the French batteries to quit.

This letter ended in a way which might have brought Ivor into considerable trouble, though in the end the affair blew over without any official displeasure being recorded against him. He finished it by commenting on the uselessness of the 15-pounder guns provided for the Territorial divisions, which he said 'have proved to be absolutely worthless and cannot be put into the line at all! They are unable to register a target in a battery of French 75s!' He went on to say that they should be replaced by 18-pounders as provided for the New Army gunners, and suggested showing this letter to Leo. Unfortunately things then began to get out of hand. Leo passed the letter to Violet; Violet passed it onto Clemenceau; Clemenceau put it into *L'Homme Libre,* the paper he owned in France; and finally it became the basis of an article in *The Times.* On 3 September Ivor found it necessary to tell Tiny that: 'You really must forbid Violet ever to send anything I write to any person connected with the press. Leo is alone trustworthy about such things. The fact that Violet "saw no harm" in it only proved that her discretion does not run on military lines.' Since it was presumably Leo who passed the letter to Violet his trustworthiness could also be open to some doubt!

For the first three weeks of August, the three brigades of the 18th Division had been under instruction with the 5th Division and 51st (Highland) Division. On the 22nd of the month came the moment they had all been waiting for, when the 18th was instructed to take over part of the front line from the 5th Division. The sector allotted was between places whose names are familiar to all students of the Somme battles, Carnoy and Mametz. At this stage, life in the line was relatively peaceful in these parts, and so ideal for new arrivals to gain confidence, an aspect mentioned by Ivor in a letter dated 5 September:

> We have just completed a fortnight in the trenches and it has done us a lot of good. Half have already been relieved and the other half are in. There has been just enough artillery firing, sniping, bomb throwing and consequent uncertainty to give the troops confidence, without too many casualties, and I should like another fortnight of similar treatment, if I could arrange it – for the second lot. Total casualties about 150 to date.

Much of the rest of the letter was devoted to the subject of mining, about the value of which Ivor was doubtful, commenting that 'I honestly do not see how either we or the Germans have bettered our situation after months of mining effort!' He also grudged what he regarded as the useless work of digging down shafts 50-feet deep and running galleries out from them towards the enemy lines for distances up to 100 yards. Of those who did the mining he wrote: 'On the face of it, the amusement seems senseless but those concerned (500 men one way and another here) are very keen on their job and so are the RE officers of the Mining companies.' On 29 September, three days after the start of the Battle of Loos, Ivor was writing to say that it was not an 'enviable situation' to be sitting in relative peace while great actions were being fought in other parts of the line. 'However', he told his troops who felt that they were being left out of winning what were still expected to be great victories, 'it is much nicer than it was when we all ran like hares from Mons to Paris!' Tiny was given some information about her husband's doings when Herbert Shoubridge, his excellent GSO1, or Chief of Staff as he would be described today, wrote to her on 3rd October 1915. Starting by telling how much the fighting qualities of New Army divisions varied according to how their commanders had trained them, he went on to say:

> I can't tell you how much all the trouble the General took about getting good Brigadiers and COs is repaying him now. He still keeps going on the same tack – whenever he asks now the GHQ people say – 'Oh we can't do that, Maxse has got all the good men!' He is extraordinarily fit and is always doing something or going somewhere. I am sure there is hardly a front line trench in our whole line that he has not visited.

Monty looks after him very well but we both find it rather difficult to keep him in order when it comes to his going to places he ought not to.

In a letter dated 19 October, Ivor told how he trained his senior officers. The previous day he had taken the commanders of his infantry brigades, Brigadier Generals Hickey, Heneker, and Martin, and his CRA, Brigadier-General Casimir Van Straubenzee, on an all-day staff tour, during which he rehearsed with them on the actual ground the main points of how he intended to fight the battle if attacked on his sector. These brigadier-generals had all been replaced, however, by the following spring. Heneker was wounded and following his recovery was in due course promoted to command a division. Van Straubenzee was also promoted, and other berths were found for Hickey and Martin. The four vacant places were filled by Higginson, to 53 Brigade; Shoubridge, from his appointment as GSO1, to 54 Brigade; Sir Thomas Jackson, Bt, to 55 Brigade; and Metcalfe to CRA. Having spent a day in each brigade area, ensuring that all commanders were fully aware of their neighbour's plans and responsibilities, the next step was for the brigadiers to take their battalion and artillery battery commanders through a similar process at a lower level. In due course battalion commanders were to take out groups of their own officers, on the reason for which Ivor then expounded:

> All this is done to get them out of the very narrow grooves in which they all live. You have no conception how greatly the British officer tends towards a minimum of thoughtfulness in war. Even on matters which affect the life or death of himself, his pals and men, the average officer, good and valiant as he is, will not of his own accord enquire how his next door neighbour proposes to defend his trench in the event of an attack.

More conscious than many of his contemporaries of the importance of co-operation between the infantry and their supporting artillery, Ivor had from the outset picked the best possible gunner officers to serve the division. His first CRA, Brigadier General Stone, had done excellent work in the early days, but had been sent home after arrival in France because he was considered to be too old, at 59, for active service. His successor, Van Straubenzee, was of similar calibre, and he was fortunate to be joined in November 1915 as his new brigade-major, or BMRA, by an officer whom many people consider to have become Britain's greatest soldier of the 20th Century. The 32-year-old Major Alan Brooke was fortunate in his turn to receive this posting, as General Sir David Fraser, his eventual official biographer, has recorded in his masterly life of the man who was to serve his country so well as CIGS in the Second World War. As BMRA Brooke had frequent contact with Ivor. Based on Brooke's own recollections of the occasion, Fraser tells the story of their first meeting:

Brooke reported to Maxse on 20th November. The meeting was typical of both men. Maxse barely said 'good morning', and looked Brooke up and down critically.

'I don't like your hat.'

Brooke was not, however prepared to be put down from the start.

'Neither do I,' he said, 'and if you give me a week's leave I shall go home and buy a new one.'

No week's leave, and no new hat, but no further testing attack until a few days later when the Brigade Major, RA accompanied his Divisional Commander to the trenches, and 'perched on a stick that was protruding out of the hurdle revetment' alongside the General, who monopolized the fire step built for a single sniper. Maxse exposed most of his upper body above the parapet and pointed out various German trenches while Brooke turned his head in the required direction. 'Keep your head still!' said Maxse, 'You're no good as a deer stalker,' an observation which somewhat stung the experienced Brooke. And, a little later as the stick which supported Brooke broke off and he dropped to the bottom of the trench – 'There you are: bobbing about like a bloody sparrow!'

Brooke came deeply to admire Maxse, as did all served him. With his gift of mimicry he also caught the great man's manner perfectly, and at the Staff College, long after the war, Brooke imitating Maxse with humour and affection was one of his most demanded acts. He was now as active and as interested as even he could wish. Not only did he serve an outstanding Divisional Commander but his immediate superior, the Commander Royal Artillery, was a brilliant Artilleryman, Brigadier-General Casimir Van Straubenzee, 'one mass of energy' as Brooke described him.[13]

Also using Brooke's recollections, Fraser provides a succinct picture of Ivor's methods as a 'trainer of the most thorough kind':

He believed in the most exhaustive explanation of every tactic, every theory. He believed in unremitting practice; every set piece attack planned by the 18th Division was incessantly rehearsed on ground specially selected for its similarity to the future battlefield. He believed in physical fitness and stamina, and made demands of calculated severity in training the units of his division, expecting and obtaining the highest standards. He believed in discipline rooted in confidence and self-respect, but did not ignore its outward manifestations on which he insisted with well-known rigour. Above all he believed in thoroughness. With his abrupt and sometimes unconventional manner he had set the indelible mark of his character upon his entire division.

Important visitors appeared from time to time. On 21 September 1915, Lord Kitchener inspected the 8th East Surreys and the 10th Essex. On 25 October, Ivor commanded a parade of battalions from the 5th, 51st

Highland, and 18th Divisions for an inspection by King George V and the
French president, Monsieur Poincaré. Also present were the Prince of
Wales and General Allenby, who had recently taken over the Third Army
from Sir Charles Monro.[14] Ivor had been sad to see Monro depart, as he
had explained in a letter on 21 October: 'It is a great blow to me because
I had complete confidence in him as a *soldier*. Having had the experience
of serving one or two generals who were anything but soldiers, I realise
what a huge difference it makes to one and all on active service.' On 9
January 1916 an old friend appeared on a visit in the form of Monsieur
Clemenceau, at this stage the head of the French Senate Armed Forces
Committee, accompanied by Generals Haig, Robertson, and Lord Cavan.
General Mangin, who was commanding the neighbouring French 5th
Division, was also in the party. Ivor had met him many years before when
he was one of Marchand's officers at Fashoda. During this visit, Ivor took
them all forward to a point where they could have a view of the enemy
lines. While they were there, the enemy began to shell the area, causing
Ivor to tell Clemenceau that he must take cover. 'But remember I am a
soldier', objected the man described by the divisional history as 'a tough
old veteran. "All the more reason why you should obey," countered
General Maxse with a bow and a smile. And Clemenceau obeyed.'[15]

As much concerned with the efficient administration as with tactics,
Ivor took steps to improve the delivery of food to the men in the forward
trenches in a way explained in a letter written on 14 January 1916:

> An immense amount of work has been put in since I took over the lines
> in August. At that date every morsel of food, water, and ammunition
> had to be carried up (one or two miles) to the front trenches by hand by
> infantrymen on fatigue. I calculated that a cooking pot actually travelled
> each day a distance of 15 miles there and back for the meals on men's
> shoulders! . . . Now I have established cookhouses very much nearer the
> front and have laid on water to each of them – thus greatly reducing the
> awful labour of carrying things for miles up and down communication
> trenches.

On 23 January he enjoyed what he described as 'a delightful and unexpected visit from Sir William Robertson, the CIGS, in whom he found
'the same simple downright way of talking as ever'. Robertson told him of
his problems with Squiff (Asquith) and other politicians, who 'lay verbal
pitfalls for the unwary' and make it 'hard to know when to say what you
think and when to keep silence'. There is a further reflection of what
might almost be called the flippancy of leading political figures in England
about the war in a letter to Tiny two months later on 17 March. Lord
Salisbury, son of the great Prime Minister who had died in 1903, and also
Violet's brother-in-law, had stayed with Ivor for two days at his headquarters. While finding him very pleasant, Ivor was caused to make the

comment that 'none of the Cecils seem to me to realise the inmost meaning of this war. They look upon it – quite unconsciously – as a break or
interlude in the game of party politics which is to be resumed when it is
over.'

Towards the end of 1915, planning had begun for a joint offensive by
the British and the French in the Somme region as part of a major effort
of all nations in the alliance against Germany and Austria, which included
Russia and Italy, as well as Britain, France and Belgium, to achieve victory
in 1916. The first disruption to these plans was the massive German
assault on the strongly defended French town of Verdun in February
1916. The slogan 'Ils ne passeront pas' became immortalised as expressing the furious determination of the French resistance. In some of the
most savage fighting of the whole war, French losses mounted to the
point where they were, before long, to have an important effect on the
projected joint operation on the Somme.

Throughout the spring of 1916, preparations for the offensive went on
steadily. On 1 March the 18th Division joined XIII Corps, commanded
by Lieutenant General W N Congreve, VC. The other division in the
Corps was the 30th, also from the New Army, largely recruited from
Liverpool and Manchester with a stiffening of regular battalions in the
brigades. While the relative calm of the division's introduction to active
service continued, and as its first year neared completion, Ivor was able to
enjoy a happy interlude at the end of April. Tiny crossed to France with
John, now 14 and at school at Eton, to stay in Paris at the Hotel Meurice
in the Rue de Rivoli. Ivor came down from Amiens by train to join them.
He then took John back to his headquarters to stay for a few days, before
returning with him to England for a short leave at Little Bognor. John was
also invited during his stay to spend a day at XIII corps headquarters with
General Congreve. It would not be long before there would be no place
for a schoolboy visitor at any headquarters in the area of the Somme.

Notes

Letters quoted in this chapter from and to General Maxse are at the
WSRO, Files 154, 210, 211.

1   Nichols, G H F, *The 18th Division in the Great War* (Blackwood, 1922), pp. 2,
    4.
2   Middlebrook, Martin, *The First Day on the Somme* (Penguin, 1984), p. 19.
3   Nichols, p. 3.
4   Nichols, p. 5.
5   Nichols, p. 8.
6   Harris, Ruth Elwin, *Billie: The Nevill Letters: 1914–1916* (MacRae, 1991), p.
    18. Quoted from IWM 69/53/5

7 Harris, p. 18. Quoted from IWM/PP/MCR/155 *Preparing for War*, unpublished account by Lt-Col H H Hemming.
8 Nichols, pp. 7–8.
9 Harris, p. 20. Quoted from IWM 69/53/5
10 Nichols, p. 7.
11 Harris, p. 26.
12 Harris, P. 27.
13 Fraser, Gen Sir David, *Alanbrooke* (Collins, 1982) pp. 68–9. Taken from notes written by Field Marshal Viscount Alanbrooke after the Second World War.
14 Nichols, p. 22.
15 Nichols, p. 33.

13

Command of the 18th Division on the Somme in July 1916

———•◆•———

As more and more troops were moved into the Somme sector in April, May, and June 1916, it was possible to take divisions out of the line for periods of training in quiet areas well away from the trenches. Welcome as these periods were, it was invariably discovered that the time available for proper training was much more limited than commanders had hoped for. The interference factor which upset so many training arrangements was the endless demand for fatigue parties to undertake labouring tasks on a multitude of projects necessary for supplying the 16 divisions in Fourth Army which would eventually be launched into battle. Ivor was to point out later that throughout the months available '. . . manual labour was required day and night, whenever battalions were out of the trenches. Railways were built, roads created and repaired, train lines laid, water pipes were put underground, cables were buried six feet deep. No rest and no training for the infantry, except during the one week'.[1] As will be shown shortly, in the 18th Division the best possible use was made of the limited time available for training.

Since XIII Corps held the most southerly section of the Fourth Army line, its right-hand boundary marched with the French Sixth Army, part of which was General Balfourier's XX Corps. On 19 May, Ivor told in a letter of going to pay his respects to Balfourier, whose corps was 'considered, in peace and war, the best corps in the French Army'. He went on to tell of Balfourier's 'brilliant intervention at the end of the first week of the Battle of Verdun', and to note that his troops had been 'reconstituted and filled up six times', having been in all the major French battles since the war began'. A few days after this visit he wrote to say that he was just off to review a French division at Balfourier's invitation.

On 15 June a letter recorded the details of a stay at the French GHQ where he was the guest of General de Castelnau, of whom he wrote:

> There is nothing in his appearance to denote 'the strong man' like K or Sir W Robertson, but they tell me that when there is a crisis and no one knows what to do, he appears on the scene, in his simple manner, makes up his mind quickly, gives orders which no one can disobey or hesitate about and leaves his subordinates with the conviction that what he has ordered *is* the best and only thing to be done. This is a great factor in any warfare. Consequently his orders come off and are translated into decisive action at once. This appears to have occurred before the 'Marne' and after the first failure to hold the front in Verdun during the week 21 to 27 Feb 1916.

The same letter ended with an account of lunching near Amiens with Generals Foch and Marchand, the latter being Ivor's old friend from Fashoda days, with whom he had much to talk about. His comment on the Army Group Commander was that: 'Foch is a man with *brains* essentially', a slightly obscure statement from which it can be deduced that Ivor did not find his personality particularly inspiring on this occasion. The mention of Verdun in Ivor's letters is particularly significant when studying the preparatory phase of the Somme battles. As originally conceived, the offensive would be a joint affair, with the French attacking on a 25-mile front similar to the British. Under the pressure of the German onslaught on Verdun, they now said that it would only be possible to do so on an eight-mile front. In addition they wanted the offensive to open earlier than Haig had intended, giving 1 July 1916 as the latest date up to which they could hold on at Verdun without some move to divert the enemy. In these circumstances, Haig's earlier hopes of a great break-out from the trenches into a war of movement began to look forlorn. With much reduced French co-operation the chances of success were lessened, and although the break-out was still hoped for, more limited aims might become necessary, and could in due course be claimed. These aims were now threefold: to draw Germans away from Verdun; to weaken enemy morale by inflicting heavy losses; and to gain ground from which to launch a massive assault in 1917 to achieve final victory.

Frustrated though he was by the limited time allowed for serious training, Ivor made full use of every available minute. In a letter written on 5 July, after the battle had begun, he referred to incidents which

> . . . demonstrate that *training* is everything. If British men know what is wanted of them they can accomplish marvels; the difficulty lies in getting them to understand, each unit its particular job. This was done very thoroughly in the 18th Division on model trenches which we dug at

Cavillon representing (from aeroplane photos) the exact Bosch trenches each company and platoon had to take. But it took time and trouble and endless conferences and rehearsals and practices day after day!

In his study of *British Generalship in the Twentieth Century*, Major-General E K G Sixsmith suggests that Ivor's methods were appreciated beyond his own division. He writes that

> . . . special attention must be directed to Maxse, commander of the 18th Division, because he was an expert trainer who was to have an out-standing influence on the development of British infantry tactics. That he had some influence on the training that went on in XIII Corps cannot be doubted. All who knew him can testify to his dominating personality and to his ability to tell both his superiors and subordinates how things should be done. Let this not suggest that he was dogmatic or pigheaded, he was above all a man who thought things out and who learnt from experience, other people's as well as his own.[2]

During May a new commanding officer for the 12th Middlesex, in 54 Brigade, joined the division. He was to have a remarkable impact on its fortunes before the year was out. On 15 May, Ivor mentioned in his letter that 'Lt-Col Maxwell VC from Viceroy's staff in India has just turned up to command one of my battalions. He is Indian Cavalry, and a bit of a "bug" out there, but seems very nice'. By this stage in the war, Maxwell at 45 was on the old side to be commanding a battalion. There were to be no complaints during the preparations for the Somme offensive about the shortage of shells for the artillery, such as had been heard so often in 1915. It was planned to open with a massive five-day bombardment of the enemy positions, which it was hoped would so pulverise their defences that the infantry could walk across 'no mans land' when it ended to occupy the shattered German trenches with virtually no opposition. And to deal with such opposition as still existed, there would be plenty of ammunition left for the guns to support the advance. At the headquarters of the CRA of the 18th Division, the BMRA, Major Alan Brooke, was working to ensure the best use of every round. Brooke's two tasks were to select and register the targets to be destroyed during the preliminary bombardment, and to prepare the fire plan for supporting the infantry advance when the actual assault was launched. A big part of the preliminary task was the cutting of the wire in front of the enemy trenches. In the 18th Division all its trench mortars were used for this purpose, supported by some shrapnel and high explosive shells, and the job was done most efficiently. Brooke's biographer has recorded the important innovations he made in respect of his second task:

> Above all, Brooke himself had proposed and gained at least partial acceptance of a new system of supporting fire. Brooke knew that many of the enemy machine guns were and would be sited in shell holes

between the main trenches. His system was based on the principle of lifting by fixed increments of a specific number of yards, regulated by the predicted rate of our infantry advance. His artillery operation order provided for the first five lifts to be bombardments of specific trench lines, and thereafter for the barrage to 'creep' by lifts, at ninety-second intervals, of fifty yards. It was the first 'creeping barrage' . . .

The idea of such a type of barrage was French. In the preceding March Brooke had taken a French Colonel Herring round the 18th Division sector. The 'creeping' or 'rolling' barrage in exactly the same form was described to Brooke by Herring. It became, as he said, 'famous and universal'. His very individual contribution, however was to develop the system by converting it into clear maps, so that the barrage could be set out, with its timings and implications 'on the artillery board and fire orders worked out from it'. This device had much occupied Brooke in the weeks before 1st July and the result became standard, with tracings given to each artillery brigade showing battery lanes, lifts and timings.[3]

If the Fourth Army front is envisaged as 'L' shaped, XIII Corps' sector was along the bottom arm, out to the right, and at the far end of it. The corp's two forward divisions, the 18th on the left and Major-General John Shea's on the right, looked due north towards the village of Montauban. The 9th (Scottish) Division was in reserve. The right-hand or western boundary of XIII Corps marched with Balfourier's French XX Corps. The map at page 141, taken from the divisional history, and widely used in several other publications, shows the enemy trenches and strongpoints facing the 18th Division. The Pommiers redoubt reinforced the formidable Pommiers trench line in the centre of the divisional objective, while to the right the boundary with the 30th Division cut through the western end of Montauban village.

Although they were not to know it at the time, there were certain aspects of the positions allotted to the two divisions in the XIII Corps sector which were to give them the advantage over those situated further north. As Fraser points out, they looked '. . . northward over slightly rising fields towards the villages of Montauban and Mametz. The terrain was comparatively straightforward, the objectives clear'.[4] Opposite such places as Fricourt and Beaumont-Hamel it was a different story. Partly due to skilful interdiction by the British gunners, the German artillery grouped opposite XIII Corps, and its neighbouring XV corps on the left, was far weaker than that ranged against formations further north. Eventually there were only 10 batteries of German field guns and 13 of heavies in the south, while 68 batteries opposed VIII Corps north of the River Ancre. Furthermore, the counter-battery tasks which continued to be fired against the reduced enemy gun sites in the south were augmented by assistance from the heavy guns of the neighbouring French XX Corps.[5]

While the famous, quick-firing French field guns, the 75s, were of modern design, some heavy pieces were antediluvian. But this did not destroy their effectiveness, as a description of them firing, by Captain Jean Pozzi, the French liaison officer attached to Ivor's headquarters, will show. In his book *La Première Bataille de la Somme*, Pozzi described how these archaic weapons 'se sauvent littéralement de cinq ou six mètres après chaque coup', but, in spite of this 'obtiennent des résultats d'une précision qui stupéfie nos alliés britanniques'.[6]

Finally, because of the relatively open nature of the terrain, the Germans had put fewer troops in their forward trenches opposite XIII Corps than was their normal custom. This meant that these trenches could be quickly taken. There would be the usual depth of defences to be tackled thereafter, but from closer starting points.

The bombardment designed as the all-destroying prelude to the Fourth Army attack began on 24 June 1916, with zero-hour for the infantry assault scheduled for 7.30am on the 29th. 'But the weather', as Martin Middlebrook explains in his splendid book, *The First Day on the Somme*, 'was a source of anxiety. A series of heavy summer storms had broken out on 26 and 27 June and it was still raining heavily in the early hours of the 28th, only 24 hours away from zero-hour.'[7] At 11am that day the decision was made to postpone the start of the attack for 48 hours, making 7.30am on 1 July the new zero-hour. All the complicated arrangements caused by such a change in plans were dealt with skilfully. 'The postponement was handled with the minimum amount of disorganization and was, for once, a triumph for the much abused staff.'[8]

Ivor had moved up close to the forward trenches on 28 June, ready for the start of operations the next day. Due to the postponement, he had time to write on 29 June: 'Here is another line from my dugout where I am comfortably lodged with plenty of blankets and a sound roof . . . it has been raining so hard that the trenches are in a bad condition.' He added: 'Everyone is in excellent spirits hoping to give the Bosch a good thump shortly.'

During 30 June the trenches in the divisional area were packed with troops, and it was fortunate that the enemy shelling was relatively light at the time. It would later transpire that in Montauban, as explained by Terry Norman in *The Hell They Called High Wood*, 'a French 240mm mortar bomb had penetrated an important dugout with devastating effect. The dugout had been a central artillery command post and every occupant was killed in the explosion, thereby substantially disorganizing the control of enemy artillery fire in that area.'[9]

At 6.30am on 1 July the artillery opened up with the first shells of the furious, one-hour barrage which reached a crescendo at 7.20, 10 minutes before zero-hour. While this was being fired some units in the division moved forward to take up positions in 'no man's land' close to where their

own shells were falling. In these cases, Ivor had warned them to be prepared to accept up to six percent casualties from friendly fire in return for
the advantage of being closer to the enemy when the final bombardment
ended.[10] There was a momentary stillness when it did, and then the
infantry assault began, while the gunners fired the first of the 35 lifts
ahead of them that were to constitute the 'creeping barrage' which proved
such a success.

All three brigades in the division were employed in the front line for the
attack: 54 Brigade on the left, 53 in the centre, and 55 Brigade on the
right. Their first objectives were the two trench lines known as Train
Alley and Pommiers Trench. Next they were to advance to take the second objectives, Montauban Alley and the strongpoint just south of the
Montauban–Mametz road known as the Pommiers Redoubt. Finally the
third requirement was to establish a defensive position on the Montauban
Ridge overlooking the narrow, winding wood 500 yards beyond, aptly
named Caterpillar Wood. As the battalions set off towards these objectives, an incident occurred which caught the public imagination at the
time. This was the kicking forward of two footballs towards the German
trenches by men of a company of the 8th East Surreys, on the right flank
of 55 Brigade. They were commanded by Captain Billie Nevill, some of
whose letters have been quoted earlier. His intention was to give his men
something to divert their minds from thinking too much about danger as
they went forward, but the gesture was to be wrongly judged in two ways.
At first it was lauded as demonstrating British 'pluck and sporting spirit'
to the Hun, and in later years condemned as foolish bravado. Like so
many incidents in the war, great and small, it would never be seen in its
true light by the public at home. Unlike the infantry advancing on most of
the Fourth Army front, men of the 15th Division, and of the 30th on their
right, discovered that most of the enemy wire facing them had been well
cut up. The main resistance during the first stage of the advance came
from an area of small craters, some 150 yards wide, on the right of the
road running south from Montauban to Carnoy. Machine-gun and rifle
fire from the determined German defenders of these craters held up 55
Brigade and the right-hand elements of 53 Brigade for some time, and
inflicted heavy casualties on their leading battalions. The progress of 54
Brigade and the left of 53 was assisted by the exploding of a massive
mine, of 5,000 pounds of explosive, under a strong enemy machine-gun
cost at Kasino point. Perhaps because the charge had not been set deep
enough, or because of some other fault, the debris of the mine, as
explained by Middlebrook, 'instead of rising straight up and falling back
around the crater in the normal manner, spread out and fell over a wide
area'. The result was that many soldiers were hurt by falling slabs of stone
and chalk, some seriously, but the overall effect was favourable, with the
machine-gun post having 'gone sky-high'.[11]

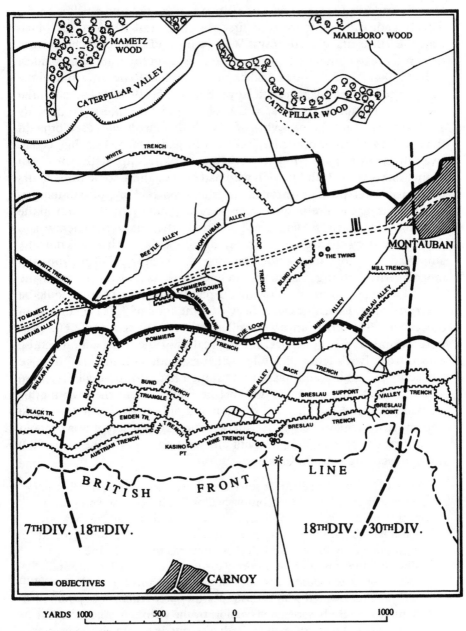

MAMETZ WOOD

MARLBORO' WOOD

CATERPILLAR VALLEY

CATERPILLAR WOOD

WHITE TRENCH

BEETLE ALLEY

MONTAUBAN ALLEY

LOOP TRENCH

BLIND ALLEY

THE TWINS

MONTAUBAN

PRITZ TRENCH

POMMIERS REDOUBT

POMMIERS LANE

MILL TRENCH

MINE ALLEY

BRESLAU ALLEY

TO MAMETZ

DANTZIG ALLEY

POMMIERS TRENCH

THE LOOP

BULGAR ALLEY

BLACK ALLEY

POPOFF LANE

MINE ALLEY

BACK TRENCH

BUND TRENCH

TRIANGLE

BRESLAU SUPPORT

VALLEY TRENCH

BLACK TR.

EMDEN TR.

DAY TRENCH

BRESLAU POINT

AUSTRIAN TRENCH

KASINO PT

MINE TRENCH

BRESLAU TRENCH

BRITISH   FRONT   LINE

7TH DIV. 18TH DIV.

18TH DIV. 30TH DIV.

━━ OBJECTIVES

CARNOY

YARDS 1000   500   0   1000

BATTLE OF JULY 1ST 1916

While the 7th Bedfords and the 11th Royal Fusiliers in 54 Brigade made good progress, reaching Pommiers Trench by 7.50am, the 7th Queens and 8th East Surreys in 55 Brigade were fighting a stiffer battle. This brigade did not arrive at its first objective until 10.15am, by which time the 7th Buffs and 7th Royal West Kents had been brought forward from reserve to compensate for the heavy losses in the leading battalions.

By 9.30am, 54 Brigade had taken the Pommiers Redoubt, while in the centre, the 8th Norfolks and 6th Royal Berks of 53 Brigade had captured the Loop Trench system, at the back of the Pommiers Trench, by 10.20am. At 11am these two brigades were in contact with each other at the north-east corner of the Redoubt. 55 Brigade reached its final objective on Montauban Alley at 1.30pm, linking up with the 16th Manchesters from 30th Division who had arrived there some three hours previously after pushing through the shattered remains of Montauban village. During the afternoon, patrols were sent out up to 500 yards in the direction of Caterpillar Wood, and reported little sign of the enemy.

A straightforward account of the events of the day such as this must be amplified to bring fuller understanding to the story. Throughout the morning the fighting was desperately confused, and the men on the ground were not aware of following the pattern of incidents that could be described later. Casualties were heavy. Of the total of 3,711 incurred, 45 officers and 871 other ranks were killed, and 103 officers and 2,692 men were wounded.[12] A better feel for the reality of the day's action can be gained from Ivor's letter of 5 July, which expanded on the brief note he had scribbled on the 2nd to say that his men had 'captured all they were asked to take'. Starting by saying that he had no idea when writing his hurried note on 2 July that 'my division and only one other in the whole Fourth Army achieved complete success and got to where it was ordered on the first day of the infantry assault', he went on to praise the men of the division, starting with the artillery:

> Those who saw the 18th Div start and those who have seen what my artillery (under Metcalfe) accomplished on 1st July, are so complimentary that we are inclined to blush when we hear them talking. My boys are still hanging on to their objective and gaining a little more ground, but on one of my flanks and still more towards the north, the progress is slow and the Bosch are stubbornly disputing every inch of ground.
>
> There were wonderful episodes of simple unadvertised pluck and determination by men who had no idea they were doing a big thing! I can quote two. Both were made possible by the strenuous training of the division whilst I was at Cavillon, both were made extremely dangerous by the Bosch fire.
>
> 1) The 8th Bn East Surreys and the 7th Bn Bedfordshire were very heavily shelled for a whole hour whilst lying out in our forming up trenches waiting for the exact minute (7.30am). One platoon of the

East Surreys lost every single officer, NCO and man except only one Private. That Private, nevertheless, advanced alone to the farthest objective (over a mile behind the front line German trench) and reported himself to the nearest officer of his battalion!

2) In the 7th Bedfordshires, there were 16 Company officers with their companies at the start of the battle. Five were killed or wounded in one dugout by one Bosch shell during our five days preliminary bombardment: eight more officers were knocked out by the Bosch barrage while waiting for the hour of assault on 1st July. Thus the battalion went over our parapets with only three officers in its four companies; yet the battalion reached its furthest objective in comparatively good order and did what it had to do on the way – namely kill the Bosches.

These episodes which are absolutely true ones demonstrate that *training* is everything.

During the first night on the newly won objective, a counter-attack by the enemy was beaten back by the men in the village of Montauban, who were mainly from 30th Division. At times the village, and the 18th Division trenches along the ridge west of it, were heavily shelled, but the ground ahead remained virtually empty of Germans to a depth of over two miles for several days. The divisional history tells how:

> On 3rd July Lieut-Colonel F.A. Maxwell, VC, reconnoitred nearly two miles in front of the new line, taking with him a Vickers gun and its gun team for emergencies. On the night of 4th July, Captain S. le F. Shepherd, of the Northants, brought in two German field guns that had been abandoned 400 yards from White Trench, while the same morning two companies of the Essex creeping stealthily down from Montauban Alley to Caterpillar Wood, found that the enemy had stolen away.[13]

While everyone who has made a study of the battles of the Somme knows how Congreve told Rawlinson about the complete absence of the enemy in the area facing XIII Corps on the first day, and how his plea for advantage to be taken of this fact was turned down, not many may realise that the land lay empty for three days or more after the fighting on 1 July.

On 8 July, Ivor wrote to say that the 18th was being relieved by the 3rd Division at 4pm, and that two of his brigades were 'already back enjoying a rest'. Near the end of the letter, which contained more reflections on the action on 1 July, he mentioned, as 'one of the most satisfactory features of our attack', the complete destruction of the German wire entanglements by the artillery heavy trench mortars. Two days later, on 10 July, he wrote again to tell how he had been inspecting all the 13 battalions in the division and 'was astonished at their excellent good spirits and happy appearance'. The period of rest in billets well behind the line was soon to end, however, when on the morning of 11 July, 55 Brigade was ordered to move forward to Maricourt to act as reserve brigade to the 30th Division, then involved in bitter fighting in an attempt to capture Trônes Wood, which stood a mile and a half east of Montauban, beyond Bernafay Wood. Due to constant heavy shelling by both sides, the wood had become a tangle of fallen trees in which the men of the 30th Division had become exhausted and had taken devastating losses. Because of the importance of holding the wood, to guard the right flank of a major attack northwards planned to start at 3.20am on 14 July, there was consternation at XIII Corps headquarters when it was learnt on 12 July that a German attack had driven the 30th Division out of all but a small portion at the southern end of it. In his report on the action, which is quoted fully in the divisional history, Ivor wrote: 'The result was that in the evening of the 12th July the 18th Division was ordered to relieve the 30th Division. The relief was completed by 10am on the 13th'.[14] Its further orders were to capture Trônes Wood by midnight 13–14 July at all costs. This task was given to 55 Brigade, which had already taken over from 89 Brigade of the 30th Division at the south-east corner of the wood. The 12th Middlesex and the 6th Northamptons from 54 Brigade were put at the disposal of the commander of 55 Brigade if he should need them.

A heavy barrage by the German artillery met the attack by 55 Brigade when it was launched at 7pm on 13 July. Neither the 7th Queens attacking from the left, nor the 7th Buffs on the west, made much progress into the wood. Scattered groups from the 7th Royal West Kents did however reach the railway line running across the middle of the wood, about 600 yards from the southern end. The situation was hopelessly confused, with no information coming back from the troops in the wood, and it became clear that 55 Brigade had achieved no more than earlier efforts by the 30th Division. At midnight Ivor was telephoned by Congreve from XIII Corps headquarters and asked what he intended to do. The answer was that he would relieve 55 by 54 Brigade, and that he still hoped to take the wood by 3.20am. He explained the extent of the task in his report: 'When it is realised that barrages of fire, both British and German, had been directed upon all parts of the wood for many hours during several days by all calibres of British and German artillery, some notion may be formed of the difficulties encountered by any battalion which had to attack it, unreconnoitred, in the night.'[15]

In the end, the wood was not cleared of the enemy until just after 9am on 14 July, but the activity in it was sufficient to prevent any German interference with the attack launched at 3.20am to the west. This operation achieved an early success against enemy second-line trenches between Delville Wood and Contalmaison, but later ran out of steam. The story of how Trônes Wood was eventually taken revolves around Colonel Frank Maxwell of the 12th Middlesex. His battalion and the 6th Northamptons were the leading units of 54 Brigade, and because of the difficulty of communicating with them once they had entered the wood, Brigadier-General Shoubridge put Maxwell in command of the two battalions and any troops of 55 Brigade that he might find and take under his wing. The method he eventually used to achieve success was described in a letter he wrote to his wife. He started by telling of his arrival at the south of the wood with two of his own companies, and his taking over command of the Northamptons, whose own commanding officer had been killed. Then came his account of the action he took:

To talk of a 'wood' is to talk rot. It was the most dreadful tangle of dense trees and undergrowth imaginable, with deep yawning broken trenches criss-crossing about it; every tree broken off at top or bottom and branches cut away, so that the floor of the wood was almost an impenetrable tangle of timber, trenches, undergrowth, etc., blown to pieces by British and German heavy guns for a week.

Never was anything so perfectly dreadful to look at – at least I couldn't dream of anything worse – particularly with its dreadful addition of corpses and wounded men – many lying there for days and days. (Our doctor found one to-day who had had no food or water for five days.)

Well, I formed a line with fragments of Northants and two companies of my own, under a job lot of about five very young officers, all the rest being *hors de combat*.

After infinite difficulty, I got it shaped in the right direction, and then began the advance, very, very, slowly. Men nearly all much shaken by the clamour and din of shell-fire, and nervy and jumpy about advancing in such a tangle of debris and trenches etc. I had meant only to organize and start the line, and then get back to my loathsome ditch, back near the edge of the wood where we had entered, so as to be in communication by runners with the Brigade and the world outside. It is a fundamental principle that commanders of any sort should not play about, but keep in touch with the higher authorities behind. But though old enough soldier to realise this, and the wrath of my seniors for disregarding it, I immediately found that without my being there the thing would collapse in a few minutes. Sounds vain, perhaps, but there is nothing of vanity about it really. So off I went with the line, leading it, pulling it on, keeping its direction, keeping it from its hopeless (and humanly natural) desire to get into a single file behind me, instead of a long line either side. Soon I made them advance with fixed bayonets, and ordered them, by way of encouraging themselves, to fire ahead of them into the tangle all the way. This was a good move, and gave them confidence, and so we went on with constant halts, to adjust the line. After slow progress in this way, my left came on a hornet's nest, and I halted the line and went for it with the left portion. A curtain may be drawn over this, and all that need be said was that many Germans ceased to live, and we took a machine-gun. Then on again, and then again, what I had hoped for. The Germans couldn't face a long line offering no scattered groups to be killed, and they began to bolt, first back, then, as the wood became narrow, they bolted out to sides, and with rifle and automatic guns we slew them. Right up to the very top this went on, and I could have had a much bigger bag, except that I did not want to show my people out of the wood, or too much out, for fear of letting the German artillery know how we had progressed, and so enable them to plaster the wood *pari passu* with our advance. So far they had only laid it on thick, strong, and deadly in the belt we had left behind. However many we let go for this reason, we slew or picked up later.

And, finally the job was done, and I was thankful, for I thought we should never, never get through with it.[16]

Ivor's views on the proper place for a battalion commander to be during an attack were well known, and in one of his earlier letters about the action on 1 July he had written: 'Our losses in senior officers are nil because I had them all dug in and kept them tight in hand.' While he could not on this occasion censure Maxwell for getting into the middle of the leading infantrymen, it was not a practice of which he normally approved. Though not incurring his 'senior's wrath', Maxwell earned from Ivor the title of 'my best platoon commander' as a result of his action. But Ivor's pride in its success was made clear in a letter written two days later on 16 July. After describing the regiments from the southern and eastern counties as 'the boys to go fighting with', he went on to say that although slow to anger '. . . suddenly in the battle they wake up and go for it like demons. They are simply splendid, The way they captured and held Trônes Wood, after about four failures by previous troops, was a magnificent feat on the morning of the day before yesterday.' The cost of success was heavy. The casualties recorded in 54 and 55 Brigades amounted to 21 officers killed and 55 wounded, with 206 other ranks killed and 1,245 wounded. In his report on the operation Ivor mentioned that: 'The Northamptons lost 15 officers and about 300 other ranks, and the Middlesex 7 officers and about 300 other ranks.' He also gave a special word of praise to the men of the 7th Royal West Kents who had . . . 'through the night of 13th–14th July maintained their position in isolated parties in the wood in which there were a large number of Germans'.[17]

After the hard fighting from 1 to 17 July, when the victors of Trônes Wood were finally relieved by troops from the 30th Division, Ivor expected to take his battered battalions out of the line for a period of reinforcement and retraining. Preparations were under way for doing so when at 7pm on 18 July a telephone message from XIII Corps called for the immediate despatch of a brigade to assist the 9th Scottish Division fighting at Delville Wood, which lies half a mile north from the apex of Trônes Wood, at the eastern edge of the village of Longueval. By this time, the three brigades of the 9th Division, 26, 27 and the South African Brigade, had been fighting in the area for four days, having been part of the 3.20am attack on 14 July for the flank protection of which the securing of Trônes Wood had been so essential. By 15 July most of Delville Wood had been in South African hands, but at 8am on 18 July a colossal bombardment had started, which went on for over seven hours, reducing the wood to a shambles of splintered trees and churned up earth, and killing many of its defenders. At 3.30pm, an assault had been launched by a strong force of fresh German soldiers who drove the remnants of the South African Brigade back into the south-west corner of the wood. Because the holding of this corner was considered so vital, the call came for a further brigade to be put in to support the South Africans. 53 Brigade, relatively untouched during the Trônes Wood action, was the obvious one for Ivor to send on what was to prove, in the words of Brigadier General Higginson, the 'grave-yard' of his brigade. Although the divisional history is right to call the operation . . . 'a triumph of individual bravery and resource – particularly on the part of the non-commissioned officers,'[18] it was in no other way a triumph. The 8th Norfolks were designated to lead the advance into the wood, and an artillery barrage was laid on to support them at 6.15am. Finding that he was not ready by then, the commanding officer asked for it to be delayed until 7.15am. His message did not reach brigade headquarters in time, and his advance therefore began without artillery covering fire. Trying to make their way to the wood through Longueval, the Norfolks were badly held up by machine-gun fire. The 10th Essex pushed through into the inferno of the wood and joined up with the South Africans. The 8th Suffolks were only able to clear part of Longueval village, although instructed to take all of it. During the night of 21–22 July, 53 Brigade was relieved, having held on to the vital corner of Delville Wood and part of Longueval, but at the cost of 12 officers killed and 39 wounded, and 181 other ranks killed and 773 wounded. With the return of 53 Brigade to the fold, after this disastrous spell under command of the 9th Division, the 15th was moved 50 miles north to a rest area in the Third Army sector near Armentières. During the first part of their six-week spell away from the front-line, the battalions were mostly occupied with taking in reinforcements. Then in the middle of August, a period of intensive training was put in hand in preparation for a return to the Somme. As the time approached for the move south, Ivor was told that the 18th Division would come under command of Lieutenant General Sir Claud Jacob's II Corps, part of the Reserve, later Fifth Army, on its arrival back in the Somme sector. Jacob was an old friend who had been in the same Sandhurst intake in 1881.

After its victories in July, apart from the Delville Wood episode when not under his direct command, Ivor's division had achieved the reputation of being one of the best in the BEF. Following the first successful fortnight, with his own flag flying so high, he felt confident enough to tell Tiny to be careful to avoid becoming involved in the increasingly popular game at home of criticising the performance of certain generals. At the end of his letter of 16 July he had warned her against 'crabbing' other commanders, saying that: 'It is all very petty and foolish and I most sincerely hope (and expect) that you will never do anything similar: . . . In this war we must *seek* for nothing: do our job in the best way we can: and recognize that there is a great element of luck, or unluck, in the whole business.' He was astute enough to know that so far his own luck had held.

Notes

Letters from General Maxse in this chapter can be found in files 210 and 211, Maxse papers at WSRO, Chichester.

1   Prior, Robin and WILSON, Trevor, *Command on the Western Front* (Blackwell, 1992), p. 156. The letter quoted was written by Maxse to Maj.-Gen. Montgomery-Massingberd, Chief of Staff, Fourth Army on 31 July 1916.
2   Sixsmith, Maj Gen. E K G, *British Generalship in the 20th Century* (Arms and Armour Press, 1970), p. 93.
3   Fraser, Gen, Sir David, *Alanbrooke* (Collins, 1982), p. 72.
4   Fraser, p. 70.
5   Prior and Wilson, p. 104.
6   Maxse papers, IWM, 69/53/8.
7   Middlebrook, Martin, *The First Day on the Somme* (Penguin, 1984), p. 102.
8   Middlebrook, p. 103.
9   Norman, Terry, *The Hell they Called High Wood* (Kimber, 1984, 1989), p. 42.
10 Middlebrook, p. 279.
11 Middlebrook, pp. 126–7.
12 Nichols, *The 18th Division in the Great War* (Blackwood, 1922), p. 48, records 3.707, but the correct figure of 3.711 is in the Maxse papers 69/53/7.
13 Nichols, pp. 49–50.
14 Nichols, p. 53.
15 Nichols, p. 55.
16 Maxwell, Mrs C., *Frank Maxwell, Brig General, VC, CSI, DSO: A Memoir and Some Letters* (John Murray, 1921), pp. 153–61. Maxwell's description of the taking of Trônes Wood has been quoted in several other books.
17 Nichols, pp. 68–9.
18 Nichols, p. 70.

14

The Capture of Thiepval and the Schwaben Redoubt during Operations from September to December 1916

———·◆·———

The main events covered in this chapter were described by Ivor in December 1916 in a lengthy report entitled *The 18th Division in the Battle of the Ancre*, which was in due course published in printed form with a red cover. At the top of his own copy he wrote 'Ivor Maxse – his book', and from here on it will be referred to as 'The Red Book' rather than by its full title. It begins with a resumé of the division's activities from 24 June to the end of November 1916. This finishes with the claim that:

> . . . the capture of Thiepval and the Schwaben Redoubt were distinct and important episodes even in a great war. They involved in each case a deliberate assault and the capture of a considerable depth of intricate trenches defended by stubborn German regiments who had held their ground against many previous attacks. After visiting the ground at leisure and in peace I am to this day lost in admiration at the grit shown by the British battalions which fought continuously from 26th September to 5th October and conquered such strongholds as Thiepval and Schwaben. I therefore deem that the story be told in some detail and with all the accuracy I can command.[1]

During the training period in the Third Army area west of Arras from 20 August to 8 September Ivor concentrated on two subjects which he considered particularly important: attack formations and consolidation on taking an objective. As usual everything was taught and rehearsed down to the smallest detail. All was done in a precise and methodical manner. Writing later to Major General A A Montgomery, Chief of Staff at Fourth Army headquarters, on 18 November he gave as one of his answers to a request for lessons learned in the Somme battles, his opinion that training directives must deal with 'methods' rather than 'principles'.[2] His men were given specific instructions on how to tackle every stage of an attack and not, as in many divisions, merely reminded of a few general principles of warfare and left to get on with it. 'As regards attack formations', he wrote in the red book, 'the doctrine in the 18th Division is as follows:–

> (a) Teach, drill and practise a definite form of attack so that every man shall know it thoroughly. On this basis of theory and knowledge common to all, any brigade, battalion or company commander varies his attack formation to suit any condition which may be peculiar to his front and to his objective. The reason for this system is that all ranks know at least one attack formation thoroughly. It can be varied according to circumstances and at short notice.[3]

On 3 September full notes were distributed throughout the division on quick consolidation on captured objectives. These were signed by Ivor's GSO1, the exceptional Lieutenant Colonel Wallace Wright, VC, of whom he was to write later, in a letter to Tiny, that he was 'A1'.[4]

The valuable spell of training completed, the division moved out of Third Army territory to join Claud Jacob's II Corps in the Reserve Army, soon to be renamed Fifth Army, under General Sir Hubert Gough. Up to this time Ivor had not, as he put it later in a letter to Tiny on 7 October, 'even seen H. Gough before I joined his Army!' Their paths were, however, to be closely linked for much of the rest of the war. In the book he eventually published about the Fifth Army in 1931, 'Goughie', as he was widely referred to throughout the army, recorded his recollections of how: 'The 18th Division came in and took over the line immediately south of Thiepval . . .'. Of the divisional commander he wrote:

> Maxse had an immense capacity for grasping the more important points in training and the new military operations which this modern form of warfare was forcing upon us. Quick and energetic, with a great capacity for work, he did not suffer fools gladly, but at the same time he never failed to encourage initiative among his subordinates; he drove them hard, but one and all, long before they had finished their experiences of fighting the Germans under his command, realised the soundness and value of his training, and thanked him for it.[5]

Every minute of the fortnight available for preparation for the assault on the remains of Thiepval village, and on the heavily defended Schwaben Redoubt 1,000 yards beyond it, was used to the full. On 1 July the 36th (Ulster) Division had taken the whole of the Thiepval plateau, a magnificent feat which Sixsmith suggests was 'inspired no doubt by the anniversary of the Battle of the Boyne'. Left unsupported, while efforts were wasted in renewing attacks which had failed elsewhere, the

Ulstermen were eventually driven off the ground, and the Germans who retook it determined to turn the whole area into an impregnable fortress. Later British assaults in July and August were beaten off with ease. In being chosen to make another attempt to take Thiepval in late September, the 18th Division was being paid a great compliment, but Ivor had no doubt that the task would be a severe test. Afterwards, he might confidently write in the red book: 'With sufficient time to prepare an assault on a definite and limited objective, I believe a well trained division can capture almost any 'impregnable' stronghold, and this doctrine had been taught to the 18th Division.'[6] Before the event he would hardly have been human if he had not had some doubts about the outcome. As he had put it in a letter on 3 September, 'I cannot get to the bottom of the prevailing optimism in high places, and as I have invariably been taken in by it in former years, I do not allow myself now to indulge in day dreams about the Bosch!'

'PREVIOUS PREPARATION', to which Ivor accorded these capital letters to stress its importance, began as soon as the division arrived on the Ancre on 9 September 1916. He recorded that:

> Arrangements were then made to acquaint all company, battalion and brigade commanders with the ground over which operations were probable. Motor cars and 'buses were placed at our disposal and parties of officers were familiarised with the ground and the approaches to it. But above all an admirable lecture was given at my request to brigade and battalion commanders by Brigadier-General P. Howell, General Staff, at Corps Headquarters on the *local* situation and on recent fighting experiences on this particular front.'[7]

The benefits of this lecture were twofold. It put 'life and intelligence' into the work of preparation by battalion commanders, and it ensured that everyone understood the importance of Thiepval, and of the high ground around the Redoubt beyond it, from which the enemy had observation over British positions as far back as Albert, four miles away.

Throughout the 'Previous Preparation' phase everyone was told in full detail about what to expect when the attack was launched. As Ivor put it:

> The system in the Division is to tell subordinates as much as possible of impending operations long before they occur . . . It is better to risk information leaking out through captured prisoners than to run the risk of ordering infantry over the parapet unacquainted with what they are expected to do or where they are to go.[8]

By the second half of September the main thrust of the Reserve (Fifth) Army's onslaught on the German positions was from ground to the south of Thiepval captured earlier in the month. Much of the line occupied by the British further north, at the top of the upright arm of the 'L' described earlier, was the same as on 1 July. The 18th Division's attack was to be part of a major effort by II corps and I Canadian Corps to take the ridge that ran from Thiepval to Courcelette, some three miles away to the east. To the right of the 18th was the 11th Division, and beyond it the Canadians. The artillery of the 18th Division had been attached to the Canadian Corps for the coming battle.

The 18th Division was not, however, to be left without artillery support. This was provided by allotting the fire of the field guns of the 25th and 49th Divisions to the 18th. These would shoot from its left flank as it advanced, making the laying of barrages across the axis of attack even more effective than when put down by overhead fire. A battery of 6-inch howitzers was placed at Ivor's disposal from II Corps artillery, and began a steady softening up of chosen enemy positions well in advance of the attack. Care was taken not to destroy trenches which it was intended to use during the consolidation phase of the battle. To ensure efficient working the 'artillery staff and that of the division were in the closest possible touch and lived in huts next door to one another. All arrangements were discussed by word of mouth, thus avoiding telephone conversations and written messages.'[9] Four tanks were allotted to the division, and Ivor told Tiny about them in a letter on 20 September:

> I have thoroughly examined our new 'tanks' and discussed them with those on board. They are weird things and have been described in the London newspapers pretty correctly. . . . But we have at last a good thing before Bosch and he will take six months to produce a better. They have already done more military damage than all the Zeppelins put together in two years.

Although not entirely successful at Thiepval, the tanks were continuously supported by Ivor when many other commanders were dismissive of them.

Some of the hardest worked members of the division, both before and during the battle were the Royal Engineers. After it was over Ivor was to describe their commander Colonel H C Joly de Lotbinière, known as Joby, as 'worth his weight in gold' and as 'the best CRE in the whole Army'. The trenches from which the attack was to be launched were taken over from the 49th Division on 21 September, when they were found to be in poor condition, with only one communication trench, called Prince Street, which was barely passable by day. Five days later, by the morning of 26 September when the operation was due to begin, 2,500 yards of assembly trenches had been dug, long, deep communication trenches had been opened up, grids had been laid, and dumps of engineer stores established well forward, ready for the consolidation phase. As well as the 79th, 80th and 92nd Field companies, RE, de Lotbinière had the divisional pioneers, 8th Royal Sussex, and sappers from the 49th division do the heavy digging and carrying required. From 23 to 25 September this work-force had to be augmented at night by men from the 8th East Surreys and 7th Queens in 55 Brigade in order to get everything done in time. Needless to say, all concerned were exhausted by the morning of the 26th, but their efforts were a vital contribution to the success of the attack. Jacob's plan for II Corps envisaged the 11th and 18th Divisions attacking simultaneously, with the 11th given as its objective the taking of Zollern and Stuff Redoubts, and the 18th the capture of Thiepval and the Schwaben Redoubt. 146 Brigade of the 49th Division under Brigadier General Goring Jones, was attached to the 18th Division. Its mission was to hold the front-line trenches immediately east of the Ancre, and to provide an infantry battalion for the attack on the Schwaben Redoubt which was to follow the capture of Thiepval. Following the first stage of the assault of each division a pause of one hour was ordered on the Zollern–Thiepval line north of the village. Within the 18th Division sector, the arrangements for the operation were clearly described by Ivor in two paragraphs in his red book. He first explained that the attacking brigades were 53, on the right, with 54 on the left, while 55 Brigade was in reserve, east of the Ancre, ready to move forward to exploit success, The task of 53 and 54 Brigades was to clear the whole network of trenches in the area allotted to each. This had to be accomplished in co-operation with the troops on their flanks, and within forward limits imposed by the artillery barrage table. The next paragraph described the methods to be employed by the infantry:

> Zero hour was 12.35 p.m. on the 26th September when a heavy shrapnel fire was to give the signal for the first wave of infantry to leave its trenches and advance straight for the main German defences south of Thiepval at a slow walk. The distance across No Man's Land averaged 250 yards, The barrage 'lifts' were to move at the rate of 100 yards in 3 minutes at the start, increasing the pace to 100 yards in 2 minutes when the shelled area was passed . . .[10]

The choice of 12.35pm for zero-hour was undoubtedly due to Ivor, who must have persuaded Jacob that it was a better time to begin an attack than the usual dawn start. Throughout the war, he persistently stuck to this theory, believing that the dawn alternative had two serious disadvantages. First, that the troops reached their objectives a few hours after dawn, and then had to hold on under artillery fire for the remainder of the day, much of the time without support. The enemy were given plenty of time to locate the British positions in daylight, and then to plan counter-attacks. His second objection was that the men got no proper sleep or food during the night before the assault, and set off from the start line more or less exhausted from the night march up to it. The consequence was that they were too tired to consolidate properly on their objectives, or to deal with enemy counter-attacks. His ideal timing was for the troops to complete the capture of their objective an hour before sunset, in as fresh a state as possible, and to have the following night available for consolidating their position. Therefore zero-hour should be roughly six hours before sunset, assuming that five were allowed for taking a strong enemy-defended locality.

Conferences were held in every battalion in the division on 25 September, using a summary of the local situation which Ivor recorded in the red book. Full details were given of the importance of Thiepval; of the enemy troops holding it; of the weight of British artillery fire poured onto it during the preceding four days, including a gas attack on the night of the 24th; and of the balance in favour of 24 battalions in the 11th and 18th Divisions against 10 German battalions. In respect of the enemy he also wrote:

> Great importance has been attached to Thiepval by the Germans who have issued frequent orders to all concerned to hold it 'at all costs'. They have even boasted in writing that it is impregnable. The 180th Regt of Wurthenburgers have withstood attacks on Thiepval for two years, but the 18th Division will take it tomorrow.[11]

The story of how this confident prediction was made to come true can be summarised briefly in respect of the sequence of events, which is less interesting than the efforts of the people who brought it about. In 53 Brigade on the right, the assaulting battalions, 8th Suffolks and 10th Essex, moved forward in six waves. The 8th Norfolks were in support for mopping up duties, for carrying forward stores, and for escorting two tanks on the brigade's right flank. The 6th Royal Berks were in reserve. The brigade machine-gun company had two sections putting overhead fire down on the remains of Thiepval at 2,150 yards range. With relatively light losses, 53 brigade had reached its first objective by the time the one-hour pause was ordered, and had killed, wounded and taken prisoner many Germans. Setting off again after the pause towards the Schwaben Redoubt, the leading companies were soon checked by enemy fire from all directions, with 10th Essex suffering heavy casualties. Little further progress was made, and at 8.30pm, orders were given for battalions to consolidate positions already gained and to wait for instructions for a more deliberate attack on the Schwaben Redoubt at a later stage.

Since its objectives on the western side of what was left of Thiepval were known to be even more heavily defended than those given to 53 Brigade, the frontage allotted to 54 Brigade was narrower. Shoubridge gave the 12th Middlesex, under Maxwell, the task of taking the remains of the village, and the 11th Royal Fusiliers that of clearing the network of German trenches and dugouts to the left of it. The 6th Northamptons were in close support, but the reserve battalion, the 7th Bedfords, was

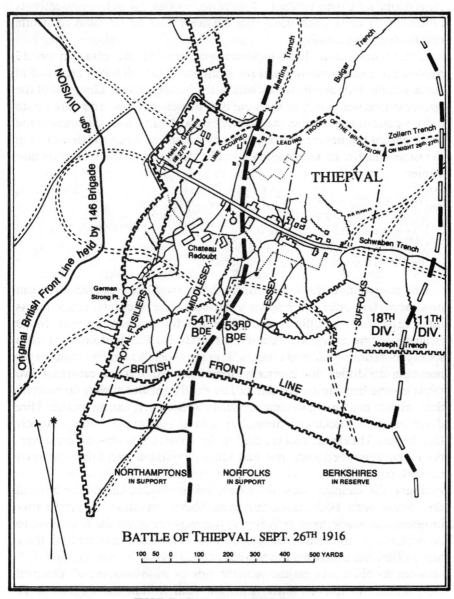

BATTLE OF THIEPVAL. SEPT. 26TH 1916

100 50 0 100 200 300 400 500 YARDS

THE BATTLE OF THIEPVAL
26 September 1916

kept well back in dugouts in Thiepval Wood. Two tanks were attached to 54 Brigade, and it had the assistance of its own machine-gun company and trench mortar battery. By 6pm, after bitter fighting, much of it at close quarters, Thiepval village and the château had been taken, but a section of the trenches to the west were still in German hands. Only remnants remained of the two leading battalions and of the Northants, who had been badly shelled as they followed the others, to hold onto the ground they had so miraculously managed to capture. Maxwell took command of these remnants and formed a defensive system of two lines, 50 yards apart, around the château. A strongpoint was made of the one tank which had reached them during the battle, but had sunk in mud after doing some good work when the struggle for the village was in progress. During the night the 7th Bedfords were brought forward to relieve the men left around the château, and their place in Thiepval Wood was taken by the 7th Royal West Kents from 55 Brigade. The next morning, 27 September, the Bedfords successfully assaulted the Germans still holding out in positions to the west, and by 11am these had been cleared and the whole of the Thiepval plateau had been captured.

Before going on to describe the efforts made to take the Schwaben Redoubt, there are several aspects of the fighting for Thiepval to be mentioned, beginning with the way in which Higginson's plans for 53 Brigade avoided an error that had been the cause of serious loss in earlier operations. It had been standard practice for men following the leading troops in an assault to come forward and occupy the leaders' assembly trenches soon after they had vacated them. The enemy soon realised what was happening and shelled these assembly trenches shortly after an attack began, with devastating results. On this occasion Higginson left them empty, so that when the Germans put down a barrage on them, which Ivor described as 'especially accurate and severe', there were no casualties, even though the trenches were practically obliterated. This barrage over, the support battalion, 8th Norfolks, 'moved rapidly forward over the open in small columns'.[12]

Though 53 Brigade's casualties were light until they had passed beyond their first objectives, 54 Brigade's leading battalions were from the outset involved in hand-to-hand encounters which Ivor described as 'severe and bloody'. Out of the 18th Division's total of 1,456 casualties on 26 and 27 September, 54 Brigade suffered 984, made up of 18 officers and 176 other ranks killed, 29 officers and 563 other ranks wounded, and 198 other ranks missing. Of these 984, the 12th Middlesex accounted for nearly half at a figure of 430, among whom 10 officers and 60 other ranks were killed. Greatly though he was admired by officers and men throughout his battalion, the fact of being commanded by such a heroic figure as Maxwell was a mixed blessing for the Middlesex. After his exploits at Trônes Wood he was bound to be chosen to tackle the most dangerous portion of the German defences at Thiepval. Some extracts from an eight-page letter he wrote to his wife about the battle give an idea of the conditions faced by his men.

> We pushed off over the most awful country that human being ever saw or dreamt of. July 1st was a playground compared to it, and the resistance small. I knew it would be, and I confess I hated the job from the first – which was only three days before we began it. So many attempts had been made, and so many failures, that one knew it could only be a tough thing to take on, and I hadn't personally any particular hopes of accomplishing it, more especially as the distance to be covered – nearly one mile – was enormous for these attacks under any circumstances, and under the special one of country absolutely torn with shell for three months, it was, I considered, an impossibility . . . I will not describe the details of the battle – they would be very difficult to understand. Briefly, we worked up and up our long journey, but left untaken, on our left, a very strong place filled with machine-guns and a determined garrison. This was a thorn in our side, indeed, and it defied all our efforts to take it till this morning, but not till it had done us in for a large number of casualties from first to last. All the regiment spent its night out, of course, either in shell holes or [a very few] in dug-outs, either bombing or engaged with the enemy at close quarters. I had a safe place in a pile of ruins, which managed to ward off shells and all the other unpleasant things of modern battle. It was a busy night for me, though, and not unmixed with anxiety – in fact, very much to the contrary. Perhaps the most trying business is to keep your generals informed of how things are going. It is extraordinarily difficult, for on a field like that of Thiepval telephone wires don't remain uncut by shells for more than five minutes. . . .
>
> This morning I had orders to clear out on relief by another regiment, but, much to the C.O's delight, I disobeyed the order and stayed on to see him through the attack on the stronghold that had beaten us till then. I was in no mind to lose what we had so hardly won by going before he had done his job. And he only did it after three hours attempt. But I have paid the penalty of a dressing down by the general, who is furious. And more furious because I don't mind, and he knows I would do it again even if the King had given me the order.

In a later letter he made a further comment:

> If there were ever an occasion when things might have gone wrong, and the attack died or fizzled out, that one occurred on the 26th. The ground was made for skulking, and every yard afforded opportunity for men to drop down unseen and stay there without being seen. . . .

The general referred to as being furious was Shoubridge, who ticked Maxwell off for remaining with Lieutenant Colonel Price of the Bedfords after being relieved. The divisional history claims that Maxwell's retort to

Shoubridge was: 'What are you grousing about? I've got you another medal.'

The skill with which the Bedfords carried out the relief during the night was given special mention in the red book: 'The problem was to extract three tired battalions from their battle positions and to put one battalion in their place. This had to be done in pitch darkness by troops who had never seen the locality but who had to get to it through a hostile barrage.'[14] Ivor regarded this achievement as a remarkable example of 'efficiency and battle discipline', which disclosed a high standard of training in 54 Brigade. The Bedfords came in for further praise as a result of their successful operation on the morning of 27 September to clear out the remaining enemy positions on a rectangular strip of ground to the west of the village. Much of this success was due to the conduct of Second Lieutenant Adlam, commanding a platoon in the right-hand assaulting company, who earned a Victoria Cross for his efforts. These included leading his men in a dash across open ground, under heavy fire, in order to deal with enemy strongpoints which he cleared by 'a whirlwind attack' using captured German hand-grenades. In the close-quarter fighting inherent in battles of this nature the example of outstandingly brave individuals, such as Maxwell and Adlam, could make the difference between victory and defeat. During the afternoon of 27 September, Haig came to divisional headquarters, and at 4.30pm a message went out to the three brigades to report that: 'The Commander-in-Chief personally called to-day on General Maxse to congratulate the Division on its success at Thiepval.'[15]

Although credit was rightly due for the capture of Thiepval, it was only the first stage of the operation, which had the second objective of the Schwaben Redoubt. When the attack was launched at 12.35pm on 26 September it had been hoped to take both objectives in one day, but the opposition had been too strong. With the first phase completed by midday on the 27th, Ivor had to decide when to set things in motion for the second. Although it was obviously desirable to do so as quickly as possible, he came to the decision after much thought that to attempt an attack on the afternoon of the 27th would be a gamble, 'whereas on the 28th we could make almost a certainty of success and arrange for an overwhelming quantity of artillery to prepare the attack'.[16]

As to the method to use, he had been coming to a decision between three possible alternatives during the afternoon of the 26th. Due largely to the fact that he had begun to have doubts about the ability of the commander of 55 Brigade, he decided to take two of his fresh battalions from his control and use them to reinforce 53 and 54 Brigades. The 7th Queens were attached to 53 Brigade, while the 7th Royal West Kents stayed with 54 Brigade, who were reinforced by the 1/5th West Yorks, on loan from 146 Brigade of the 49th Division. The two remaining battalions of 55

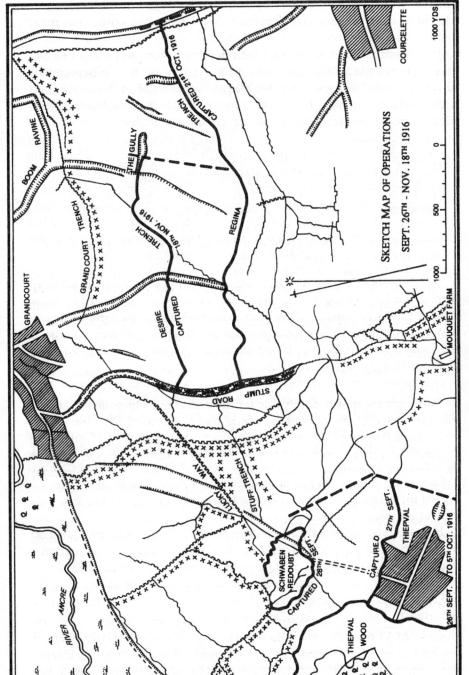

SKETCH MAP OF OPERATIONS

Brigade, the 7th Buffs and the 8th East Surreys, were held in divisional reserve under their commander, Sir Thomas Jackson, Bart, who was 'degummed' or 'dégommé', to use the terms in common use at the time, shortly afterwards.

In accordance with his strongly held theory on the subject, Ivor ordered zero hour for the Schwaben assault to be at 1pm on the 28 September. Due to the lie of the land Ivor was able to observe much of the action from high ground a mile away to the west. Among others, he took Maxwell with him to observe the scene, which he described in this way:

> From this post the sight of our artillery on the German lines was quite remarkable. The whole place was literally rent by bursting shells and it seemed impossible to believe that human beings could survive under it and fight . . . Our lines of infantry could be distinctly seen moving and disappearing over the broken ground close up to the barrage. But when the German guns also opened up one realised how difficult it must be for our men to distinguish their own barrage from the barrage put down upon them by the enemy.[17]

Watching beside him, Maxwell was equally impressed by the artillery fire, which he mentioned was produced by 600 guns.[18] But both knew from bitter experience, as Ivor also explained in the paragraph quoted above, that even the heaviest barrage did not 'obliterate men and things to the point of annihilation'. There were always some who survived and came up to fight as soon as it lifted.

A month after watching this battle Maxwell was promoted and appointed to command 27 Lowland Brigade in the 9th Scottish Division. Just under a year later, on September 1917, he was killed by a sniper near Zonnebeke during the Third Battle of Ypres. As the divisional history put it: 'He was a mighty fighter, a man among men, and the 18th Division was proud to have its name associated with his.'[19] It might be added that his influence on events during the capture of Trônes Wood and Thiepval played a significant part in achieving Ivor's growing reputation as a successful commander.

Following close behind the barrage, both 53 Brigade on the right and 54 on the left covered the first 600 to 800 yards towards their objectives in good time. By 2.30pm, the Queens and Suffolks in 53 Brigade sector had achieved a footing in the eastern corner of the Schwaben Redoubt. By 1.42pm, a Lieutenant-Colonel G D Price of the 7th Bedfords had reported that his battalion was moving onto its final objective. Of the 1/5th West Yorks, following the Bedfords, Ivor was later to record that: 'It did very well; the men were better than the officers who were not trained like ours and could not direct or form up or get started.' In the same letter he noted that the battalion had been sent to him 'for disciplinary reasons'. It was to be withdrawn soon afterwards to rejoin the 49th

Division, so the good conduct of the men during this action may have expunged whatever transgression had been committed earlier.

The fight for the possession of the redoubt went on for eight days after the first strongpoints around its perimeter were reached following zero-hour on 28 September. There were frequent close-quarter struggles with the enemy, and positions changed hands time and again. Hand grenades were much used: Captain H R Longbourne of the 7th Queens was awarded a DSO, and a full paragraph in Ivor's red book, for a particularly effective 45-minute grenade duel with the Germans, following which he '. . . led his company into Schwaben Redoubt and assisted his battalion in capturing its southern face with the minimum of loss to themselves'.[20]

By 10pm on 28 September, Ivor had a clear enough picture of the situation to give preliminary instructions for the relief of 53 and 54 Brigades during the night of 29–30 September by 55 Brigade. When this had been completed, Jackson was left holding the front with his own four proper battalions plus one, the 6th Royal Berks, attached from 53 Brigade. All these five units were regarded as 'fresh', but Ivor put the use of the word into perspective in his report:

> When, however, we speak of 'fresh' battalions during an operation I think we should realise that they are only fresh as regards actual fighting. They are far from being untired, because their nights have been mostly spent in the exhausting labour of carrying rations, water, ammunition and R.E. stores over terribly rough ground to their comrades in contact with the enemy.[21]

Jackson's orders were to 'complete the capture of the Schwaben Redoubt and occupy all the high ground to the north of it'. Between 30 September, when the first attempt to achieve this aim was made by the 5th East Surreys, and 5 October when the 18th Division was relieved by the 39th, a series of 'ding-dong' battles were fought with the Germans over the northern quarter of the Redoubt. Although the British front line had been pushed forward a little by 5 October, the enemy still held onto some of their strongpoints on the northern edge. Ivor was extremely disappointed by this untidy end to what was otherwise such a successful series of advances, and made it clear that he blamed the unfortunate Jackson. Not only did he have him 'degummed', but he also had his shortcomings recorded in print in a slightly spiteful way: 'In my opinion the 55th Brigade was not handled with firmness and the attacks were too partial. The situation should have been grasped more firmly by the brigade commander concerned and he was so informed.'[22] On Jackson's departure Lieutenant Colonel Price of the Bedfords was rewarded for his good work during each of the stages of the fighting by being promoted to Brigadier General to take his place.

The dismissal of Jackson was deeply resented by his brigade. Private

Robert Cude, later a sergeant with MM and bar, was a battalion runner with the 7th Buffs during the Schwaben action. In his diary he wrote on 29 September:

> Just now an interesting situation arises, for Maj. Gen. MAXSE Officer Commanding 18th Div, gives order that Buffs are to make a frontal attack on the system of trenches held by Jerry. This order our Brig. Gen. JACKSON refuses to carry out under the plea that he had insufficient troops at his disposal, and that it is impracticable.

The diary went on to describe a second refusal to attack by Jackson, though he did organise a bombing raid which was unsuccessful and produced what Cude called 'a fair number of casualties'. Out of the line on 6 October, Cude recorded that:

> Brig. Gen. JACKSON is relieved of his command and returns to England. For what – being a human man. He will carry with him the well wishes of the whole Bde and we can never forget the man who would wreck his career rather than be a party – however unwilling – to the annihilation of troops under his command. What would the Bde like to do with Gen. MAXSE, the man with a breast full of decorations – not one earned!

The bitterness felt about Jackson's treatment spilt over into Cude's comments on his successor:

> In place of our General we have another thing sent to us to take command. Words fail me to describe it, if it had a label around its neck and hung in a shop window one could say it was in its right place. Its name is Brg. Gen. PRICE and whatever price was asked for it would have been dear?[23]

It was hard to avoid the impression that Ivor's disappointment at the failure to capture the whole of Schwaben Redoubt may have caused him to be less than fair to Jackson and the men of the 55 Brigade, and certainly Cude's vivid phrases show how much those men resented this treatment.

Having been relieved by the 39th Division the 18th was withdrawn for a much-needed, though all too short, period of rest and reorganisation. On top of the total of 1,456 casualties suffered during the Thiepval phase, a further 1,990 had been incurred during the Schwaben fighting. Of these 1,204 came from the battalions of 55 Brigade. Although the grand total of 3,446 killed, wounded and missing is horrific enough, it was spread over a period of eight days, and by First World War standards was not an unduly costly price to pay for the capture of an important enemy stronghold. Between 26 September and 1 October 1916 eight German officers and 839 other ranks were captured and counted into the prisoners' cages. Estimates made on the ground put enemy dead at 900 at Thiepval and 600 at the Redoubt. Based on a calculation of three wounded to one killed, Ivor extrapolated these figures into an optimistic overall figure of 5,500 Germans 'incapacitated' as a result of the two operations.[24] Back in a rest area, Ivor wrote on 7 October to describe his billet:

> I am back in a rest area in a little sort of humble villa, the abode of a very nice French country doctor whose whole family seem to live in one room, in order to give me and our mess all the accommodation we require! He is a very intelligent man and is deeply interested in what he calls 'les vainqueurs de Thiepval'. He says it has been his lot hitherto to house 'les vaincus'. He is also taken with the fact that Clemenceau just now sent a message to say he would call upon me this afternoon . . .

Four days later, on the 11th, he sent an apology to Tiny for being 'remiss in writing these past few days because I have such a lot to do, re-organising and training. It takes *me* more hours of work to train than to fight . . .'

'October and November 1916', in the words of the divisional history, 'were months in which the staff proposed and the weather disposed'. What it goes on to describe as 'the persistent rain and the virulence of the shelling' gradually turned the whole region into a morass, with trenches becoming ditches of liquid mud.[25] Under these conditions aims could only be limited. What was actually achieved can be briefly described, though the discomfort, and steady losses, of those taking part in the various actions must not be forgotten. About 1,000 yards east of the Schwaben Redoubt, in the sector given to the 11th Division during the Thiepval battles, was the start of a long, well-prepared, enemy defensive line known as Regina Trench. Five hundred yards north of it, also running west to east, was Desire Trench. A further 1,500 yards beyond Desire Trench lay the village of Grandcourt. On return to the front after its short period of rest, the 18th Division was put into the line opposite the western end of these trench systems, with the Canadian Corps on its right, or eastern, flank. On 23 October a successful attack by 53 Brigade, with the 10th Essex and 8th Norfolks as assaulting battalions, took Regina Trench. Six German officers and 309 men were taken prisoner, and 250 were killed. Between 21 and 23 October, 53 Brigade incurred only 269 casualties in all, being 48 killed, 189 wounded, and 32 missing.[26]

Ivor's letters during the ensuing month touch on two matters he thought significant. On 30 October he told how the men in the trenches were 'having a bad time all round' because of the cold and the mud, but in spite of it refrained from grousing and had 'absolute confidence in themselves and their own capacity to beat the Bosch'. On 15 November he wrote at length about German morale, which he felt was much lower than it had been at the start of the Somme battles. Unlike the enemy tactics three months earlier he could report that: 'Not even one serious infantry counter-attack in force has been launched during the month we have occupied Regina Trench.'

On 18 November, the day of the first snowfall in the winter of 1916–17, 55 Brigade put in an attack on Desire Trench. On the right were the Canadians, and on the left the 19th Division. While the Canadians and 55 Brigade gained their objectives, the leading elements of the 19th Division swerved off line and left a sap into which German machine-gunners were able to move, and to inflict heavy casualties on the 7th Royal West Kents, 55 Brigade's left-hand battalion. Though the operation was a success, with the whole of Desire Trench reported clear of the enemy on the morning of 19 November, it had become obvious that any further attacks in the Somme area were out of the question until the weather improved. The 18th Division was relieved in early December, and sent to a rest area near Abbeville, where it remained until 16 January 1917. However to quote the divisional history again: 'When it came back to the Somme it was to fight under a new leader.'[27]

Ivor's reputation, and that of his division, stood high after the actions of 1 July and Trônes Wood. The Thiepval success enhanced it even more, and congratulations poured in from many quarters, starting with Haig's visit, already mentioned, on 27 September. As well as receiving messages of praise from his own two immediate superiors, Jacob at II Corps and Gough at headquarters Reserve Army, Ivor was sent letters from senior commanders elsewhere in the BEF sector. Lieutenant General Sir Charles Fergusson, a Grenadier commanding a Corps further north, wrote to say that: 'It is a tremendous feather in the cap of the Div to beat the Bosch in a fair fight in spite of his defences elaborated during such a long time, and it will give everyone tremendous confidence.'[28] Perhaps most pleasing of all, given the high opinion Ivor held of the sender, was a letter from General Sir Herbert Plumer, commanding Second Army, which asked him to '. . . send me a few lines describing your attack and how you carried it out – as you say trouble in training and careful organisation of the smaller units pays over and over again'.[29] It is safe to assume that all this interest in the Thiepval operations inspired Ivor, never a man to hide his light under a bushel, to have his report published in the form of the 'red book', which has been so freely quoted throughout this chapter. Given that it was produced in December 1916, so soon after the events with which it is concerned, it reflects a remarkable amount of work done in a very short time. Having seen the book printed, Ivor returned home to spend December on leave. Although nothing was announced about his future until he came back to France on 1 January 1917, it is probable that he had been given notice that he could expect promotion and a further command at corps level on his return.

Notes

Letters quoted from Maxse to his wife can be found in WSRO, file 212.

1 Maxse, General Sir Ivor, *The 18th Division in the Battle of the Ancre* (Hereafter shown as RB for 'red book'), p. 3, para 5. There is a copy of the book in IWM 69/53/8.
2 IWM 69/53/7.
3 RB p. 5, para 13.
4 IWM 69/53/7.~
5 Gough, General Sir Hubert, *The Fifth Army*, (Hodder and Stoughton, 1931), p. 147.
6 RB p. 3, para 6.
7 RB p. 4, para 7.
8 RB p. 4, para 9.
9 RB p. 17, para 67(a).
10 RB p. 5, para 10(e).
11 RB p. 5, para 11(b).
12 RB p. 6, para 15.
13 Maxwell, Mrs Charlotte, *Frank Maxwell, Brigadier-General, VC, CSI, DSO: A Memoir and some Letters*, (John Murray, 1921), pp. 174–8. A long extract was included in Nichols' divisional history.
14 RB p. 11, para 40.
15 RB p. 13, para 47.
16 RB p. 18, para 50.
17 RB p. 14, para 55.
18 Maxwell, p. 180.
19 Nichols, Captain, *The 18th Division in the Great War* (Blackwood, 1922), p. 101,
20 RB p. 15, para 57.
21 RB p. 16, para 64.
22 RB p. 17. para 65.
23 Some of the diary of Robert Cude is in an IWM publication by Malcolm Brown called *The Imperial War Museum Book of the Western Front* (Sidgwick & Jackson, 1993). The whole original ms is held by the museum.
24 RB p. 13, para 47 and p. 17, para 66.
25 Nichols, p. 130.
26 Nichols, p. 131.
27 Nichols, p. 136.
28 IWM 69/53/7.
29 IWM 69/53/7.

15

Command of XVIII Corps in 1917 and Early 1918

———— • ◆ • ————

Being a firm believer in the importance of leave, as will have become clear in the record of his service so far, Ivor took full advantage of his time at home in December 1916. Judging by the comments in several of his letters home during the war about ensuring that his billhook and other tools were kept well sharpened, he put in many hours tackling the still overgrown garden at Little Bognor. His periods at home were as important to Tiny as they were to him, bringing her inspiration to carry on with renewed vigour what her biographer refers to as her 'innumerable activities' connected with wartime life. He describes her work:

> It demanded constant sacrifice and infinite labour. She never spared herself. The children would hear the type-writer clacking at high pressure for long hours every day. She was chairman of a score of committees, the controlling influence of a large part of the local war effort. Her practical intelligence, her courage, her human sympathies inspired willing co-operation. It was now that she established herself in the hearts of her neighbours, and none of her wartime activities did more to gain the affection and respect of the village folk than her labours to trace the missing and prisoners-of-war by liaison with the War Office.[1]

At the end of December Ivor returned to France. On 1 January 1917 he was officially promoted to Lieutenant General and his CB was upgraded to KCB, so that he now became Sir Ivor. The same day he wrote to report on a visit to 'nose around' at GHQ, where he discovered, though it was not yet official, that 'I am to get the XVIII Corps about the 15th inst:. It is a new corps altogether and I am to form it.'

166

The two weeks that followed were taken up with finding out as much as possible about where and how his new command was to be established, and with farewell visits to the formations and units in the 18th Division. On 7 January 1917 he wrote to say that '. . . I simply hate leaving this division – far more than leaving a battalion, the Regiment or the 1st Guards Brigade. I suppose because it has been much more my child than any of them, and because it has had such a series of unbroken successes in battle.' The man to whom Ivor handed over command of the 18th Division was Major General Richard Lee, a Royal Engineer serving at the time as Chief Engineer to the Reserve Army, and a close friend of Gough. Lee remained in command throughout the rest of the war, only leaving the division after the Armistice, not long before it was finally disbanded in March 1919.

Ivor arrived at his new headquarters at 4pm on 15 January 1917, announcing in a letter written the following day: 'At that hour therefore this Corps was born! It is a microscopic infant today, a mere lump of flesh which can scarcely articulate.' His staff were all new apart from two important people who came with him from the 18th Division; Captain Montagu, his ADC, and 'Joby', his CRE, now promoted to Brigadier General. Also holding appointments in the rank of Brigadier General came S E Hollond, known as 'Tom', as B-GGS or in more modern terms Chief of Staff; D J M Farson as CRA; and L H Abbott as QMG. As a corps commander, Ivor was now entitled to a second ADC. Tiny was given the task of searching for a suitable man whom he insisted should be over 30 and in some way incapacitated for service at the front, as well as being capable of keeping up the official War Diary. He did not want a young man who would be terrified whenever spoken to! In the end an excellent choice was made of a Captain Williams, in civil life a jobber on the London Stock Exchange, and a fluent French speaker. While all these officers busied themselves collecting together the equipment necessary for the running of the headquarters, Ivor described his own part in this activity, in his letter of 16 January, as 'sitting still and doing nothing'. Although he wondered, half seriously, whether a corps commander's main job was to 'make everyone else work and apparently do nothing yourself', he knew that there would soon be more than enough to keep him occupied.

The role of a corps headquarters differed entirely from that of a division. A corps was a formation with an ever-changing structure, while the units which composed a division remained the same, even if the individuals in them did not. A corps might be composed of anything from two to five divisions, and the headquarters staff rarely had time to get to know their opposite numbers at divisional level as well as they would have liked. At times a corps headquarters was little more than a regulating link set in the chain of command between an army and the divisions fighting a battle. At other times, when conditions were relatively static and divisions remained with a corps for some months, the corps commander could have considerable impact on the actions of the divisions. Due to the enormous size of the BEF, army commanders could not possibly control operations without having corps headquarters to act as a link between them and divisions.

Although infantry and cavalry divisions constantly passed from one corps to another, there were units permanently attached to the corps itself. Heavy artillery, engineer stores depots, Royal Flying corps squadrons, field hospitals, supply depots, and prisoner-of-war cages were all permanent elements of what were known as corps troops. Tasks were allocated to them by the corps commander in support of his battle plans.

On 4 February 1917 the Germans began their withdrawal to what became known as the Hindenburg Line, a strongly fortified defensive system which they had been secretly building since the previous September. It stretched 25 miles from opposite Arras to the River Aisne, passing through St Quentin. The withdrawal was completed by the end of March, about which time XVIII Corps was put under command of General Allenby, whose Third Army was preparing for an operation in the Arras area as part of the ill-fated Nivelle offensive. Although Ivor was to mention in a letter at a later date that Allenby 'had billed me and my Army Corps for a big push in his original scheme', in the event XVIII Corps remained in reserve during the battle of Arras, which opened on 9 April with considerable success in the early stages. Due to lack of flexibility, these advances were not followed up as successfully as they might have been. Then the battle was prolonged until 14 May, with attacks continuing to be pressed when there was no hope of a further breakthrough. This was partly to relieve pressure on the increasingly mutinous French Army. In a letter written on 12 April, when things were still going well, Ivor explained that since 'the battle on 9th and 10th was such a complete success', the reserves were not needed. Instead, because some divisions in other corps had been involved in heavy fighting, he was ordered to exchange his fresh divisions with them. His task was to take over these exhausted divisions, and then, as he put it, 'my business now is to patch them up, re-equip them, re-fill them with men etc, and get them ready for another fight. What they will most want is SLEEP after four nights out!' He was able to add that fortunately casualties were 'very small compared with those we had during the first few days on the Somme'.

On 13 April Clemenceau paid Ivor another visit, this time on his way back from a visit to the Arras battlefield. 'C was in splendid form', he reported to Tiny. He was always very conscious of his connections with France, and only shortly before had written in a letter of 26 March about how beneficial his father's efforts to have him taught French had been to him. He went so far as to claim that: 'It has been through my great facility in talking and reading French that I trained the whole 18th Division on

the lines which have made it famous and are now being copied by others.'
Humility, whether real or false, was not a word in his vocabulary!

Divisions joining XVIII Corps were quickly made aware of its commander's ideas on training. One of Ivor's first actions after setting up his
headquarters in January had been to print what he called 'a system of
leaflets' as part of 'a *new* method' for training platoon commanders.
Sending a sample to Tiny with his letter dated 28 February 1917 he went
on to say:

> Some people think me flippant and therefore disapprove; but Gough has
> had them all printed and sent them out to all the Divs in his army!
> Fortunately he sends them out anonymously! I know the jokes are bad
> and that the language is vulgar . . . BUT my four Divs are training hard
> and the stuff is remembered by Platoon Commanders who forget most
> other things!

The real value of the leaflets lay in the way they explained how things
should be done in practical detail, reinforcing his constant insistence on
methods and not principles. The one on MARCH DISCIPLINE has 25
paragraphs, but most are only one sentence long. Some examples are:

> 3. A BATTALION WHICH MARCHES BADLY IS LIKE A MAN
> WHO DOESN'T WASH.

> 13. Every man's equipment off WITHIN 30 SECONDS of order for
> ten minute halt. Time this on company marches until perfect.

> 24. The more tired the men are at the end of a long march, the more
> strictly must you enforce march discipline, and cheer on your platoon by
> a kindly word.

> 25. INSPECT FEET IMMEDIATELY AFTER EVERY MARCH.

The leaflet on INTENSIVE DIGGING has only eight paragraphs,
but these are longer, and they go into great detail. For example, paragraph
3 explains how digging should be carried out by three-man teams:

> An average man can work intensively for TWO MINUTES only, that is
> if he really puts his whole heart, head and muscles into his digging and
> sweats like a pig. He should then REST FOR FOUR MINUTES, dig
> again for two minutes, and so on for two hours. The essential point is
> that the relief of one man by another must be effected with lightning
> rapidity.

The digging leaflet ends with a warning to any young platoon commander hoping to win a Military Cross: '8. *MOTTO*: "NO DIG NO
DEC."' In case the message was not clear, at the bottom of the page
comes: 'N.B. "DEC" is short for "DECORATIONS".'[2]

Each corps in the BEF established a training centre known as its Corps

Battle School, and naturally Ivor took a great interest in the one in XVIII Corps. Regular courses were held there, and he lectured to the course students whenever possible, seeing the opportunity to do so as an important way of putting over his ideas to large groups of officers and NCOs. His carefully prepared and typed notes for his lecture to a course on 14 May 1917 for platoon and section commanders end with a return to two of his favourite themes: 'Keep sections together – have conferences.' By 'conferences' he meant telling the men as much as possible about forthcoming operations. He also stressed another of his maxims, that there is always an opportunity for training soldiers 'on any bit of odd ground near any billet in any odd quarter of an hour on any day in the week without any facilities at all, if you only make up your mind to do something with them and do it quick'.[3]

On 23 May he paid a visit to another corps when invited to give a series of talks to officers of the Guards Division on the battle of Arras. He described his two-day visit in a long letter to Tiny, telling her how he met many old friends, whom he found

> . . . keeping the whole thing going on its splendid morale side – and quite convinced that the Great War really revolves around the Guards Division and is in fact merely a setting or framework within which the Guards Division can display its inherent quality – to its own satisfaction – no one else's opinion of it being sufficiently acquainted with it to carry weight.

Going on to say how the same characteristics are found in other regiments, 'sometimes more or often less', he ended his letter with the comment that: 'It has taken them two years of hard knocks to discover that the Gds Div has flanks!! and that some "other" Division has to be trusted to safeguard those flanks in an attack.' Generated by his interest in the garden at Little Bognor, Ivor took every opportunity while in France to investigate the fruit and kitchen gardens in the many parts of the country through which he travelled in his duties. On 25 May 1917 he reported that:

> I have been having some most interesting talks with the gardener here – in the Château of Monsieur de Fosseux, who is a very rich man indeed, but like so many Frenchmen won't spend much on improving his place! He is however very fond of fruit, and the gardener is evidently a highly competent fruit grower and loves talking about it.

Other letters include lengthy, detailed descriptions of wind protection, planting distances, pruning, and similar matters.

In June 1917 XVIII Corps moved north to join Gough's Fifth Army in Flanders. The corps was to remain part of it for the next ten months, until the army was finally broken up and reorganised during the great German offensive in March 1918. Since he worked well with Gough, in spite of the latter's well-known 'short fuse', this arrangement suited Ivor well.

Following the termination of the Arras offensive in mid-May, the next major effort of the BEF was the successful action of Plumer's Second Army at Messines Ridge from 7 to 14 June, which showed what could be achieved when an attack was thoroughly prepared and its objective limited. About this time, the failure of Nivelle's offensive in May, coming on top of the appalling losses at Verdun, led to serious mutinies in the French Army, which were somehow kept secret from the Germans. Their result, however, was in Sixsmith's words, 'to put the burden of the western front firmly on British shoulders. For this and other reasons, Haig decided on an offensive in Flanders.'[4] This offensive was to become known officially as the 3rd Battle of Ypres, but is often referred to by the name of one of its objectives, the Passchendaele Ridge. Preparations for the battle went on throughout July. On the 2nd, Ivor was lecturing to company commanders of the 39th and 51st Divisions at the start of a special course lasting 'for three strenuous days', during which he told them: 'We mean you to dwell in the ATMOSPHERE of this battle and allow no interruptions.' His notes for the lecture record many of his usual themes, stressing the need for detailed training in the practice trenches for all their men, and warning of the danger of German counter-attacks 'as soon as you become disorganized after your fight' to gain an objective.

A long letter dated 23 July told of a visit by Haig on the 21st, when he held a conference at Ivor's headquarters for his staff and his divisional commanders and their staffs:

> D.H. was in great form, better than I had ever seen him – full of confidence and – for him – communicative and genial. Though it must have bored him, he consented to go round all my Staff Officers and crack suitable jokes with the humbler members of the staff including all the NCOs and clerks . . . Some were in shirtsleeves and no one was standing too rigidly to attention – and D.H. did his part excellently well and produced a very good impression on all.

The same letter reported a visit next day by Gough, 'also in a most genial mood', and ended with a description of the new crest which had been produced for XVIII Corps. This had been devised by one of the officers on his staff, and Ivor sketched it in:

An air offensive was launched against the enemy as early as 11 July, and the preliminary artillery bombardment began on the 16th. These operations had been planned with a view to the main attack starting on 25 July, but in the event it was postponed until the 31st. Inevitably, the Germans realised what was happening: never had they been provided with such good warning of an impending offensive.

The four corps in the Fifth Army occupied a sector of the front lying east of Ypres, facing a ridge of slightly higher ground running north-east from the area of Messines to a flat plateau near Gheluvelt, from where it descended gradually northward through Passchendaele until merging with the low-lying plain of Flanders at Staden. On the southern flank of Fifth Army was the British Second Army, and on the north General Anthoine's First French Army. Within his boundaries Gough placed his corps in the order, reading from north to south, of XIV Corps (Lord Cavan), XVIII (Maxse), XIX (Watts) and II Corps (Jacob).

XVIII Corps' position in the front-line lay opposite St Julien, a village some one and a half miles away, at the western edge of which flowed the small river or 'beck' to use a Yorkshire term, called the Steenbeek, following a north-westerly course across most of the Fifth Army area of operations. Several other small 'beeks' or 'becks' ran into it from the ridge of higher ground described above. To capture St Julien and establish crossings over the Steenbeek was the task allotted to Ivor in the first phase of the coming battle. Having secured the river, his right flank was to be pushed forward towards the enemy trench system on the ridge ahead.[5]

Ivor's two leading divisions were the 39th and 51st Highland. The 11th and 48th Divisions were held in Corps reserve. He was allotted 24 tanks from 'G' Battalion Tank Corps. Artillery support consisted of 441 guns in all, of which 288 were field pieces, to be used for the creeping barrage ahead of the infantry assault.

Support had been given in many quarters to a paper widely circulated by Ivor in June to explain his objections to dawn attacks, but in spite of it the Fifth Army went into action on 31 July at 3.50am. This first action of 3rd Ypres lasted until 2 August, and was officially named the Battle of Pilckem Ridge. Heavy rain set in on the evening of the 31st and lasted on and off for the next four days. In a slightly optimistic letter, written on 1 August while waiting for a visit from Haig, Ivor claimed that as well as capturing 1,700 prisoners, actually counted into the corps cage, his divisions had taken all their objectives 'precisely up to time'. He went on to mention the heavy shelling and fierce enemy counter-attacks which followed the advance, but suggested that only one brigade on the extreme right of his front was driven back from its objective, while in fact in that region the Germans had recovered a lot of ground. In the St Julien area the Steenbeek crossings were successfully seized, including an important

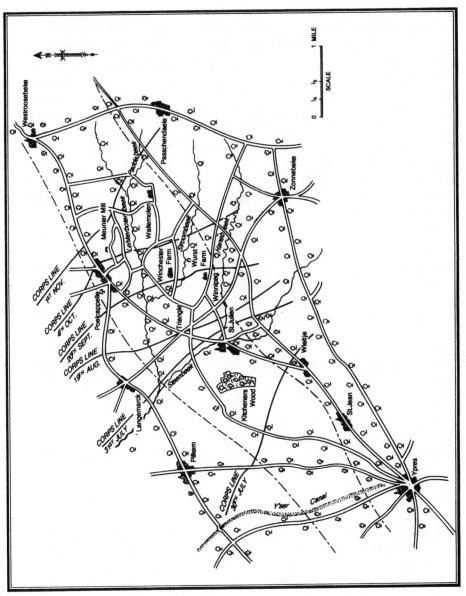

BATTLES IN FLANDERS, 1917

stone bridge, but within the village itself there was confused fighting for some time.

One incident during the struggle for the village caused Ivor considerable amusement when he heard about it sometime later, and he told the whole story at length in a letter on 27 August. On the evening of 31 July a company of the Royal Sussex Regiment had received a warning that heavy guns were going to bombard enemy strongholds in the village in ten minutes' time, and that the company should evacuate it immediately. Fortunately the Sussex had just taken some magnificent, concreted German dug-outs beyond the bridge over the Steenbeek, and there was enough time to move the company into them before the shells came down. A second company from the same battalion joined them soon afterwards. The spacious dug-outs had been used as a field dressing station, and were full of good rations, stocks of soda water and other comforts. These proved essential, because it was assumed that the companies had been captured when contact was not made with them after the bombardment, and so no further supplies were sent forward. Ivor ended his letter by saying:

> . . . meanwhile the whole world outside was pulsating and throbbing with excitement as to the fate of the 'Fortress of St Julien'. The Bosch claimed St Julien because he kept on re-occupying a few of its northern houses. Finally, D.H. had somehow to account for our possessing it when I reported that we held it.

Early in August the 58th Division was posted into XVIII Corps. Commanding 173 Brigade in the division was the young Brigadier General Bernard Freyberg, VC. In his biography of his father, Paul Freyberg tells of his first meeting with Ivor:

> Maxse's first words to Freyberg after they met were, 'I hate you bloody gallant Brigadier-Generals – what the devil do you know about training men?' Maxse had a disagreeable technique for imposing his will, but militarily he was extremely able, and the well trained New Zealand Division of the Second World War owed much of its excellence to the methods devised by General Maxse and taught to Freyberg in 1917. 173 Brigade spent the first three weeks of August in the training area under Maxse's direction, commencing early in the morning and carrying on until it was dark, often until the men almost dropped with fatigue.[6]

About the same time, another officer whose initial impressions were far from favourable met Ivor for the first time. The story is told in another book by a son about his father, in this case David Fraser's edited edition of the diaries of Colonel the Honourable William Fraser, Gordon Highlanders, who attended a parade on 21 August at which Ivor presented medals to members of the 51st Highland Division. Fraser noted that: '. . . my opinion of the Corps Commander did not improve. I'm certain he's efficient but in a nasty hole and corner sort of way. Would not trust him a yard . . .'. As editor, his son has followed this entry by noting that his father's strictures on Ivor are surprising, since 'Willie later took the view that he was among the best, if not the best, corps commanders on the western front; and came to work with him very closely, and to like him very much'.[7]

Leo Maxse was invited by GHQ to visit the BEF in August, in his capacity as editor of the *National Review*, and fitted in a short stay at XVIII corps headquarters. During a trip to Ypres, the brothers watched two exciting examples of aerial combat. First a 'dog-fight' in which an aircraft from Ivor's own corps supporting squadron shot down a German fighter, and second the escape by parachute of two men from an observation balloon set on fire by an enemy aeroplane.

XVIII Corps took part in the next Fifth Army operation, known as the Battle of Langemark, from 16 to 18 August, and made only slight progress against a number of strongly defended German bunkers and fortified farms. While two of these farms were captured, it was a costly and frustrating action, fought in the dreadful conditions which were so much part of the story of 3rd Ypres. A combination of the incessant rain which fell that August and the damage done to the drainage system of Flanders by heavy artillery shelling from both sides, turned the battlefield into a morass of mud. To set against these unsatisfactory two days for his corps, Ivor was able to give his support soon afterwards to an original system of attack, using tanks, which had far-reaching effects. On 19 August what was regarded as a small effort by the standards of the time produced results beyond the wildest expectations of those who planned it. Ivor wrote about it the next day:

> We have had two successes in the Corps, one on the 16th inst, in the big battle, and another one yesterday in a minor operation with tanks and smoke screens . . . This last little operation was run on a new plan invented partially by myself. At any rate, if it was not invented by me it was carried out for the first time by this Corps at my instigation. The British dislike of new ideas is so tremendous that one has to fight a lot of people to get any new idea seriously considered! However, a Corps Commander who means to do something definite can easily break away opposition *once* or perhaps twice. Then he can start a new idea but it must be a humble one! I cannot go into detail but the result was my Corps advanced to a depth of 500 yards on a front of over a mile, did in a lot of posts of picked Hun machine gunners and carried all our objectives with a loss of *15* Infantrymen and *16* men in tanks. The alternative plan put forward and which I refused to sanction involved deploying at least six Bns. of Infantry and incurring perhaps 800–1,200 casualties to

obtain the same results. When the results became known yesterday, my Corps H.Q. became a centre of interest from GHQ down to the humblest Platoon Commander.

The action concerned was fought by a composite company of 11 tanks from 'G' Battalion Tank Corps and eight platoons of infantry from the 1st Worcesters and the South Staffords. The aim was to clear four concrete blockhouses, lying alongside the St Julien–Poelcappelle road, which had disrupted attempts to advance further during the battle three days earlier. Although by the end of the operation only four tanks were able to return to base, all the four so-called 'impregnable' blockhouses had been taken with the minimal losses so proudly recorded by Ivor in his letter. When the news of this remarkable success was received at GHQ, General Kiggell, the Chief of Staff, anxious to know how it had been achieved, rang XVIII Corps headquarters. Commenting at the end of the letter above that this call was 'for the first time in the war', Ivor's immediate reply was the one word 'Tanks'. However when 'Kig' as he called him pressed for more details Ivor soon gave up, because, in his words, 'as if one could explain common sense down a telephone to someone who has never commanded even a humble Company!' In command of the tanks supporting XVIII Corps was Colonel, later Brigadier General, C D Baker-Carr, a leading tank expert and a promoter of the plan. Knowing the low opinion of the value of tanks in most parts of the army before the St Julien action, he believed that its importance was such that, without the faith in the potential of tanks which it restored, the Cambrai operation might never have been launched. And in his opinion:

> If the Cambrai battle had not been fought, it is certain that tanks, if not actually abolished, could never have played such an important part in the final stages of the War, when tens of thousands of valuable lives, by their aid, were mercifully preserved.[8]

Ivor was developing his own theories on the most effective use of tanks, which he linked to his ideas about employing aircraft in the ground-attack role, and about types of artillery fire that would avoid cratering the ground across which the tanks and infantry were due to advance. An opportunity to explain his theories came when a captured enemy document, describing their new methods of defence in depth, was sent to him from Fifth Army for his comments. In his lengthy reply dated 21 August 1917 he included these paragraphs:

(a) The ideal to which we should work is to obtain temporary command of the air in front of our offensive with sufficient aeroplanes to attack strong points, nests of machine guns, infantry advancing or massing for counter-attack, and the personnel of enemy's batteries.

(b) Three conditions are requisite for the more effective use of Tanks in large numbers:-

    (i)   Sufficient aeroplanes to deal with the enemy's anti-tank guns and forward batteries.

    (ii) The area to be traversed should not be made impassable by our own heavy guns during the preliminary bombardment.

    (iii) Smoke to blind enemy's artillery observation posts.

If these conditions obtain, Tanks should be used in sufficient numbers to neutralize strong points, nests of machine guns, and generally to facilitate the task of the infantry. Tanks should be given definite objectives, and definite infantry units should be told off to co-operate in attacking each tank-objective, but not necessarily to accompany the Tank. A suitable formation for Tanks would be in several echelons according to the depth of the objective. The infantry formation (already practised) aims at stalking the tank-objective under a barrage and assaulting it simultaneously with the Tank.

He went on into detail on the correct types of artillery fuses to use, on suitable formations for the attacking infantry to employ, and on the requirement for battalions to be followed by mechanical carriers, enabling 'our infantry to carry less weight and thus convert them into mobile fighters'.[9] While attaching due weight to all these tactical concepts, Ivor did not lose sight of the preponderant role of the 'Queen of the battlefield'. In an earlier paper put up to Fifth Army he had explained on 12 August that: 'I hold the view that ground is gained by artillery, that ground is defended by artillery, that battles are won by artillery, and that battles are lost by lack of artillery.'[10] All his theories assumed the need for powerful support from the guns as a first essential.

At the end of August 1917 Haig put Plumer in charge of the main thrust of the campaign, and all corps in Fifth Army, apart from XIV and XVIII Corps, came under command of his Second Army. Sixsmith suggests 'that Haig would have done better to have left the leading role in Plumer's hands throughout and to have made the Messines attack part of the main operation'.[11] An unfortunate result of this reorganisation was a three-week delay, while it was taking place, during a period of dry weather in September.

Still part of Fifth Army, Ivor's corps operated on the northern flank of Second Army during the next phase of 3rd Ypres, which opened with the Battle of the Menin Road Ridge from 20 to 25 September. The corps enjoyed what he described in a letter written on the 20th, soon after operations began, 'as a really great day for the XVIII Corps, and we have thoroughly proved ourselves. It has in fact been a "devil" of a battle for us all day long, and we have completely defeated the Hun, not only in our original advance of 1,000 yards but in numerous counter-attacks which we have successfully defeated in detail.' Two days later, on 22 September, he wrote to describe an aspect of the battle which gave him great satisfaction:

> We are holding all gains in spite of further counter-attacks yesterday
> evening at 6 p.m. There is one thing and only one thing I am really
> proud of within myself. It is that ever since fighting commenced in this
> corps in July I have attained my objectives with fewer casualties than
> other Corps, have used up fewer Divs than any other Corps, and that
> my Divs remain less tired now than most others!
>
> In this last battle, I put in only two brigades on a front of 3,700
> yards – that is I put in only two Brigades for my original attack. Nearly
> all others put in double that amount or more. I had to resist all sorts of
> advice (to get my own way) but as we came off on my plan I am now 'a
> blue-eyed boy' and listened to with attention – at any rate for the time
> being! It won't last however because nothing lasts in war: but Divs like
> being in this Corps very much.

Further satisfaction came from the conduct of the two Territorial divisions from which the leading troops were drawn. These were the 51st
Highland and the 58th Division, the latter a second-line formation in its
first big battle, though, as already described, it had been given a rigorous
period of training since joining the corps. In the 58th Division, drawn
from London, the men Ivor particularly praised were the Post Office
Rifles, whom he had mentioned in a letter on 21 September:

> Just think of the second-line Post Office Rifles standing up to the flower
> of the German Army and mowing them down with machine guns and
> rifle fire after themselves being subjected to one half-hour of the most
> furious enemy shelling which has ever been borne! As evidence of the
> Post Office valour is entirely derived from the Highlanders on their
> immediate left I feel I can accept it as absolutely correct.

Three days later, on the 24th, he recorded the return of these men from
the front-line in a letter which also reflects the deep division at this stage
of the war between senior army officers, known as 'the hats', and leading
politicians, 'the frocks'. Although he is mentioned in the following passage
from the letter, it was one of Churchill's greatest achievements in the
Second World War to avoid this bitterness and distrust among the same
groups. Ivor wrote:

> Yesterday I went out to greet my second-line Post Office Rifles on the
> way out of the trenches and you never saw such faces, never! They were
> all heroes and they had all killed Huns *themselves*. No description can
> possibly convey what those men feel and what all our men *know*, and the
> miserable Bonar Laws, Squiffs, Churchills and Harcourts, Balfours or
> Bob Cecils don't live in the same world as men who know what this war
> is. Nor do the blighters deserve to be fellow countrymen to my Post
> Office Rifles.

Ivor's letter on the following day, 25 September, was written at 10.30pm when he had 'a moment before my electric light wagon will cease fire for the night'. A dinner party had just finished at the headquarters at which: 'My guests were the Prince of Wales and Le Général Anthoine [commanding the French First Army] and the whole thing was a most hilarious gathering with Tom Hollond's delightful personality at its best.' He was pleased to note that the Prince talked French well and was not the least shy.

In the same letter, he told of a trick which he had developed to fool the enemy. This was clever enough to make Ludendorf report in his communiqués on three occasions that the Germans had repulsed British assaults east of St Julien. These assaults were really 'sham attacks by "pole targets" and painted figures which rise and fall with a string'. For three months Ivor had been training 100 men from the Cyclist Corps to make these 'Chinese' or sham attacks, and they deceived each new German division as it arrived in the battle zone.

The commander of the 51st Highland Division, Major-General Harper, known to his troops as 'Uncle', was due to go on leave about this time. Tiny received instructions in a note written by Ivor on 23 September to try to see him when he was at home, since his is 'now one of the two or three best divisions in France and it has been made (from a poor one) by General Harper'. Similar instructions to look after officers, of whom Ivor had a good opinion, while on leave frequently crop up in his letters home. It was another aspect of Tiny's war work.

Under command of XVIII Corps, as preparations were made for the next attack, came his beloved 18th Division. The history of the 10th Essex records members of the battalion taking particular satisfaction 'in encountering the Black Man again', and that they were 'all happy to know that he was to be presiding genius' in their next action. The authors of the history go on to comment that:

> Maxse was not a commander who attained position by rigid orthodoxy and impeccable respectability. The winds of controversy have blown in alternating gusts around his reputation as they have about those of all men of strong individuality. But among the mass of men who came beneath his military sway he had the all important capacity of inspiring confidence, and that means very much to an army in the day of battle. The familiar clenched fist, and his 'Gentlemen what I *wahnt* is . . .' got right there with his hearers at many a pregnant address.[12]

What he '*wahnted*' on this occasion was the capture of the village of Poelcappelle. The western end of the village was taken on 4 October, but it was not until the 22nd that Higginson's 53 Brigade of the 18th Division finally drove the enemy out of all of it – or out of what little was left standing in it. On 24 October Ivor was able to mention in his letter that:

The XVIIIth are again 'blue-eyed boys' in consequence of being the only ones to capture all their objectives on the 22nd and to hold them definitely. They even did more and advanced their front beyond what was demanded. I never know how long the "blue-eyed" phase may last? Sometimes only for a day! . . .

D.H. spent an hour with me yesterday and was most pleasant as he always is.

On the 26th, he told of continuing efforts to advance under almost impossible conditions. 'Another attack took place this morning. Again that d . . d weather played us just the same trick.' After three dry days the rain came at 2am, which was too late to stop the assault. It was however reasonably successful in spite of the conditions. By 1 November the corps front was established on a line running from a point roughly 600 yards beyond Poelcappelle at the north, down towards Passchendaele to the south. These operations at the end of October were part of what was to be given the official title of the First Battle of Passchendaele. They marked the end of XVIII Corps' involvement in 3rd Ypres, and it did not take part in the Second Battle, when the Canadians in Second Army finally took the village of Passchendaele and secured the ridge of that name on 10 November.

Throughout the following months those on both sides who continued to live in the battle-zone did so in a fashion described in the 18th Division history as '. . . crouching in icy wind, drenched with pitiless rain, shelled day and night. The acme of filthy hideousness, a Calvary of misery, and none could foresee the end!' Of the stinking mud it recorded that '. . . when the rain ceased the nostrils had to accept a faded musty smell that hung in the air five miles behind the line – a smell that told of desolation and decay, of gas shells, of dead men.'[13]

On 5 December 1917 Ivor wrote to tell Tiny of the arrival of her brother Charles Leconfield to stay at his headquarters, and told how the two of them had taken a walk over 'the ground won by the XVIII Corps during the Flanders Offensive'. At Wurst Farm, which had been captured on 20 September, they were, as he explained, '. . . amongst scenes which were of intense interest to me during August and Sept. last'. He went on to make a comment which should be borne in mind by everyone bold enough to attempt the description of First World War operations: 'Now they are in our possession they become less interesting day by day and are losing their battle characteristics so rapidly that I quite understand why no historian can ever reproduce any accurate description of anything but the broad lines of any battle.'

On 9 December Ivor was writing again, this time to Brigadier General Charles Bonham-Carter at GHQ on a subject in which he took a great interest: platoon organisation. He had touched on this in his report, already quoted, to Fifth Army on 21 August, when he had suggested that each section should be a self-contained fighting unit including riflemen, rifle grenadiers and a few bombers, with a Lewis gun section an integral part of each platoon. Now in December, in his letter to Bonham-Carter, he wrote:

> Why not consider the future organisation of platoons in 1918, when we shall be worse off for manpower, *now*. Rather than cut numbers in platoons why not double Lewis guns. Train companies to operate on wider fronts and have intervals between fire units. Scrap the idea of shoulder to shoulder. Substitute waves for worms which deploy quickly to fire or to avoid the enemy's fire. Teach each fire unit to keep together and support its neighbour with fire.[14]

As 1917 drew to a close, the future employment of XVIII Corps was decided by two separate events, the first being of only indirect significance at this stage. This was the armistice arranged at Brest-Litovsk, which brought to an end the war in Russia, and so released German divisions to be transferred to reinforce their armies on the Western Front. The second event, of more direct import, was a decision made on 14 December by the Supreme War Council in Paris that the British Army should take over more of the Allied front line from the French. The result of this decision was that Gough's Fifth Army was instructed to withdraw from Flanders and move south to the Somme sector, to hold a line opposite St Quentin, allowing the French Sixth Army on the Aisne to considerably shorten its front. This move took place between 10 and 30 January 1918.

Back in October, at the time he was writing about being a 'blue-eyed boy', Ivor had taken advantage of being temporarily in good favour with his superiors and had put in for leave over Christmas. Therefore, during the lull before his headquarters started to move south he was at home with his family. On his return he was to learn how popular the corps Christmas card had been, with some 60,000 copies printed. With the move of Fifth Army came more reallocations of divisions to the four corps which were eventually to come under Gough's command, as he took over a stretch of the line from the French Sixth Army on the Somme. XVIII Corps was the first to arrive in its new location, and Ivor's headquarters was in position by January, with the 30th, 36th, and 61st Divisions now placed under command.[15] Ivor asked Gough to let him have the 58th Division instead of the 30th, but received a long letter dated 13 January 1918 to tell him why this request was not granted. Starting by saying 'I hate refusing you anything as you have always been out to help the Army', Gough went on to explain why he had little faith in the 30th, which was no longer the formation it had been on 1 July 1916. He claimed that 'they want discipline badly and they want training. They are a "political" Div and Derby has been allowed to interfere.' So he continued: 'Then unfortunately I am convinced that you are one of the very few who have any idea how to train a Div so I said "Give the 30th to Maxse and he will make something of them" – it is very bad luck that your virtues should come back on you but consider the good of the service.'[16]

Ivor could hardly demur at this decision, since he undoubtedly shared his army commander's view that he was himself one of 'the very few' with any idea how to train a division. This opinion he was to record in an interesting document written soon afterwards, when he was appointed a member of the Court of Inquiry convened to investigate 'The Action fought South of Cambrai on November 30th'. One of the best remembered and most written about actions of the war, the Battle of Cambrai, opening on 20 November was the occasion when tanks were first used in large numbers in conjunction with a carefully planned surprise attack by infantry, for which the supporting artillery bombardment did not begin until zero-hour. The most important task for the tanks was to flatten the German wire, a task normally undertaken by preliminary artillery programmes which always destroyed the chance of surprise.

It was at first a huge success, with gains of up to four miles on the first day. Then the impetus of the attack was lost; the Germans counterattacked on 30 November; and not only was much of the ground retaken by the enemy, but in the south they even penetrated the original British start line. This disaster after the original victory was what the Court was required to investigate.

The president was Lieutenant General Sir Alexander Hamilton-Gordon of IX Corps, and Ivor and Major General Pinney, 33rd Division, were the members. Although he signed the report of the Court's findings, Ivor was not satisfied with that, and produced not only what William Moore in his book *A Wood Called Bourlon* has described as a 'grumbling appendix', but a 'mini-report' of his own as well. Both contained some vintage Maxse comments. As might be expected, inefficient training drew his sharpest criticism. Drawing attention to widespread lack of understanding of the rudiments of successful defence, he wrote: 'The ignorance arises from the fact that our officers are not taught elementary tactics and that those whose business it should be to instruct them are themselves uninstructed.' In a further damning reflection on standards of training, which also shows how frequently divisions were moved from one corps to another, he recorded from his own personal experience: 'The writer of this note is acquainted with one corps which during the past twelve months happened to have thirty divisions in it. Of these, two were splendidly trained, a dozen were trying to train and the remainder had little if any system of training at all.'[17] In spite of these strictures, Ivor felt that the overall picture of the Cambrai outcome was becoming unbalanced, and wrote home on 28 January 1918, while the Court was sitting, to tell Tiny that:

> The nonsense talked about Cambrai, both here and at home, makes me despair of British intelligence. The whole battle was a ten days British

success which was only marred by one incursion, on one date, at one place. Everywhere else on the same date on a front of ten miles in violent fighting the Hun was badly done down – but to hear people talk one would suppose the Hun had really won a great victory! What he did on 30th was to gain a local success.

Just under two months later, he was to have his own experience of an enemy assault which became rather more than an incursion.

Notes

Letters from Maxse to his wife can be found at WSRO, files 439, 442, 483.

1 Gore, John, *Mary Maxse* (Rolls House, 1946), p. 76.
2 IWM 69/53/8 – Cyclostyled copies.
3 IWM 69/53/8.
4 Sixsmith, Maj Gen E K G, *British Generalship in the 20th Century* (Arms and Armour, 1970), p. 104.
5 There is a buff folder in IWM 69/53/8, with papers about XVIII corps operations during 3rd Battle of Ypres, from which this is taken.
6 Freyberg, Paul, *Bernard Freyberg, VC* (Hodder & Stoughton, 1991).
7 Fraser, Gen Sir David, *In Good Company* (Fraser Publications, 1990), p. 149.
8 Baker-Carr Brig Gen L D, *From Chauffeur to Brigadier* (Benn, 1930), p. 255.
9 IWM 69/53/8 Letter to Fifth Army dated 21 Aug. 1917.
10 IWM 69/53/8 XVIII Corps letter G.S.69 to Fifth Army dated 12 Aug. 1917.
11 Sixsmith, p. 109.
12 Banks, Lt-Col T M and Chell, Capt R A, *With the 10th Essex in France* (10th Essex Old Comrades, 1921), p. 192.
13 Nichols, Capt G H F, *The 18th Division in the Great War* (Blackwood, 1922), p. 24.
14 Quoted in Bidwell and Graham, *Fire Power: British Army Weapons and Theories of War 1904–1945* (Allen & Unwin, 1982), p. 127.
15 Edmonds, Brig Gen Sir James, *Military Operations: France and Belgium 1918*, Vol I (Macmillan, 1935), p. 47.
16 This letter from Gough is in File 502, WSRO.
17 Moore, William, *A Wood Called Bourlon* (Leo Cooper, 1988), p. 194. Quoted from documents attached to the Cambrai Report file in PRO WO/54/53. Maxse's own notes are in IWM 69/53/8A.

16

Command of XVIII Corps during the Battles of March 1918

———•◆•———

Knowledge of the build-up of German strength, as divisions released from fighting the Russians were transported from the Eastern to the Western Front, overshadowed all activities of the BEF in the first two months of 1918. On 18 January, four days after XVIII Corps headquarters was established at Ham, 12 miles south-west of St Quentin, the young Brigadier General Freyberg, on a brief attachment to Fifth Army, was present at a meeting between Gough and Ivor. He listened as they talked about 'the sudden change of policy and the taking over from the French of the front down to La Fère'. He later recorded that:

> The conversation between General Gough and General Maxse made a great impression on me. I had never before heard a plan of campaign discussed by two such senior commanders and I gathered from their conversation that:
> (a) The Fifth Army had been given an impossible task to do. That they had too few men either to hold the line in its present condition, or to put it in a satisfactory state of defence before the Germans launched their attack in the spring, and
> (b) That even if we had sufficient men to dig the necessary defences, we hadn't sufficient engineers', material (i.e. wire and pickets. etc,).
> I learned also that the British General Headquarters Reserves available in event of a crisis, after the Fifth Army moves were completed, would not be more than seven weak divisions.[1]

For mainly political reasons, which there is not space enough to explain here, nothing was done to reinforce the BEF on the scale required to counteract the growing power of the enemy. There were reckoned to be 449,000 category 'A' men waiting in home depots, ready to be sent to France, but less than a quarter of them were posted to the BEF, even though Haig estimated that his infantry would be 40% below establishment by 31 March 1918 without further drafts.[2] To cope with the shortage of infantry, various measures were introduced, the most drastic being the reduction of battalions in all brigades from four to three, and hence in each division from 12 to nine. Men from disbanded battalions were either posted around others within their brigades or used to form composite units in army reserve, sometimes causing a serious loss of morale. Given the extent of the known German threat, the failure to send the necessary reinforcements to the BEF was inexcusable.

Back in London, Sir William Robertson, the CIGS whom Ivor so much admired, continually strove to persuade the War Cabinet of the need to build up the strength of the British forces. However, as he explained in his book *Soldiers and Statesmen 1914–1918*, published in 1926:

> The warnings with respect to the continuous arrival of German reinforcements on the Western front, and the prediction that a desperate attempt to snatch victory would probably be made by the enemy on that front not later than February, were, for all practical purposes, disregarded.[3]

Robertson's uncompromising resistance to the suggestions put forward by Lloyd George, the Prime Minister, for directing troops to other theatres of war than the crucial Western Front, in the end led to his fall. Sir Henry Wilson was brought back from a liaison post in France to become CIGS, and Robertson was offered the chance to take Wilson's place. This he refused to do, and on 19 February he resigned rather than accept a course of action which would imply abandonment of his principles. Tiny was one of the many people who wrote to sympathise with him. He replied on 25 February, telling her in his letter that: 'I thought over things a great deal one night when I should have been asleep. I made up my mind then as to the course I would adopt, and I had a perfectly easy time afterwards.'[4] The general opinion of the whole affair among senior officers of the army in France was summed up by Ivor in a letter to Tiny on 17 February: '. . . we all feel that Lloyd George is quite untrustworthy and perhaps dishonest. Whether Robertson or Wilson or someone else moves, the fact remains that no soldier can ever feel that he can trust to the "ay" or the "nay" of Lloyd George or of any prominent politician.' Much as the Prime Minister would have liked to have brought about the downfall of Haig as well, he was fortunately unable to achieve this double 'degumming', for which the army and the nation would be thankful before 1918 was over.

Of the 42-mile front allotted to the Fifth Army, XVIII Corps was responsible for covering nine miles, which included the semicircle of some 3,000 yards radius described by Edmonds in the Official History 'as passing through the outskirts of St Quentin, and enclosing that town on the west.'[5] III corps, to the south of XVIII, was given almost twice as long a stretch to cover, but its right included the marshy ground along the River Oise, which was not regarded as a likely enemy line of advance. On Ivor's left flank, XIX Corps had a front of seven miles, which took in the headwaters of the Omignon and Cologne rivers. Within the XVIII Corps boundaries, the 36th Ulster Division was on the right, the 30th in the centre, and the 61st South Midland Division on the left.

Back in the middle of December 1917, GHQ had issued instructions to all armies on the way in which their defences should be arranged. 'Three Zones of defence, the "Forward Zone", the "Battle Zone", and the "Rear Zone", were to be prepared, each organized in depth . . .'.[6] Due to shortages of labour for constructing these defences, the Rear Zone was rarely more than a piece of ground reconnoitred and marked out, and was usually referred to as the 'Green Line'. Put briefly, the Forward Zone was based on the existing front-line trench system, duly strengthened and well supplied with machine-guns. Behind it the Battle Zone was to be 2,000 to 3,000 yards in depth, with mutually supporting positions prepared on the best ground available from which to destroy the enemy. GHQ rather optimistically suggested that: 'If the enemy penetrated [the Battle Zone], and the immediate attacks of local reserves did not succeed in expelling him, a deliberate counter-attack by the corps or army reserve was to be launched at the first possible moment.'[7] Such comments would have been more helpful if there had been enough reserves in existence.

One of the sketch maps in the Official History shows in detail the layout of the XVIII Corps' defences in March in the 30th and 36th Divisions' areas, opposite and south of St Quentin. Nearest the enemy there were numerous forward posts with a mass of wire linking them, and also running back along likely lines of advance for the enemy. At distances varying between 1,500 and 2,000 yards behind these forward posts there were bigger defended localities, joined by a line of trenches and more wire. Machine-gun emplacements and observation posts were sited throughout the forward zone. There was next a gap of anything from 1,500 to 4,000 yards, depending on the terrain, before the first defences of the Battle Zone were reached. A further long bound of several miles was then needed to reach the Green Line. General Farrar-Hockley has described these defences in his book, *Goughie*:

> The south centre sector was held by Sir Ivor Maxse and XVIII Corps: three divisions in line from a point immediately below the Omignon stream to the St Quentin canal, which it straddled. Two of the three divisions looked daily into the town, the majority of whose buildings

were still standing behind the broken outer edges. The tough, shrewd and energetic Maxse knew every square yard of his positions and the range of his preparations was immense. Every unit had spent at least ten days in training and rehearsals for its role; yet the defences were as far advanced as any others.[8]

Haig came at least twice to inspect Ivor's preparatory work and to discuss his plans for holding his sector. His diary for 14 February 1918 records arriving in XVIII Corps' area near the devastated village of Entreillen and lunching in a field close by:

> General Maxse met me here and our horses having joined us we rode along the defences on the S and E of Holman Wood and continued our ride on the north side of the wood overlooking the River Omignon.
>
>   I was greatly pleased with the general plan of the defences . . . I also discussed with Maxse the possibility of the enemy avoiding the wood and turning the flanks.[9]

He was back again on 7 March, as described by Farrar-Hockley:

> 'Every detail had been thought out', Haig recorded, '. . . I thought that they were taking it too much for granted that the enemy would do what they had planned he should do.' Though this was a sound general criticism, it disregarded the slight experience of Maxse's units in their current role. Events were to show the value of their preparations.[10]

Ivor's training methods, and the reasons for adopting them, were very clearly explained in a letter to Tiny on 22 February:

> It is ten minutes to post time and I have realised that I have not written for several days – all of which have been continuously and successfully employed on an important conference which I ran. I had all Bn. Commanders of the whole Corps and all officers above them, present here for four days. We thrashed out a great many subjects and I feel convinced did a great deal of good. Goffie attended two days and played up splendidly. I now expect to get a real move on at training for the battle.
>
>   Soon, in two batches or three, I am also going to have all the Company Commanders for a similar conference – and this will again be followed up by batches of Platoon Commanders! It entails a lot of work on your humble servant, but all my staff as well as all those who attended this week are unanimous that it creates an esprit de corps such as none of them have ever seen previously in France. As I have no difficulty in running such shows and as they are obviously desired, I think it is only my duty to go in for this quite new form of soldiering. We are in fact a democracy. The reason they are so much wanted is that our Bn. Commanders [and lower ranks] are all practically civilians with a khaki uniform on – and I am the 'party leader'.

From the notes for his lecture at the start of this four-day course on 19 February, the essential elements of his teaching can be extracted. They were greatly influenced by his study of what had gone wrong at Cambrai while he was a member of the Court of Enquiry:

> The main lesson learnt was the futility of putting all your eggs into the front line basket and of neglecting distribution in depth. For two years GHQ and others preached depth. The French learnt it. We British agreed to it in principle, but not one division in ten carried put depth on the actual ground. But you shall. Many commanders cling to the silly idea that successful defence implies firing every weapon into no man's land.[11]

The notes go on to stress the importance of each part of the forward Zone holding on as long as possible, with battalion redoubts doing so for several days even if surrounded by the enemy. To avoid surprise, forward companies must patrol No Man's Land every night, going right up to the enemy wire to see if it has been cut. 'If it is not cut their infantry cannot attack through it. That is your best safeguard against a surprise attack.' Finally arrangements must be perfected for signalling news of the enemy from the forward outposts, and plans made for ensuring messages arriving in a fog. In respect of the likely enemy tactics, Ivor used his Cambrai study as well, and set out his deductions from it in further notes:

> The Bosche is managing his attack another way; he is practising it very much like he did at Cambrai. Creeping Barrage – Smoke Barrage (hand grenades) – then all eggs in the Storm Truppen basket. Storm Truppen are specially trained: They and the machine-gunners are the only good people in the German army. Storm Truppen and light machine guns go right ahead and do not stop for anything. They are followed 200 yards behind by masses of infantry. The Hun idea is that these Storm Troops will make holes and continue their advance past our strong points. They have been training to go 12 Km (7 miles) the first day.[12]

His description of the enemy's methods was to prove remarkably prescient.

The venue for Ivor's training sessions was the Corps Battle School, where the new commander, specially selected by Ivor, was the Willie Fraser of the Gordon Highlanders who had made such disparaging remarks about him the previous autumn, but was now coming to appreciate his qualities. How much the training courses were needed is shown by the entry in Fraser's diary on 20 February 1918:

> We have been holding a training conference of Brigadiers and Bn. Commanders and any amount of generals on the subject of training, and we made them enthusiastic. But it's no good – they are not organised, the battalions are not organised, and they CAN'T train. The state

of affairs within battalions in this matter is incredible. I have never been so astonished in my life.[13]

By the middle of March it became clear that the German attack might come at any moment, so that the colossal artillery bombardment of the British positions which began at 4.40am on Thursday 21 March was not unexpected. Five hours later, the infantry assault led by storm troops, followed at 9.40am and for the next week furious fighting took place on a 50-mile front, with over 60 British and German divisions involved, a number increased when French formations began to join the battle. The inevitable confusion that surrounds all major battles was heightened on the British side by the fact of withdrawing all the time, and doing so over such big distances. Although XVIII Corps had left Fifth Army before the front was eventually stabilised on 5 April, the British had by then fallen back to a point 35 miles west of St Quentin.

Before turning to an assessment of its commander's actions during the fighting, it is necessary to give a resumé of XVIII Corps' moves from 21 to 28 March. The following map shows the extent of each day's withdrawal. It should be mentioned here that the XVIII Corps' war diary, as with most other formations in Fifth Army, was written up sometime after the various actions described had taken place, since only what the official historian, Brigadier General Edmonds, describes as 'meagre' notes were recorded while the withdrawals were in progress by the majority of units.[14]

Throughout 21 March savage fighting took place in the Forward Zone. While the outposts nearest the enemy were quite soon overrun and suffered heavy losses, the redoubts in the defended localities at the rear of the Zone held on successfully in the 61st and 30th Divisions' sectors. On the right, the 36th Ulster Division was obliged to retire during the night behind the St Quentin Canal in order to keep in contact with the 14th Division of III Corps on its flank. Orders for this retirement were passed down from Gough, who also put the 20th Division from army reserve under command of XVIII Corps during the day.

During 22 March orders were given for two extensive withdrawals by the formations in XVIII Corps: first to the Green Line during the afternoon, and then to a new line of defence on the west bank of the Somme during the night. The newly arrived 20th Division acted as a rearguard while the 30th and 61st retired through it, the 36th Division keeping further south in touch with III Corps. The need for, and the timing of, these moves back to the Somme were strongly criticised in some quarters, though there were good reasons for them. Some aspects of the argument on the subject will be discussed shortly. At 2.30pm, the corps headquarters were moved from Ham to Nesle. During the evening the French II Cavalry Corps and V Corps arrived in the south of III Corps area, the first of the reserves which would soon move up to take over part of the British

GERMAN ADVANCE BY DAYS
March 1918

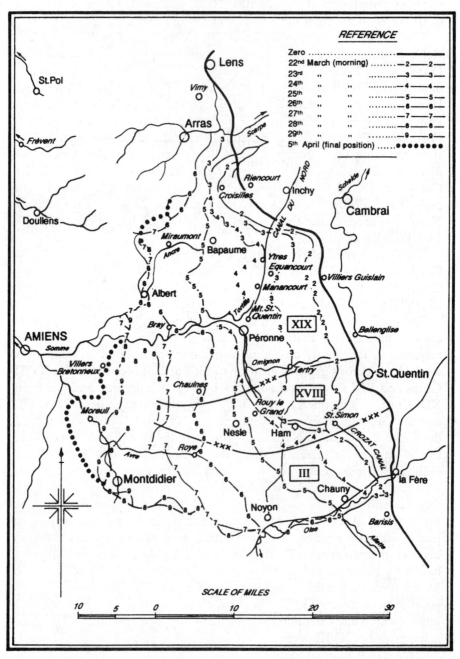

line. XVIII Corps held firm on its Somme defences throughout 23 March, though to the south parts of the 30th Division and the 36th Division were obliged to pull back up to four miles. This was partly caused by a German penetration of the line near Ham, and partly by the withdrawal of III corps on the right flank from its positions along the Crozat Canal.

The official history records that XVIII Corps 'found itself in an unenviable position on the morning of the 24th except that its left, the 20th Division, still held the line of the Somme'.[15] The 61st Division, greatly depleted, had been moved back into reserve. The enemy penetration near Ham had been extended to form a dangerous wedge between the 30th and 36th Divisions, forcing the 30th to fall back north-westwards. Fortunately French help was at hand. During the night four French divisions had come up to occupy a thinly held support line behind these two divisions. Eventually, after a day of fierce fighting the whole of XVIII Corps was forced to withdraw, and by the morning of 25 March had pulled back another five miles from the Somme to the line of the Canal du Nord. To the south the French filled the gap which had opened with the 14th Division of III Corps.

With the arrival of the French in strength, command of the XVIII Corps area passed on the 25th to General Robillot of the II Cavalry Corps. Since the French divisions had arrived without their own artillery, all XVIII Corps field guns had been detached to support them.

The confusion on 25 March was not lessened by having French generals in command of British units; though the spirit was willing, the response to frequently changing instructions in another language was weak. A dangerous gap was growing to the north of Nesle between XVIII Corps and XIX Corps, and an attack by a French division and one from XIX Corps was planned to close it. Although planned, it never came off, and the Germans swept on. Although the 20th and 30th Divisions held the line of the Canal du Nord until 5pm, both the British and French were forced once more to retire during the night. Noting that Robillot was pulling his troops south-westwards, and thereby increasing the gap with XIX Corps, Ivor at this point ignored French instructions and took back direct command of the sadly depleted and exhausted, but still battleworthy divisions of his Corps. He moved them north-westwards, keeping in touch with the French, but preventing a complete break occurring between the two armies. By the morning of 26 March they had dropped back a further seven miles, and corps headquarters was at Moreuil. On 26 March there took place, some 30 miles from the Fifth Army area of operations, the conference at Doullens which was to have such a devastating impact within a few days on both the army and its commander. The main achievement of XVIII corps on 26 March was to consolidate in the neighbourhood of Roye, and to fill the five-mile gap on the right of XIX Corps. Steps were also taken to recover the artillery units which had been loaned to the French, and which Robillot's corps had taken away with them when they moved off south-west.

Although fighting continued on 27 March the crisis on the Fifth Army front, in the words of the official history, 'can be said to have ended',[16] During the afternoon, Gough visited Ivor to tell him that orders had been received from General Foch, now Commander-in-Chief of both the British and French forces, that XVIII Corps was to be relieved in the line by the French First Army, and to be withdrawn to become part of a reserve formation in the process of being created behind the front line.

On 28 March, the relief of XVIII Corps was carried out, and it took no further part in the fighting. The German advance was slowing down, and made little progress after the 29th, with the allied front line finally stabilised 10 miles from Amiens on 5 April. With this brief account of the events of the period 21 to 28 March in mind, it is now time to consider Ivor's handling of his command in more detail.

In spite of the pressure he was under, Ivor managed to write two letters home during the battle on 23 March and 26 March. In the former he told Tiny of how the week of combat had begun: 'Before 5am on 21st the Hun opened up on us the most terrific bombardment I have yet heard and deluged all our front system with shells for five to six hours – including a lot of poisonous gas shells.' He was pleased to mention that the use of gas was not entirely one-sided. Being forewarned of the attack on 21 March from German prisoners and deserters, XVIII Corps heavy guns had poured 'a dose of 3,000 gas bombs of the most deadly sort' onto the enemy the day before, which Ivor believed 'took excellent effect on the big town St Quentin where huns were collecting in cellars'. When the infantry assault came in at the end of the bombardment, he reckoned that it was in such strength that each of his forward battalions had to fight almost a whole division of Germans, adding with pride mixed with sorrow that 'they did it, though few remain, very few to tell us what happened'.

On the evening of 20 March a ground mist had started to rise over the whole Fifth Army area, and by dawn on the 21st had thickened into a dense fog, limiting vision to a few yards in many places. The situation was made particularly baffling because gas masks had to be worn, due to the gas shells used in the enemy bombardment. The fog was a great advantage to the German storm troops at the start of their assault on the British Forward Zone for two main reasons. First, it prevented observed artillery fire being brought down on them from the British guns, and second, it negated much of the effectiveness of the defensive outposts that relied on mutual support by interlocking belts of rifle and machine-gun fire. Although the attacking storm troops suffered many casualties, the presence of the fog ensured that these were much less than they would have been in clear weather.

The XVIII Corps war diary tells how the first line of resistance in the

Forward Zone was pierced in many places during the morning, although the enemy were frequently checked by local counter-attacks. 'By mid-day, however, the whole line of resistance was overwhelmed by numbers. The redoubts in the FORWARD ZONE, however, continued to hold out long after they were surrounded.'[17]

During the afternoon of 21 March, Gough visited his four corps head-quarters. Leaving III Corps, where he had given permission for a withdrawal to the Crozat Canal, as long as contact was kept with flanking formations, he moved north. Farrar-Hockley tells of the next call:

> XVIII Corps headquarters was on the Somme Canal at Ham. Its proud and confident commander, Sir Ivor Maxse, was happy to tell Gough that the corps battle zone was still intact after fierce fighting in which four of his outpost battalions had been totally destroyed. Five others were still fighting on in the forward zone. But the penetration of Butler's left flank had inevitably opened Maxse's right. He understood also that his left had been laid open due to a penetration into XIX corps. Gough told him to adjust both his flanks, if necessary making use of the 20th Division which had been allotted to his sector. When they had left Ham and were travelling to XIX Corps headquarters at Le Catelet, Gough's ADC remarked that XVIII Corps seemed confident that they could hold their positions against any odds.
>
> 'My dear boy', said Gough, 'quite apart from their casualties in the battle zone, they have lost the better part of nine battalions forward. General Maxse has now [with the 20th Division] twenty-seven battalions. How long do you think he can go on taking casualties like that?'[18]

Gough's own recollections of the visit were recorded later in his own book, *The Fifth Army*:

> I found Maxse and his staff cheerful, active, and confident, and thus they remained throughout the whole of the battle. His XVIII Corps had done magnificently, and after desperate fighting still held its Battle Zone intact.

After mentioning that nine battalions in the Forward Zone had sacrificed themselves, and had been almost annihilated, Gough went on to tell how he had discussed the threat to XVIII Corps' flanks. He agreed that Ivor

> . . . should continue to hold his Battle Zone as long as possible on Friday, 22nd, but that he should draw back his right flank, to keep touch with III Corps, which was withdrawing to the line of the Crozat Canal, and that he should also throw back his left to cover the Omignon valley and keep touch with the XIX Corps.[19]

A further visitor to appear in the evening was Paul Maze, whose book *A Frenchman in Khaki* is one of the classics of the war, giving a vivid picture of conditions during the March disaster. Starting in 1914 as an unofficial interpreter attached to the Royal Scots Greys, Maze, who was a gifted artist, had become by 1918 a trusted member of the Fifth Army staff, used by Gough as a liaison officer, though ostensibly only a sergeant. In this rank he was to earn a DCM, MM and bar, and the Croix de Guerre. In a foreword to the book, Winston Churchill, a painting companion in later years, wrote that: 'Under Gough, and upon his supersession, under Rawlinson, Sergeant Maze became in the words of Sir William Robertson "an institution". He was unique and indefinable . . . this anomalous figure, neither French nor English, neither officer nor soldier, nor indeed civilian . . .'.[20] Maze's recollections of his arrival at XVIII Corps headquarters were that:

> I found General Maxse absolutely calm and apparently happy, as was his wont; he asked me for news of the other parts of the front. His had stood the strain. His look of satisfaction was no doubt due to that. He had held the line of his battle zone, having only lost a few of his outlying posts and some of his redoubts. Although he was satisfied, he didn't deceive himself as to what the following days had in store for him and the rest of us. He told me that General Gough had been in and told him he was not to count on receiving any help from army reserves for some time.[21]

In his book on *British Generalship in the Twentieth Century*, mentioned already on several occasions, Sixsmith, normally a Maxse admirer, is critical of Ivor's preparations for the defence of XVIII Corps sector. After telling of his insistence on defence in depth, and in prepared and rehearsed counter-attacks, Sixsmith then states: 'When the German attack came on 21 March Maxse's was one of the three Corps on which the brunt fell. Maxse's methods in the attack had always been justified by comparative success, but there is little evidence that his defensive teaching bore any fruit on this occasion.'[22] Though there is some justice in this verdict, its slight unfairness lies in the failure to stress two important factors which precluded the teaching being put into effect properly: shortage of manpower and the lack of time to construct defensive positions of sufficient strength. In a masterly assessment of the action on 21 March, the official history explains how British teaching was based on 'the principles laid down by the German General Staff after nearly three years experience of the defensive on the Western Front', but then goes on to show how these principles could not be followed satisfactorily:

> Had the Battle and Rear Zones been elaborated by a labyrinth of trenches and switches, tiers of wire, and hundreds of 'pill-boxes', machine-gun nests and deep dugouts, after the German model, they could no doubt have been capable of a prolonged defence; but time and labour had been lacking to do in six weeks what had taken even the Germans months if not years.[23]

There was fog again on the morning of 22 March when further enemy attacks were launched all along Fifth Army's front. As explained earlier in the resumé of the week-long battle, this was the day, and night, when XVIII Corps made a nine-mile withdrawal to the west bank of the Somme; a move for which Ivor has often been criticised. His own version of what happened, along with a comment indicating that he was already aware of some of this criticism, came in a letter written eight days later on 30 March.

> Please recollect that the Hun never broke through any part of my Corps. All sorts of rumours are prevalent about every action and every Senior Officer, as is usual on these occasions. Also scapegoats are being searched for all round! My Corps only retired from its original battle-post because it was ordered by me to do so. And the only reason why it was so ordered was that both its flanks were completely turned. I don't blame my neighbours for this, but it is nevertheless an absolute fact. The choice for me on 22nd March lay between fighting it out on the spot and losing four Divs complete, or retiring hand in hand with my neighbours on the right and left. I did the latter after a personal conference with my immediate superior. If I had done the former we would have killed many more Huns but should ourselves have been completely surrounded and thus left a big gap empty on the British battle front. Two days mist, (21st and 22nd) greatly assisted the enemy's assault and saved them many casualties.

The corps war diary, which notes that the headquarters closed at Ham at 2.30pm and 'reopened at Nesle at the same hour', gives this explanation of the reasons for pulling back on 22 March:

> By noon on the 22nd March it had become evident that a further withdrawal to the left bank of the SOMME would have to take place as the troops at the disposal of the Corps Commander, with the exception of two brigades of the 20th Division, had all been heavily engaged from 4am the previous morning. The 61st Brigade had been in action since the previous evening. The fighting had been continuous against enormous odds, and consequently the losses were heavy. In addition the corps front on the SOMME was stretched out from 16,000 yards when the battle commenced to 22,000 yards. The troops were becoming exhausted. The REAR ZONE was a poor line of defence as the trenches had only been dug 18 inches deep, but the wire in front of it was good. At the best it was but a position suitable for a rearguard action.[24]

There are two main grounds on which XVIII action is criticised. First, that it was too precipitate, and second, that it left a big gap on its northern flank with XIX Corps, which in turn affected the operations of other corps of both Fifth and Third Army further up the front-line.

Edmonds, the official historian, blamed Ivor on both scores. At various points in his narrative of the events of the day, he makes comments which lead up to the penultimate paragraph of his 'Remarks on the Retirement':

> The over-hasty withdrawal of the XVIII and the very heavy numerical superiority of the enemy opposite III Corps, proportionately heavier than elsewhere, made it a serious problem whether direct French help could arrive in time, especially if the habit of the British soldier to stand and fight it out – whatever the odds might be – was it seemed to him, to be changed into a habit of 'skedaddle'.[25]

Farrar-Hockley tells how around noon a message came through from Fifth Army about impending French reinforcements, coupled with the mention of Gough's plan to hold briefly on the Somme river and canal. He suggests that Ivor understood that 'he was required to retire to the Green Line as a preliminary to withdrawal to the River Somme'. He then comes to his critical assessment of Ivor's handling of the retirement.

> As he knew that the Green Line was, for the most part, a succession of signboards and a line of wire he did not believe that any stand could be made along it. If they were to go back, he decided, they must go back all the way to the water line. On this basis his forward divisions, 61st, 30th and 36th – the 20th Division was in rear – were ordered to disengage during the afternoon.
>
> It is not difficult to understand how Maxse and senior members of his staff came to make the first error. The enemy was pressing in front; the right flank, formed by the 36th (Ulster) Division, was thrown back awkwardly to the south along the St Quentin canal; they were absorbed in fighting a complex defensive action. What is extraordinary is that a commander of Maxse's experience and ability should have decided to disengage a force in close action during daylight, and without due care for the junction of his flank with Watts XIX Corps on his left.
>
> The forward infantry had lacked fire support during the morning because enemy bombardment had now cut the majority of buried telephone cables. In any case, all batteries had long since shifted to new positions distant from artillery cable heads. But there were plenty of equipments still in action, including medium and heavy guns and howitzers. A corps fire plan ought to have been made, arranging that heavy fire should fall forward of a given line at a stated time. All troops to be withdrawn from the forward zone should have been brought back behind that line and the opening of fire on and beyond it would have permitted the defenders to break clean from the enemy. Nothing of the sort was attempted and the embattled troops, infantry, entrenching battalions and field engineers, ran the gauntlet of fire as they came back, losing heavily in the process.[26]

Gough's own version of the events of 22 March, as recorded in his book, began by stating that fighting started earlier on XVIII Corps' front than III Corps' and went on later, until midnight, with battalions holding on, but suffering very heavy casualties. His account goes on to say that: 'He [Ivor] had also received the army order to fight a rearguard action, and therefore by 1pm he issued an order to his corps to retire behind the Somme.' Gough makes no direct criticism of the handling of the withdrawal, covered by the 20th Division 'at the cost of much severe fighting', but does say that XVIII Corps was no longer in touch with XIX Corps when it finally took up new positions on the Somme, and this 'caused Watts grave anxiety, which was naturally reflected in my headquarters'.[27]

Claims have been made that XVIII Corps' long retreat had serious effects on formations nearly 30 miles north in Byng's Third Army. The biographer of Byng makes this assertion:

> During the same night an event took place on the Fifth Army front which was to have a profound effect on the operations of the next few days and create an appalling risk to Fanshawe's 5th Corps [in Third Army]. Gough had indicated to his Corps Commanders that in the event of 'serious hostile attacks' they were to fight 'rearguard actions back to the forward line of Rear Zone [Green Line] and if necessary to rear line of Rear Zone,' [in 18th Corps, the River Somme]. It was left to corps commanders to decide if an attack was serious and to act independently, reporting their actions to army headquarters. In the south the 18th Corps withdrew to the Green Line during the afternoon, but Lt-Gen Sir Ivor Maxse, the corps commander, had already decided that his troops could not possibly hold any position between it and the River Somme to the west. At 12.30 pm he ordered his divisions to continue their withdrawal during the night 22–23 March. By next morning they were on the west bank of the Somme, leaving a huge gap between them and the 19th Corps to the north. Neither it nor the 7th corps were prepared for such an extensive withdrawal and the strain of maintaining touch with their more nimble footed comrades while hanging on to the right of Third Army proved to be too great.[28]

A particularly severe criticism of Ivor, though it lacks credibility, comes from the pen of Professor Travers in his book *The Killing Ground*. He asserts that: 'None of what follows here is intended to reflect unkindly on the participants involved.' However, he then moves on to tell how Edmonds laid the blame for problems of the retreat entirely on XVIII Corps, causing Ivor, when he read drafts of the Official History many years later, to say how shocked he was to be selected 'for the role of "scapegoat" in one of the greatest battles of the war'. Turning next to a brief resumé of the corps war diary, a paragraph from which has been quoted earlier in this chapter, Travers then makes a surprising claim:

> This document was XVIII Corps' reasonable defence of its actions, but in a private letter to Edmonds, Maxse admitted that although Lloyd

George, Henry Wilson and Foch were all seeking scapegoats, only the official historian [Edmonds] had actually detected him! What this specifically meant was only revealed in 1937 in a private conversation when Edmonds told Liddell Hart that Maxse had actually been away from his Corps HQ from 22 to 24 March. These were the crucial days of XVIII Corps' abrupt withdrawal to the west of the Somme thus creating serious gaps for Fifth Army. The absence of the GOC XVIII Corps seems partly to account for the confusion at Corps HQ and the issuance of the XVIII Corps' order to withdraw to the Somme. Edmonds kept his information out of the Official History in order not to be harsh and damage the reputation of an otherwise excellent officer, who in May 1918 was appointed Inspector General of Training.[29]

The first point to make is that Travers has read the comment in Ivor's private letter to Edmonds in the wrong way. Far from being an admission of some form of guilt, of being a justified 'scapegoat', it is intended to mock Edmonds, and to make fun of his judgment. As to the suggested absence from corps headquarters from 22 to 24 March, the facts of Ivor's presence there on the 23rd will shortly be demonstrated, while it could have been his proper duty on the 22nd to have spent much of the time out and about, visiting the headquarters of the divisions under his command and assessing the state of his troops for himself. In spite of odd theories put forward by Edmonds to Liddell Hart this is what Ivor was doing: the 30th Division War Diary tells of him giving instructions to the divisional commander twice during the morning of that day.[30]

Although perhaps unfairly, Ivor certainly suffered a good deal of unpopularity in many quarters as a result of the events of 22 March. Due to his readiness to criticise other commanders at all levels, and his reputation for being very pleased with himself, he had many enemies who were only too ready to pass stories around of his mishandling of the withdrawal on that day.

On the morning of 23 March, XVIII corps headquarters withdrew eight miles from Nesle to Roye, and during a slightly quieter day than the previous two Ivor was able to write the letter to Tiny already referred to earlier in the chapter. He also wrote that day to Fifth Army headquarters with a special report:

(1) During the last three days of severe fighting many heroic acts have been performed and many Germans have been killed in consequence. These acts will be described in detail in due course, but I venture to select the following units for immediate recognition in the next communiqué and beg that the Army Commander will forward them for consideration:-
(a) 61st Division
(b) 1st Battalion Royal Inniskilling Fusiliers
(c) 2/4th Battalion Oxford & Bucks Light Infantry

    (d) 9th Battalion The Royal Scots
    (e) 179th Army Brigade R.F.A.
    (f) 306th Brigade R.F.A.

The letter then went on to give brief details of the actions of each formation and unit mentioned.[31] The 61st Division war diary notes that at 5.15pm on the 23rd, Ivor called at divisional headquarters to explain the latest situation.[32] At nightfall he returned to his own temporary base at Roye, where he was joined by Paul Maze, sent to him by Gough who had 'asked me to remain with the XVIII Corps and keep in touch with the French troops that were coming to its help'. Maze went to describe his doings that night:

> As I rode on to the XVIII Corps, lorries with supplies for the troops and ammunition for the guns were crawling past me; the organisation for the feeding of the army never once broke down even in the face of our increasing difficulties. I unlaced my boots and rested for a few hours in a room next door to where General Maxse sat enveloped in his heavy coat, his cap pulled over his eyes, puffing at a cigar and facing his map like a professor studying a problem. Now and again a shout for 'Tom' would bring forth his Chief-of-Staff, General Hollond, who was calmly dealing with all the intricate problems of the anxious situation in another room. The green bed valises rolled up in the room indicated that sleep was out of the question for anyone that night.[33]

During Sunday, 24 March, the Germans greatly extended a small bridgehead they had made across the Somme on the previous day at Ham. Seven enemy divisions were launched against XVIII corps, eventually driving the 20th and 30th Divisions back four miles to the Canal du Nord, and making it difficult for the 30th to keep contact with the 36th Division on its southern flank. The condition of the troops after three days' and nights' heavy fighting with virtually no rest is well described in the Official History:

> The physical and mental strain of the struggle against overwhelming odds, the heavy losses, the sinister rumours which were rife, all contributed to depress morale. Yet never did the men lose heart or think of abandoning the combat; when they strayed from or lost their units, they would rally on any officer who called upon them . . . In such circumstances, when a unit was ordered to occupy position, a number of men, so tired that they appeared to be unconscious of their surroundings, would be pushed into a shallow trench by an equally tired officer, and most of them would fall asleep under fire, as the Old Army had done at 'First Ypres'.[34]

The arrival of Général Robillot, commanding the French II Cavalry Corps, brought promise of some relief on XVIII Corps front. However, it was soon discovered that his two mainly dismounted divisions, the 22nd and 62nd, had no artillery of their own, and only 50 rounds of small arms ammunition per man, while at all levels staffs were deficient of the equipment necessary for carrying out their proper function. Paul Maze joined Ivor and Robillot soon after the latter appeared on the scene, and described them in his book: 'No two men could have presented a bigger contrast than these two Generals; General Maxse, very quiet, sitting grimly at his table, and the rather exuberant French General dressed in the palest blue with two rows of medals tinkling on his broad chest.'[35] Under discussion were the arrangements for moving the French divisions into the line, and for a proposed counter-attack to be made the following morning by Robillot's 22nd Division in the area of Nesle. At this point, command of all British troops passed officially to the French, although the limitations noted above made the exercise of control by Robillot's staff somewhat haphazard. Though plans were made for the attack in the Nesle area, and were confirmed by Gough at a conference late in the evening of the 24th, when the time came for it to be launched on the morning of 25 March it failed to materialise. Since the French divisions had no artillery of their own, the guns of the British divisions were attached to them, a move which was to have unexpected results shortly afterwards. Returning to XVIII Corps after visiting other formations, Maze discovered that:

> General Maxse was in a bad mood when I found him, for Nesle had been lost early that morning and the counter-attack had failed. First of all the, French had been obliged to postpone the hour as they were not ready and then at the appointed hour something had gone wrong . . .
>
> This was the result of the French staff taking over the command of our troops immediately theirs were pitched forward into the battle. General Maxse said that he was not going to allow his divisions to take orders from anybody but himself in future and that he would keep firm control over his troops.[36]

This decision was to have important results, when, after another day of hard fighting, the French began to withdraw during the evening of Monday the 25th in a south-westerly direction. In a more friendly passage than usual, the official history tells how Ivor had been warned during the morning that 'in the event of a withdrawal becoming necessary, the direction of the French retirement would be south-west towards Roye'. It goes on to point out that if the British remained with the French the gap between XVIII and XIX Corps, already three miles wide, 'would be still further increased and would offer an opportunity to the enemy to separate the bulk of the British Army from the French'.[37] In the event, Ivor did not conform to Robillot's movements, but ordered his divisions to move north-west, rather than south-west, and to make contact with XIX Corps. Gough in his book gives generous praise for this decision:

Eventually, as evening came on, our divisions were withdrawn behind the French 62nd and 22nd Divisions, and – contrary to French instructions owing to Maxse's firm orders – all his divisions were concentrated in the neighbourhood of Roye. Meanwhile Robillot's corps continued its retirement south-westwards during the night, and by Tuesday morning it was standing on the line Laquy–Roye facing north-east, having fallen back during the previous 24 hours a distance of about seven miles.

Maxse's firmness and decision in keeping his corps together and moving it westwards and north-westwards saved the Fifth Army, and in fact the whole British Army and the Allied cause, from a disaster: for a complete separation of the French and British Armies would have been nothing else.'[38]

Gough was particularly generous in giving all the credit to Ivor for saving the Fifth Army, since his actions were the result of discussions between the two commanders, and the XVIII Corps war diary states that 'a ten mile gap was only avoided by the firmness of purpose displayed by General Sir Hubert Gough, Commanding the Fifth Army'.[39]

Having gathered his divisions together to the north-west of Roye, Ivor gave orders for them to move into position on the morning of Tuesday, 26 March to fill the vital gap between Robillot's Corps and XIX Corps. Although this was the day when the German advance first showed signs of losing steam, they had by no means given up the struggle, and were still probing for weak points in the British front. XVIII Corps were still fighting hard, but without their artillery support. This was one of the reasons why Gough found Ivor on the morning of the 26th 'in no sweet mood'. Although Gough had himself asked urgently for the return of XVIII Corps guns from the French in the previous day, they had still not been sent back. Ivor then decided to make use of the ubiquitous Paul Maze, going over Robillot's head and sending him direct to the French Third Army commander, Général Humbert, to get him to order the return of the guns.

Maze's own account of this difficult commission starts with his 25-mile ride on his motorcycle to the French Army headquarters. There his 'sudden entry into a luxurious panelled room where sat a hyper-military French Army Commander, acted like a cold douche'. Eventually, his turn came to put his case to Humbert, who, after some questioning, gave him a written order to pass on to the person responsible for control of the borrowed artillery, instructing it to be released. 'With a smart salute', Maze recalled, 'I shook the dust off my boots and rushed into the night to look for our artillery; it started that same night on its long detour round Montdidier to rejoin the XVIII Corps.'[40]

While the men on the ground still struggled on wearily, a meeting was in progress 35 miles away on the 26th which was to have important, but not altogether happy, results for the Fifth Army. In the French town of

Doullens were gathered some of the most powerful political and military leaders from the two allied countries, among whom the most significant were to be Clemenceau and Général Foch for France, and Lord Milner, about to become Secretary of State for War, and Haig for Britain. While it is not the place to describe the full course of the meeting here, its vital consequence was the placing of Foch in a position succinctly recorded in the resolution agreed by both parties at the end of it: 'Général Foch is charged by the British and French governments to co-ordinate the action of the allied armies on the western front. He will arrive at an agreement, to this effect, with the generals-in-chief, who are invited to furnish him all necessary information.' Much of the success of this conference was due to the excellent rapport between Clemenceau and Milner, which had its roots in an unusual source: their mutual affection for Ivor's sister Violet, at the time still Lady Edward Cecil, but in due course to become Lady Milner. After an earlier meeting with Milner in December 1916, Clemenceau had told the French president why they both got on so well together. 'I like him a lot,' he said of Milner. 'He is an old friend of mine. We admired and loved the same woman. That's an indissoluble bond.'[41] Foch wasted no time once his new authority had been granted to him. The official history reports that:

> He first went to Fifth Army headquarters at Dury, where he arrived at about 4 p.m. There he asked a number of questions of General Gough, reiterating that there must be no more retirement, and that the line must be held at all costs. He offered no advice as to how this had best be done, and did not mention reinforcements. Subsequently General Gough was informed that his right-hand corps, the XVIII, would be relieved as soon as possible by French troops and put at his disposal to serve as first reserve to his Fifth Army.[42]

Gough was appalled by the way Foch treated him, and resentful of the fact that no help of any sort was offered. By this time, gossip and rumour had created a picture of the Fifth Army which was epitomised in a disgraceful outburst by the pessimistic General Pétain during the Doullens conference, when he said of Gough's command that 'Alas, it no longer really exists', and even claimed that his men had 'refused to engage the enemy' and had 'run like the Italians at Caporetto'. Though Foch may not have agreed with so damaging a judgment, he clearly shared an unfriendly, disparaging view of the Fifth Army, failing to give deserved credit for its continuing readiness to fight in spite of the long retreat and heavy losses.

Notes

Letters from Maxse to his wife can be found in WSRO, files 207, 209.

1 Freyberg, Paul, *Bernard Freyberg, VC* (Hodder & Stoughton, 1991), p. 117.
2 Barclay, Brig C N, *Armistice, 1918* (Dent, 1968), p. 11.
3 Robertson, Field Marshal Sir W, *Soldiers and Statesmen, 1914–1918* (Cassell, 1926), p. 290.
4 This letter is in the possession of the Maxse family.
5 Edmonds, Brig Gen. Sir J, *Military Operations, France and Belgium*, 1918, Vol I (From here OH), p. 128.
6 OH, p. 41.
7 OH, p. 42.
8 Farrar-Hockley, Gen Sir A, *Goughie* (Hart-Davies, 1975), p. 265.
9 Haig Papers, Accession 3155, No 130.
10 Farrar-Hockley, pp. 266 and 391.
11 Copies of these notes are in the possession of the family, and also in the Maxse papers, IWM.
12 Sixsmith, Maj Gen E K G, *British Generalship in the 20th Century* (Arms and Armour, 1970), p. 130.
13 Fraser, Gen Sir D, *In Good Company* (M Russell, 1990), p. 215.
14 OH, p vi. Copies of the XVIII Corps diary can be found in the PRO, Ref WO 95/953, and in IWM 69/53/10.
15 OH, p. 404.
16 OH, p. 532.
17 IWM 69/53/10, File 45, p. 13.
18 Farrar-Hockley, p. 280.
19 Gough, Gen Sir H, *The Fifth Army* (Hodder & Stoughton), p. 267.
20 Maze, Paul, *A Frenchman in Khaki* (Heinemann, 1934), Introduction by W S Churchill.
21 Maze, p. 287,
22 Sixsmith, p. 131.
23 OH, p. 56.
24 War Diary, p. 19, para 53.
25 OH, p. 302.
26 Farrar-Hockley, p. 286.
27 Gough, pp. 273–4.
28 Williams, Jeffrey, *Byng of Vimy* (Lee Cooper, 1983).
29 Travers, Tim, *The Killing Ground* (Allen & Unwin, 1987), p. 233. Liddell Hart recorded the comment on Maxse's absence in his notes on *Talk with Brig Gen J.E. Edmonds, United Services Club 11 November 1937* (11/1937/88 in Liddell Hart Centre, King's College, London.)
30 War Diary of 30th Division, PRO Ref WO95/2313.
31 One of the original carbon copies of this letter is in the possession of the Maxse family.
32 War Diary of 61st Division, PRO Ref WO95/3035.
33 Maze, p. 295.
34 OH, p. 400.

35 Maze, p. 297.
36 Maze, p. 303.
37 OH, p. 462.
38 Gough, pp. 295–6.
39 War Diary, p. 28, para 76.
40 Maze, p. 306.
41 Dallas, George, *At the Heart of a Tiger* (Macmillan, 1993), p. 524.
42 OH, p. 543.

17

XVIII Corps' Movements from 27 March to the End of May 1918

———•◆•———

Although the French First Army received its orders to relieve XVIII Corps during the evening of 26 March, the relief took time to organise, so that Ivor's battered divisions were still in the line on Wednesday 27 March, the seventh day of the battle. Calling at Ivor's headquarters, now at Moreuil, in the evening, Maze found that: 'His corps had held its own throughout the day and had hardly given any ground.' To the north the British, and to the south the French, had both fallen back distances of several miles, but XVIII Corps found that in spite of his opportunities 'the enemy did not break through. He advanced feebly and even the counter attack of our weakened troops checked him.'[1] The Germans were now paying the price for the devastation they had caused during their withdrawal to the Hindenburg line in 1916, as they struggled to follow up their advancing troops with supplies across the barren, broken wasteland they had themselves created. The German difficulties were described in the letter Ivor wrote during the night of 26th–27th. Starting by stating that: 'We have had the very devil of a week's fighting . . .', leaving him without the time or mental energy to describe it in full, he went on to say: 'The difficulties of the Bosch are commencing. He has not broken our line nor has he separated us from our allies. He has caused us great losses undoubtedly but he has not broken our spirit. and my men are wonderfully cheerful though sadly reduced in numbers.' He ended by telling how the British had been 'well fed throughout – which is a great thing – and now the Hun is so far from his supplies that he must be getting hungry'.

The manner in which XVIII Corps was relieved in the line on Thursday, 28 March, was not what had been expected. 'It will be recalled', states the official history, 'that the Groupement Mesple [named after its French commander] should have relieved the remaining portion of the XVIII Corps (20th and 30th Divisions) during the night of the 27th–28th; but by dawn only a small part of the relief had taken place . . .' In an attempt to tidy up an increasingly confused and untidy situation, the French Third Army commander, General Humbert, now gave orders for a reorganisation which cannot have pleased Ivor. The official history goes on to tell how '. . . by his orders from midnight of the 27th–28th, the 30th and 36th Divisions were placed under General Mesple, and the 20th and 61st Divisions under XIX Corps, thus depriving Lieut-General Maxse (XVIII Corps) of any command, and increasing Lieut-General Watts's responsibilities . . . The transfer ordered by General Humbert took effect in the course of the day's operations.'[2]

Ivor was not the only one to be deprived of his command at this time, though he was more fortunate than his superior officer in that his deprivation was only temporary. Poor Gough's fate was worse. He had been with Ivor on the afternoon of 27 March before returning to Fifth Army headquarters to be greeted with the news of his immediate replacement by Rawlinson. For the next few days until 4 April, Gough was held in limbo, making a defence plan for Amiens, and then finally sent back to England where he retired rather than take up the inferior posting offered to him. When Rawlinson arrived he renumbered the Fifth Army the Fourth, and brought in many of the staff officers who had served with him in the earlier Fourth Army.

Later, on 28 March, the 20th and 30th Divisions went into reserve, but two days after that had reverted to XVIII Corps command, so that Ivor was able to write on 30 March to say that he would 'be back for some time but reorganising and training and tremendously busy with it'. In the same letter, part of which was quoted in the previous chapter, he also insisted once more that 'the Hun never broke through any part of my Corps'. Although this may have been the case, the price paid in loss of men was high. The corps war diary records losses of 910 officers and 20,975 other ranks up to 27 March[3], but the official history takes the figures up to 5 April and records a total of 24,031, made up as follows:

	Officers	Other Ranks
Killed	110	994
Wounded	467	6,038
Missing	485	15,937 [4]

It is suggested that when assessing the numbers shown as missing it can be assumed that 10% eventually returned, 10% were killed, and 80% were prisoners of war. As an example of what these casualties meant at the unit level, the 2nd Scottish Rifles in the 20th Division lost 19 officers and 619 other ranks between 21 March and 2 April, leaving a battalion of four officers and 60 men to be reconstructed and trained for further action.[5] That Ivor was 'tremendously busy' is hardly surprising.

The movements during April 1918 of the four divisions that originally made up XVIII Corps provide a good example of the 'to-ing and fro-ing' that went on between corps in the First World War. Only the 20th was still under command by 28 April, where it had been joined by the 24th Division, while the corps itself had been moved into the First Army sector a little south of Arras as part of the GHQ and Army Reserve. On the 28th, of Ivor's original divisions the 30th could be found in XXII Corps in Second Army; the 36th in II corps in Second Army; and the 61st Division in XI corps in First Army.[6]

On 13 April, Tiny sent a press cutting about the recent fighting to which she attached a note asking: 'Is it accurate? I wish our correspondents would not make out that the French did it all.' Returning her note, Ivor scribbled on the back: 'Keep your hair on. It is written to please the French. There is enough truth in places to make the story plausible, but it does not contain the real truth at all, at all.' The next day he wrote again at length to give his view of the situation in general: 'The Hun is all out to destroy the British Army at any cost to himself. If he cannot do it pretty soon, i.e. this summer, he will never do it. This is quite a fair military proposition from his point of view. I think he will fail. We shall muddle through somehow.' The letter then went on to explain his views on the German advantage in '*superior training*', with his usual criticisms of the British 'inherent national characteristic to be unprepared always'.[7]

It had been on 11 April that Haig had issued his famous 'backs to the wall' Order of the Day, and the theme was taken up in the notes Ivor prepared for a corps commanders conference on 19 April.[8] He found it necessary to warn against 'crabbing your commanders', and against 'pessimism in messes', and exhorted those present to: 'Catch hold of your battalions. Get a grip on your company and Platoon commanders. Mean business. Create leaders. The men are a good lot and keen.' His first long paper headed 'Lessons from the Recent Operations of the XVIII Corps' was issued on 28 April 1918. 'The chief lesson', the paper began in expected style, 'is the absolute necessity of having divisions properly trained.' Three pages of closely typed, detailed comments ensued, much attention being paid to gaps in the British defences, mostly along river valleys and in low ground, and the German skill in penetrating and exploiting them.[9]

During May, the 52nd Lowland Division joined XVIII Corps,[10] and early in the month the corps moved out of GHQ reserve to come under command of First Army, which covered a sector of the front stretching from near Hazebrouck, where it marched with Second Army, to south of Arras, where Third Army was on its flank. Due to the heavy losses

incurred during the fighting which had been going on since 21 March, the
BEF was desperately short of manpower. On taking over a part of the First
Army front from the Canadian Corps, Ivor once again found himself
holding an extended line with minimum resources, and was none too
pleased about it.

Notes

1 Maze, Paul, *A Frenchman in Khaki* (Heinemann, 1934) pp. 306, 308.
2 OH, 1918 Vol II, p. 45.
3 IWM 69/53/10, File 45.
4 OH, Vol II, p. 420.
5 Story, H H, *History of the Cameronians (Scottish Rifles) 1910–1933*, Gale &
   Polden, 1961), p. 277.
6 OH, Vol III, p. 25.
7 Letters in the possession of the family.
8 One of the original duplicated copies is in the possession of the family.
9 Ditto.
10 OH, Vol III, p. 193. An order of battle shows 20th, 24th, and 52nd Divisions
   in XVIII Corps.

18

Inspector General of Training

————·◆·————

Joining First Army was not a happy experience for Ivor. Its commander, General Sir Henry Horne, was a gunner who had started the war as BGRA in Haig's I Corps. He was a sound, if slightly obtuse, commander, with a conventional mind and a different approach to new ideas from Ivor's.[1] The two were soon at loggerheads, as Haig noted in his diary on 14 May 1918:

> . . . had a long talk with Horne (1st Army) . . . He spoke to me about Maxse who commands 18 Corps. When he arrived he made difficulties; and after his troops had been in line a few days he said he would not be responsible for the front. Horne told him that his corps was considerably stronger than the Canadians whom he relieved and that there were no more troops to give him. If his dispositions were not satisfactory, it was his (Maxse's) fault and if he still felt he could not hold his front line let him say so and another corps commander would be put in to relieve him at once! Maxse's tone at once changed! I asked Horne not to judge Maxse too quickly but if he found he could not work in sympathy with Maxse I would arrange to change him.[2]

Although Ivor was to remain with XVIII Corps for another five weeks, this meeting between Haig and Horne may have had a bearing on his appointment to a new post at GHQ as Inspector General of Training (IGT) for the whole of the BEF. Haig was already considering the creation of such a post, with Ivor as the obvious incumbent and perhaps the Horne-Maxse clash speeded up his decision to implement it. Ivor went on leave in early June, and must have already had unofficial notification of his move, because on returning to France he wrote to Tiny on 19 June to say that '. . . thére is no longer any need to keep secret about myself'. A further letter on 23 June reported that:

> I have said goodbye to-day to the XVIIIth Army Corps with great regret, have handed over command to Hunter-Weston and am about to depart for GHQ. It is a bit of a wrench and the end of a very strenuous 1½ years of fighting command.

Accusations of incompetence, and even cowardice, were still at this stage being showered on the Fifth Army for its part in the March retreat, and Ivor's next letter, written the following day, reflects his realisation of this fact. It starts by telling that his ADCs are searching for a 'residence within ten miles' of GHQ, and that he is to dine in the evening with Haig. Then he refers to current rumours before explaining how he is to operate in his new role:

> My appointment has appeared officially and has been conveyed to everyone in France who cares to hear so you need not sit on it any longer. You will no doubt hear that I have been 'ungummed' as a Corps Commander through having failed in the Fifth Army at St Quentin or some such similar yarn? But don't pay the least attention to that or any other story you may hear from gossip. Nor is it worth your while to contradict them or their tales! But to your friends you may state that training here and at home has proved to be insufficiently supervised, and that I and my staff are to devote our whole attention to training methods, training organisation, training tips etc. etc. Moreover, we are to go about and insist that training shall be carried out in a methodical manner.
>
> Thus we inspect and help and advise – through the local Commanders on the spot. We are not to command but we expect to STIMULATE THOSE WHO DO.
>
> P.S. I ought to be a Savonarola or a LUTHER!

A suitable base for the team was in due course found near Crécy, scene of the great English victory in 1346. To work with him came Major General Uniacke to supervise artillery training, and Brigadier Generals Dugan, Marshall and Guggisberg, with Tom Hollond remaining his chief of staff. Before long he felt it necessary to make representations on behalf of these and of himself, in respect of their career prospects and pay. A personal letter of 5 July to General Wilson, now CIGS in Robertson's place, suggested promotion for the brigadier generals, all of whom had been recommended for divisional commands. Next came his own case:

> I hear the Army Council have marked their appreciation of my services by cutting down my pay by £500, and Uniacke's by £300. These reductions of pay will not diminish our energies nor damp our training ardour, but they give us a glimpse of the estimation in which we are

held by our superiors! I venture however to suggest that the Inspector General of Training, who has to deal on about equal terms with Army Commanders, re training, should be a substantive Lieutenant-General. Also, I think you will find, if you inquire at the W.O. that I have already, on two previous occasions, been recommended for that rank, yet I have had no substantive promotion since the war started. If the promotions are granted to my staff, I trust the whole thing can be announced in *one* gazette, so as to start everyone in France with the notion that TRAINING is *it* for 1919.[3]

Ivor was in his element in his new job, and soon his team was working at full pitch. Visits were being made to formations and units throughout the BEF, and were planned for training establishments in England as well. A stream of pamphlets and leaflets were printed, and by the time the inspectorate was dissolved in December 1918 no less than 202,287 leaflets had been issued, out of which 41,496 copies of the one on 'Attack Formations for Small Units' had gone out.[4] As might be expected, many of Ivor's favourite themes appeared in these publications: the importance of the platoon commander; the need for leaders to train their own men; the keeping together of sections; and the proper use of every minute available for training.

That he was well aware of the worst failings of most units when out of the line was made clear in a leaflet giving a suggested address for a 'Battalion Commander's Conference on the 1st day after coming out of the Line for 10 days'. The paragraph which begins 'Now we can discuss our *training programme*' shows how well he understood the way soldiers usually thought about such matters:

I have already given out the lines on which I want training carried out. You must remember that the men are tired after a trying time in the trenches – as a rule they don't look forward to a spell out of the line because they think they will never be left in peace, and that each day and all day will be spent in some *tiresome or boring drill* or exercise which they have done over and over again – how are you going to get over this? Have any of you thought it out? There is only one way in which we can put this nightmare out of the men's minds. Take the men into our confidence – explain to them the reason why we do every exercise, let them know that each item will only last a short time and that it is up to them to pay attention to their work and think out what they are doing. When they do anything well – tell them so. If they do not do it well, explain how they could have done it better, and put them at it again. Don't make any scheme too long – knock off as soon as you see that the men have got the hang of it – then go on with something else.[5]

A young officer posted to Ivor's staff, whom he described in a letter on 11 August as 'very capable and even brilliant' was 'Major Barrington-Ward,

DSO, MC, and I spotted him in Flanders fighting', when he was a brigade major in one of the brigades in XVIII Corps. Barrington-Ward had worked on *The Times* before the war, and was to become its editor in the 1930s, though his reputation was then clouded by his role as a Neville Chamberlain supporter. While working on the IGT's staff he wrote a long skit on its work, in what can best be described as inspired doggerel, which so delighted Ivor that he sent a copy home. It starts with some lines to set the scene, and then has four parts, each headed with a word from Ivor's constantly repeated slogan of 'Explanation, Demonstration, Execution, Repetition.' A few lines are worth quoting. To tell how throughout the BEF before the IGT was appointed, everyone had their own contrary views on training, while GHQ poured out written instructions which nobody read, Barrington-Ward used these lines:

> And while the mad medley was gaily galumphing
> The persons Above them were steadily bumphing
> Shades of St Rollox, of Castor & Pollux,
> You never espied such a powerful tide,
> Such a merciless flow of grandiloquent bollocks.

Then under the heading of Execution we find:

> The Colonel Commanding the Bollockyboos
> Has strictly revised all his previous views . . .
> He keeps his battalion, untiring, approving,
> All moving and firing and firing and moving;
> They know about guns, they know about tanks,
> They'll take any risk that you like with their flanks;
> They're perfectly sound on the use of the ground,
> They all are at one that training is fun
> And there's nought they don't know about killing the Hun.[6]

The verses end with a forecast which was to prove more accurate than was probably realised as the words were penned:

> Enough and no more. This terrible war
> Was timed for three years and has now taken four,
> But this is now certain – it cannot last long
> With twenty-two officers singing this song.

The post of IGT had only been in existence for three weeks when the last, and unsuccessful, German offensive of 1918 was launched against the French between Reims and the Marne. It was followed by General Mangin's counter-attack on 18 July between the Marne and the Oise, which has been referred to as the turning point in the saga of the war. Soon after the French victory, Haig began planning an offensive by the British Fourth Army south of the Somme, and this was opened on 8

August. For the next three months the Allied armies, joined in increasing numbers by the Americans, fought a series of battles which, although often fiercely contended and heavy with casualties, were generally successful. The German army began to fall apart as it retreated towards its homeland, and on 11 November the Armistice was signed and the long and terrible war was over.

How much the work of the IGT and his staff affected these final operations of the BEF is not easy to assess. Professor Brian Bond has suggested that 'the speed and efficiency' with which the British learned to cope with open warfare as the period of continual advances began 'was chiefly due to Haig's newly appointed Inspector-General of Training, General Sir Ivor Maxse, "a man of imagination, originality and drive with a wealth of battlefield experience behind him"'.[7] Bond quotes this description of Ivor from Major-General Essame's book *Battle for Europe, 1918*, in which it is also claimed that:

> The influence of Maxse and his staff, freed from the responsibility for the daily conduct of operations, with a roving commission to go where they wished, was now felt throughout the Army. A new spirit seized the Army and Divisional schools.[8]

Certainly Ivor roved far and wide in his new role. On 7 August he was lecturing in Poperinge, where one of his audience from 19 Brigade in the 33rd Division was Lieutenant Colonel (later Brigadier General) James Jack, commanding 1st Cameronians (Scottish Rifles), whose published diary, edited by John Terraine, is one of the classics of the First World War. Jack's comments on the lecture bring out some of the problems connected with putting Ivor's teaching into practice:

> The Inspector-General of Training, General Maxse, delivers a very sound address and appears anxious to help us. It is, however, curious to hear him lay such stress on the need for carrying out orders, which we had imagined to be the foundation of military discipline, and the first thing to be impressed on all ranks when they join the Service. Another point of the General's is: that every platoon commander should have his men at his disposal for a short period of training every day when out of the Line. This is entirely sensible in theory; but few of the present platoon commanders are professionally fit to instruct their men, and we prefer to educate them first, so that they shall teach correctly and not spread false doctrines among their subordinates.
>
> Secondly, the greater part of platoons is not available for parade when companies are in reserve. Many men are on duties and working parties . . .
>
> Thirdly, after a tour of four to eight days in the line, almost the first essential is a day's rest, and not too much work in the little remaining time in reserve . . .[9]

That it was always a problem for units to follow the IGT's precepts fully, for the reasons Jack explains, is brought out by reference to an extract from one of Ivor's own reports, which he thought sufficiently important to retain with his personal papers after the war. Visiting a division on one occasion he found that in 'one or two battalions the men appeared tired, and took little interest in the morning's work'. However, 'in the 15th Battalion Cheshire Regiment quite a different spirit prevailed'. The report went on to explain how training was 'thoroughly well organized' and 'by units'. It ended by commenting: 'But what struck me most about the 15th Battalion Cheshire Regiment was the fact that its commander and his officers had overcome all the difficulties commonly complained of by other officers in similar circumstances.'[10]

While it is certain that the creation of an IGT and his staff had a considerable impact on the training philosophy of the BEF, extensive claims for their influence on the conduct of operations are unrealistic. They never had enough time. In the few months available to them they did the ground-work which would have been invaluable had the war dragged on into 1919, but in the event the end of hostilities in November came before the full effect of their teaching had been felt. Ivor maintained his close contacts with the French Army, and wrote to Tiny on 25 August with details of a visit where he 'was more than ever thankful that my French powers of conversation did not desert me':

I returned last night from a most interesting trip to French – or rather International – GHQ where I dined alone with Field Marshal Foch and one or two of his staff including General Weygand. Foch, whom I have known now for six or seven years, does not look a day older. On the contrary – though 66 years old – he is positively younger looking since his great success as Generalissimo of the Allied Armies! He received me with the greatest kindness and talked freely about the campaign – as we were alone at dinner and afterwards on some chairs in the garden on the hottest day we have had this year, Friday 23rd August. The news coming in all that day was very good indeed both for the French and the two British Armies engaged and Foch had every reason to be satisfied. Apart from the morale effect on the German Armies, which is great, we have captured over 100,000 German prisoners and over 1,600 guns since Foch launched his stroke on 18th July. These figures represent the combined efforts of both British and French attacks and also certain American successes since 15th July. Foch had received from Clemenceau – at an official function – on the day I dined with him – his baton as Maréchal de France which I handled on his writing table. To revive the baton – once so famous throughout Europe – Foch told me they had to copy that of one of Napoleon's Marshals. It had his name on it in an old fashioned character and merely the words 'Maréchal de France' and 'Ferdinand Foch'.

Foch's view of French politicians was in accord with that of British generals about their own national leaders, but with one big exception which Ivor was no doubt delighted to record:

> He notices how little all French and British politicians think about beating the enemy, but declares that now at last in Clemenceau France has found a true PATRIOT. He sees a great deal of Clemenceau and says that he *alone* of all the British and French 'statesmen' appears to be whole hearted and single minded. He begged me to try and name him one single man who could possibly be considered as 'un grand anglais'. He says France has only one and he was only found after three years of mediocrities!!

While Ivor was enjoying his evening with Foch, the British First and Fourth Armies were resuming their attacks on the Germans, inspired by the instructions given to all army commanders on 22 August, in which Haig told them:

> The enemy has not the means to deliver counter-attacks on an extended scale, nor has he the numbers to hold a continuous position against the very extended advance which is now being directed upon him. To turn the present situation to account, the most resolute offensive is everywhere desirable. Risks which a month ago would have been criminal to incur, ought now to be incurred as a duty . . .[11]

Impressed by the success of these latest British operations, Foch wrote to Haig on 26 August to say that he could 'only admire the resolute manner in which you press the business forward', and to mention that 'the Armies of General Pétain are about to recommence their attacks, using similar methods'.[12] All the Allied troops were now following Foch's famous exhortation of 'Tout le monde à la bataille', and the end of hostilities was approaching, but this fact was not then as clear to those fighting in France and Flanders as it would soon become. Avid for news, Tiny was constantly showering Ivor with questions. On 8 September, he wrote a letter which shows what a variety of opinions could be found throughout the BEF at this stage:

> You frequently ask my opinion about the war. . . . but I can say very little beyond what you read in the official telegrams. We British have been fighting strong German rearguards ever since 21st August. . . . Half our Generals don't know or realise what is happening to the Hun. According to their several temperaments, they think either (i) The Hun is about to collapse altogether & chuck it, OR (ii) the Hun has got something cunning up his sleeve and will let it out at the right moment. Thus between a totally 'demoralized' Bosch and a sort of 'superman' Bosch one can find any degree of optimism or of pessimism one wishes to discover. The truth is both are wrong inferences.

One paragraph shows how the success of the German armies in advancing so far into France earlier in the year became their undoing as they were forced to withdraw:

> My own opinion is that Hindenburg and the Gt Genl Staff must have definitely decided to retreat very soon after Foch attacked and defeated the Hun on 18th July between Chateau Thierry and Soissons. That was the crucial week. You cannot retire huge armies which have been on the offensive & have accumulated stuff . . . you cannot retire them like you do a rearguard in the Long Valley at Aldershot and get it home for TEA.

The disintegration of the German army was the inevitable price to be paid for failing to defeat the Allies in its great offensives between March and June.

The work of the IGT's team went on throughout the autumn, and Ivor himself was involved in arranging visits to home-based training establishments in England and Scotland in September and October. As the speed of the Allied advances accelerated during these months it became hard to keep in touch with the fighting troops. On 1 November Ivor noted in a letter that: 'The distances are getting so enormous owing to our victories that I expect soon to move forward myself.' Two days later, on the 3rd, he was writing about the question of the armistice terms being worked out for Germany, and fearing that they might be too weak. To crush the nation completely was in his opinion the only proper course:

> It would be strict justice, but it would also be safe. The Hun is only wishful for peace in order to recover military power and be ready to launch a more successful attack at some opportune moment in the dim future. His heart is by no means altered. That is his nature. Recognise it. It is no use blaming him for his natural temperament, but it is wicked not to recognize what it is. His history during four wars proves it – i.e. 1864, 1866, 1870, 1914 – covering altogether a period of 64 years, two generations! He had but one objective and said so – world power . . .
>
> To prevent it we must crush and humiliate his Army which means his motive . . . let no sentimental gush be expended on the dirty Hun.

On the day the armistice was announced Ivor mentioned that: 'This is a great day, too great for the French people of Crécy to do more than be thankful quietly.' However, he was planning to entertain the Mayor of Crécy and 15 of the principal inhabitants to a 'déjeuner d'Honneur' two days later, after attending a service of thanksgiving in the church during the morning. A letter on 15 November thanked Tiny for complimenting him on his efforts throughout the long wartime years:

I am much touched by the thought that you at any rate think that I have done my bit before and during this war. For really if one knows one has done it, and those we care about know it also, the opinion of outsiders does not amount to much, does it?

This comment about the opinion of outsiders indicates that he was aware of his unpopularity in certain circles: partly due to the cloud that still hung, however unfairly, over all the members of Gough's Fifth Army, and partly due to his trenchant criticisms of the standard of training he had found in many formations while acting as IGT. Fortunately, he was sufficiently tough and self-confident not to let this bother him, and he had one priceless advantage over several of his contemporaries: his request to Henry Wilson in his letter of 5 July eventually paid off when he learnt that he was to be made a substantive lieutenant general on 1 January 1919. The significance of this was explained to Tiny in a letter of 17 November, when it was obvious that the IGT's inspectorate would soon be dissolved:

In reply to your natural enquiry about my future employment I can only say – like that rotter Asquith – 'wait and see'.

There are literally hundreds of Major-Generals, Lt Generals, full Generals and swarms of Brigadier Generals and Colonels, all mentally 'waiting to see'. More than half will not find employment at all. Another half of those who do find some, will be on lower jobs than they had in the war. Thus many feel naturally depressed or vaguely uncertain about themselves, though all are delighted with the splendid results of their combined efforts.

Being among the lucky ones, Ivor was appointed to a temporary command in January 1919, and took over IX Corps in Cologne in the army of occupation in Germany. While waiting to see what, if any, permanent employment was to be offered to him Ivor reported in a letter on 13 February that 'my policy is to lie "doggo"': a different tactic from the one employed when angling for command of 1st Guards Brigade nine years earlier. It proved to be a successful tactic, and in April 1919 he was appointed to take over as GOC-in-C Northern Command in York in June. This was one of the five major commands in the home forces at the time, and was one of the 'plums' among the jobs available to a senior officer. Even if he had his detractors, his reputation clearly stood high in the circles where it really mattered, and his contribution during the war was well rewarded.

Notes

Letters from Maxse to his wife can be found at WSRO, files 209, 272.

1 Bond, Brian, *Liddell Hart: A Study of his Military Thought* (Cassell, 1977), p. 20. Liddell Hart found Horne obtuse when trying to explain the use of a sandtable to him in 1922.
2 Haig Papers, Accession 3155.
3 An original carbon copy of the letter is in the possession of the Maxse family.
4 The pamphlet *Training Leaflets*, September 1918–February 1919, contains a list of 14 leaflets, of which 12 are included. A copy is in the possession of the family.
5 *Training Leaflets*, pp. 2–3.
6 An original duplicated copy of these verses is in the possession of the family.
7 Bond, p. 25.
8 Essame, Maj Gen H, *The Battle for Europe, 1918* (Batsford, 1972) p. 46.
9 Terraine, John (ed), *General Jack's Diary 1914–1918* (Eyre & Spottiswoode, 1964), p. 252.
10 A copy of the report on 15th Cheshires is in the possession of the family.
11 Marshall-Cornwall, Gen. Sir J, *Haig as Military Commander* (Batsford, 1973), p. 282.
12 Marshall-Cornwall, p. 282.

Last Army Appointment
and Retirement

19

GOC-in-C, Northern Command

———•◆•———

Arriving in England in April 1919, Ivor had two months leave based at Little Bognor. Much of his time was occupied in arranging suitable accommodation in the York area before assuming his new appointment in June. A battle had to be fought with the War Office to have it accepted that the so-called 'General's House' in York was not suitable, being last occupied by a GOC-in-C 12 years previously, and used in the interim as a record office. Eventually he found a delightful house to rent called Middlethorpe Manor, lying two miles south of the city at Bishopsthorpe. For the first three weeks in his new job Ivor lived in the Yorkshire Club, while Tiny stayed in Sussex until the new house was ready for occupation. Then on 7 July he was able to report that 'I am just arrived this evening . . . and found everything arrived and in order. Very few breakages of furniture en route.' He went on to say that the quiet of Middlethorpe Manor was delightful, since 'the Yorkshire Club is not restful for a new GOC! Yesterday – church, luncheon, tea party. Today, Mayor's *breakfast!!*'

Tiny's biographer suggests that the four years that the family was based at York were some of the happiest in her life. With the war over, and all her family safe, she could settle down to enjoy once more a normal existence, and she threw herself into all aspects of it, making Middlethorpe the centre of a busy, but relaxed, social life as well as a family home. The Maxse children completed their school years during the York period, with John, the eldest, passing from Eton to Sandhurst; Fred from Eton to New College, Oxford: and Violet from a school at Scarborough to a 'finishing' establishment in Paris.

Tiny took her responsibilities as a senior general's wife seriously. Some of these are explained in her biography:

221

In 1919 many of the soldiers were newly home from the war; the staff and garrisons were in a process of settling in; their wives did not know each other; so breaking the ice was uphill work. Mary never flagged in her efforts. The Army Mothers Union and the organization of hospital services soon came under her leadership, as later on did the Girl Guides . . .

In addition to an afternoon party, a garden party and 'official' entertainments, they kept open house to those commanding officers in the distant parts of the command who had come to Command Headquarters for official purposes. They generally stayed in the house and sometimes brought their wives. Ivor would never let them go to an hotel.[1]

While the Maxses were living in Yorkshire they kept in touch with the progress of extensive improvements which were being carried out at Little Bognor. The scheme of work had been prepared in May 1919, soon after Ivor's return from Germany, by a young man who was later to achieve considerable fame in his chosen profession. In a letter written on 4 May, Ivor described him thus:

Major Williams Ellis, soldier and Tank Officer, Staff and Welsh Guards – *Architect* by nature and profession is here now for a couple of days. He is going to be an even greater help than I anticipated because he is a gentleman with a place of his own in Wales and has the right sort of artistic and practical temperament.

A description of some of Williams Ellis's suggestions followed, and the letter ended by saying that: 'He will have a definite plan to scale by the time you return. He is a delightful companion . . .' The plans put forward dealt with the garden as well as the house, and it was the garden aspect which particularly interested Ivor.

Still firmly convinced of the danger of Germany, Ivor had written on 29 January 1919, near the end of his time in Cologne, to express his fears of the future even though the spirit of the nation appeared to be broken: 'They are incapable of fighting but I am still more convinced that they will quickly recover – say in ten years? And that when they do recover they will be just the same Huns as they have been, with the result that they will revert to militarism which is the only thing they do really understand.' Not long after his arrival in York he was asked to speak on 28 November 1919 at the annual dinner of the York Gimcrack Club, where he expressed his doubts about the possibilities of international peace in terms which were highly unpopular in many circles. *The Yorkshire Post* reported his speech, in which he talked of the 'bosh' being 'emitted' about the League of Nations, and quoted one sentence verbatim: 'For myself, I don't understand it, and I prefer a League of Tanks to a League of Nations.'[2] Protests followed from many high-minded, peace-loving groups, and when he made similar comments two years later at St Peter's, York, School Speech Day complaints even reached the War Office. He was obliged to explain his conduct to the Secretary of State for War, but did so in a slightly off-hand manner without showing any signs of contrition.[3] Although criticised for demonstrating both ignorance of world affairs and the limitations of 'the military mind', he was sadly proved only too right when the League collapsed in 1937, and little had been done to provide the British Army with enough tanks, while the Germans were building them on a massive scale.

Ivor might not be able to do much to persuade the British Government to keep a strong, properly mechanised army, but in two ways he was able to improve the efficiency of the basic arm, the infantry. The first aspect to consider is training doctrine. Here he worked through three gifted subordinates: Brigadier General (later Sir) Winston Dugan, a future Governor of South Australia and of Victoria, who had been with him on the IGT's staff; Captain (later Lieutenant General Sir) Jack Evetts of the Scottish Rifles; and Captain (later Sir) Basil Liddell Hart of the KOYLI (King's Own Yorkshire Light Infantry). Their achievement was to rewrite the volumes of the *Infantry Training Manual* in easily understood language, incorporating new ideas based on the lessons of the recently ended war. Much of the actual writing was done by Liddell Hart, who was to become a well-known, and at times highly influential, military commentator both in the years before and after the Second World War. He first made his mark with Ivor by sending him a copy of an article he had written on 'the combat unit'. Commenting on it, Ivor wrote on 8 November 1919: 'What is difficult, and will require ten years of strenuous endeavour, will be to get the doctrine understood, adopted, and actually practised over a scattered Empire page like ours! It is a big *training* task – and implies a mental effort on the part of a number of officers who dislike thinking. But we can do much to *start* on good lines.'[4] Following a week of discussion in York in April 1920, to which Liddell Hart was invited, Ivor arranged for his posting to the staff of Dugan's brigade, based in Lichfield as part of North Midland Area, one of the five subordinate districts answering to Northern Command.

In his *Memoirs, Volume I*, Liddell Hart gives much credit to Ivor for helping him both in his shortened military career, due to unfitness following in the war, and in his eventual calling as a military correspondent. Telling of the period when he was working under Dugan in 1920, Liddell Hart recorded his impressions of his two masters:

> Maxse and Dugan were strikingly different – both in appearance and personality. Maxse was short and dark, with a sallow complexion, small deep-set eyes, and a long drooping moustache, which gave him the look of a Tartar chief – all the more because the descriptive term 'a Tartar' so aptly fitted his manner in dealing with lazy or inefficient seniors and

subordinates. Dugan was tall and fair, with finely chiselled features. He 'looked every inch a soldier', but without any of the stiffness that phrase implies. He had a leisurely way of moving and talking that was a piquant contrast to Maxse's electrifying manner, and had a twinkle in his eye that expressed his subtle, and very Irish sense of humour. In temperament, the contrast between Maxse and Dugan was no less apparent – which explains why they got on so well together, and formed such a good combination. Maxse seized the salient points of any idea with lightning quickness, although occasionally misjudging some point because of too hasty examination. His fierce manner concealed a very warm heart, and he particularly liked people who showed that they were not afraid of him. He was always ready to encourage and make use of new ideas.[5]

In 1921 Ivor again made use of his team when invited to contribute the article on 'Infantry' in an updated edition of the *Encyclopedia Britannica* to replace the previous, pre-war one. The *Memoirs* show how the work was done:

Jack Evetts wrote the preliminary section on subsequent changes in the organization of infantry, and I wrote the three sections dealing with the role, tactics and future development of infantry – emphasising the need for revived mobility by lighter equipment and wider use of mechanical transport, as well as by new tactics. My piece came to some eleven thousand words, filling seven pages of the encyclopedia, and finished it well inside a week. Maxse was delighted with it, and with characteristic generosity inserted a note at the end of the article acknowledging my help – which brought my name to the notice of the editorial staff, with beneficial effects.[6]

Ivor's other achievement in the improvement of infantry training was the reorganisation of the regimental depots. This took him a long time, and required much patience and persistence in order to make the necessary changes without damaging important aspects of regimental pride. The first problem was the varying speed at which recruits were enlisted into the 20 different infantry regiments with depots spread throughout Northern Command, and consequent upon this, the time taken to build up squads of sufficient numbers to start meaningful training. A few strongly supported regiments in well-populated, urban areas could build up squads quickly, while in some rural parts the trickle of recruits was so slow that men might hang around for weeks before being squadded for the start of their recruit's course. Ivor's solution was to arrange the depots into regional groups, within which all recruits who did not specify a definite choice of regiment were sent to one selected depot in which a 'Standard Squad' of 30 men was being built up. This was usually achieved in two, or at most three, weeks, after which recruits would be directed to another depot in the region.

The second problem was the varied quality of the training at the different depots. With approval of the War Office, certain definite standards were set, so that the printed 'Shorthand Notes of a Conference on Reorganization of Infantry Depots held at York – Wednesday, December 8th, 1920' included in bold type the sentence: 'The depot exists to supply trained men fit to take their places in the platoons of their battalions and thus relieve commanding officers of all recruit training.' Having established definite training criteria, Ivor's next task was to tour his command to ensure that his instructions were being properly carried out. An officer on his staff, with a skill in writing doggerel similar to Barrington-Ward's, described a typical Maxse visit in rhyme, laying stress on his aversion to finding too many men employed on administrative chores rather than proper training. A few selected verses tell how:

> Sir Ivor Of Eboracum,
> The Chieftain of the North,
> To reconstruct the Depots
> Upon his quest set forth.

Arriving at his destination he goes to:

> The dark and inky portals
> Of the Quartermaster's store.

> What Ho! Sir Quartermaster
> I see a goodly throng
> You must have half the Depot here
> To help your work along.

The unfortunate quartermaster being unable to persuade him of the importance of all the tasks the men are carrying out, Sir Ivor turns on him:

> Know'st thou not my watchword
> O man of pigs and boots
> The watchword of the Depots
> 'Our job's to train recruits'.

Leaving the chastened quartermaster, Sir Ivor is better pleased when he can point out some recruits on the barrack square:

> See yonder stand in serried ranks
> Just thirty men aligned
> The Standard Squad, our blessed hope,
> That I alone designed.

> Just thirty men, no more no less,
> In Standard Squads are placed,
> And on this sacred principle
> The Depot system's based.[7]

With the organisation of the depots put onto satisfactory lines, Ivor
turned his attention to standards of instruction. Using the same sort of
language which had upset many more conventional contemporaries in
respect of his wartime leaflets, he coined the maxim: 'Teach the trainer
how to teach before he teaches Tommy.' In support of his aim he insti-
tuted an annual inter-depot competition for the Maxse Cup, which was
run at Strensall Barracks, York, over two days, and was a test of training
methods rather than military knowledge. There were two valuable side-
effects of the competition: the meeting of instructors from all over the
command, while the competition was in progress, allowed good ideas to
be circulated, and it caused an improvement in the quality of NCOs sent
to the depots from regular battalions. The commanding officer in the
habit of off-loading his duds onto his regimental depot – a far from
unusual custom – could be shamed, by hearing of its dismal showing in
the Maxse Cup competition, into sending better men in future.

The family's pleasant domestic life was temporarily upset when
Middlethorpe Manor had to be returned to its owner, who wished to sell
it, at the end of its lease. Another house called Ousecliffe was found not
far away and this was purchased by the War Office to become the official
GOC-in-C's residence. While the move to the new house was being
arranged, Tiny returned for a time to Sussex.

In 1923 Ivor's four-year tour in Northern Command ended in June,
when he handed over to General Sir Charles Harrington. At the same
time he was promoted from Lieutenant-General to General, in which
rank he remained on the strength of the army until his official retirement
in 1926, although he went onto half pay and held no further active
appointment.

Shortly before his departure from York, he was invited to write a piece
for the magazine produced by the staff of his headquarters. An extract
from it epitomises his military philosophy: the title chosen was *Look
Ahead!*

> Science had gripped the fighting services and is shaking them closer and
> closer together. We see even now looming on the horizon one combined
> defence service with one combined staff, controlled by the brain of one
> Commander under one Defence Ministry.
>
> The curtain which veils future warfare can only be penetrated by a
> few gifted thinkers possessing vision and imagination. We have seen
> our skins replaced by armour; guns of low speed and low power
> replaced by those of high speed and high power; muscular movement
> supplanted by mechanical energy; and a larger part played by chemistry.
> During peacetime we should explore every avenue which leads to
> improvement in our weapons, in their antidote and in our tactics to suit
> them. Every invention should be tested on the off chance that one may
> prove of practical use in a war to come. But above all, our peace training

must be based not merely on the lessons of the last war but also on the probabilities of the next. The necessity which produced gas, Tanks, Bombs, Lewis and other guns, wired trench systems and an immense Air Force, might possibly have been foreseen before 1914? A genius did perhaps prophesy some of them but no one heeded him and he remains unknown.

We might at least see that it shall not be said of us after our recent war experiences that we allowed our sons to embark upon a campaign unprovided with the appliances and inventions which forethought can produce and test in the immediate future.

To achieve this result we require to watch and kindle every spark of imaginative genius we find, keeping it down to practical tests and within a reasonable financial limit. But don't be afraid of attempting new methods of teaching old lessons. A private soldier is as likely as a General to produce the kind of fertile ideas we seek, especially in his own sphere of military activity. I say this because I observe a tendency in some battalions to revert to pre-historic notions and antiquated training methods.'[8]

In 1921 he had been appointed Colonel of the Middlesex Regiment, an honour he much appreciated because of his close contact with its splendid 12th Battalion in the great battles at Trônes Wood and Thiepval in 1916. Shortly after becoming Colonel, he persuaded the Prince of Wales to become the regiment's Colonel-in-Chief. His own appointment he retained until 1932, while the Prince surrendered his in 1936 on his abdication from the Throne so soon after becoming King.

Notes

1 Gore, John, *Mary Maxse, 1870 to 1944* (Rolls House, 1947), pp. 82–3.
2 Quoted in an article attacking 'The Military Mind' in *The Arbitrator: Organ of the International Arbitration League*, Jan. 1920. A copy of this journal is in the possession of the Maxse family.
3 A carbon copy of this letter is in the possession of the Maxse family.
4 Bond, Brian, *Liddell Hart: A Study of His Military Thought* (Cassell, 1977), p. 27, from LH 7/1920/56.
5 Liddell Hart, B H, *Memoirs, Vol I* (Cassell, 1965), p. 43.
6 Liddell Hart, p. 54.
7 A copy of these verses is in the possession of the family.
8 A carbon copy of this short article is in the possession of the family.

20

The Fruit Grower, 1923 to 1958

———•◆•———

Plans for the creation of the orchards at Little Bognor had been maturing in Ivor's mind for some years before he left York in 1923. The preliminary steps had been taken in 1922 ahead of his departure from the north, with the result that his second career began as soon as the active years of his first ended. His friend Lord Selborne was to write about his entry into the commercial fruit-growing business many years later, in his obituary in a horticultural journal:

> Maxse had seen that the French grew their best fruit on cordons and espaliers, and when he retired from the Army he planted five acres of Cox's Orange Pippin grown in this way with some experimental rows of Doyenne du Comice pears. It is the most intensive method of horticulture and the capital investment of purchasing and planting many thousands of fruit trees, and erecting the furlongs of wire fences to carry them, was a very considerable one for an amateur's first venture. But no one worked so intensively on this intensive system as did Ivor Maxse, and he made an outstanding commercial success of it.[1]

Although occasional military duties still came his way, in his capacity as a General still shown in the Army List and as the Colonel of the Middlesex Regiment, his preoccupation with his orchards left him little time for consideration of any other military affairs. His boxes of papers were put away under the staircase, and apart from the occasion already mentioned of his disagreement with Edmonds, the official First World War historian, in the 1930s, they remained untouched until near the time of his death. However, in one respect there was a carry-over from his army days into civil life. His passion for passing on information to other people made him delight in showing his orchards to visitors, who were, in Selborne's words '. . . subjected to a brilliant exposition of the mysteries of pomology, in just the same way that had made Maxse famous as a trainer of infantry'.

John, the eldest of the Maxse's three children, served in the Coldstream Guards as a regular officer for 17 years until 1937, when he left the army for a short time before being recalled in 1939 to do various staff jobs in England. He was more suited to academic life than to a military career, in which he was overshadowed by his father's reputation. In due course, he was to take over the running of the orchards when Ivor had a stroke in 1956. John was the only one of the three to marry. His three children were born between 1932 and 1942. Tony, the eldest, is the collaborator in this biography. Martin, the next, followed in the footsteps of his grandfather and was Regimental Lieutenant Colonel of the Coldstream Guards from 1981 to 1984, while Christopher, the youngest, is a schoolmaster.

Neither of Ivor and Tiny's two other children, Fred and Violet, ever married. Fred served in staff jobs in the Second World War before settling in Spain, and then in Cyprus, where he died in 1970. Violet was a naturalist and bird-lover who lived at Little Bognor until 1939, when she joined the ATS. After the war she settled a few miles from home in a cottage at the foot of the South Downs, where she died in 1986. She travelled widely to photograph birds, and edited her films to a professional standard to show to schools and other audiences.

In 1929 the sudden need for Leo Maxse to go into hospital for a major operation caused a crisis over production of the *National Review*. His sister Violet, now the widowed Viscountess Milner, stepped into the editor's chair and called in Tiny and her son John to help. This experience was invaluable when in 1932, following a brief period of recovery during which he resumed his full duties, Leo died. The family then became fully involved in keeping the '*Nat*' going. Now permanently in control as editor, Violet started the literary side of the journal, putting Tiny in charge. This fell into two divisions: one part was a signed article on a literary subject, and the other a series of anonymous book reviews. Tiny wrote the main article every other month, while both she and John produced regular book reviews, taking an average of five books each month. Ivor also became part of the team, as described by Tiny's biographer:

> Her husband was dealing with the whole business and financial side of the '*Nat*'; her sister-in-law was the Editor, and her son was her right-hand man in her own department and also a member of the Board. It all made for family unity and active co-operation. It followed logically out of her marriage and the political activities of her younger married life.[2]

The *National Review* was kept going for many years until in 1948 it was sold to Lord Altrincham whose son John Grigg kept it going for a number of years. Tiny kept up her reviewing of books into the war years, writing one of her last reviews in October 1943 shortly before her own death.

The outbreak of war in 1939 brought changes to the way of life at Little Bognor. A boy of seven at the start, Tony Maxse has several memories of the later war years:

> When I was seven my parents moved into Little Bognor with my grand-parents at the end of 1939 to avoid evacuees being billeted on Grandfather, as it was felt this would not go down well. He was then 77 and we all remained at Little Bognor until the house was sold in 1956.
>
> My memories really start from the last year or two of the war. People were in some awe of him, but it was very rare that he was actually angry, and I think the awe was partly due to his age and rank which was much more respected in those days. People said that he had mellowed. He had not been an easy parent for my father – he would tease a lot, but I remember him as warm hearted, always with a sense of fun. He would always look for the humorous side to items in the newspaper and every-day events in the orchard and the family. A typical comment about someone might be 'I like his mug'. The stories he told were just like those in the play *My Father Knew Lloyd George*, where everyone had nicknames. In fact some of the tales in the play were identical! Like many people who achieve senior rank he would never accept anything at face value without questioning the motives behind it or wondering what might go wrong.
>
> The day followed a routine. Following a serious illness in the mid 1930s he always breakfasted in bed, two poached eggs brought up by Potter, and then shave, and I remember when quite young often going to his bedroom and watching him shaving with a proper old cut-throat, while he would chat away to me. During the day he would spend some time at his desk, but he was mostly outside, down in the orchard, prun-ing the trees, looking round and speaking to the staff. He was keen on the garden and grounds, especially the extensive yew hedges. He hated the weeds and brambles that grew under the hedges and would attack them vigorously. We know from his letters that he took a close interest in all the family's finances from early days. He had most of the money invested in equities long before this was normal and he always followed the stock market, and when I was older he would frequently discuss shares with me. Much of his advice still applies today.
>
> Grandmother was a keen churchgoer and churchwarden, but Ivor only went on Remembrance Sunday when he would lay a wreath. When I knew him he was always fairly deaf and followed the progress of the war in the newspapers. My parents had their own sitting room with a wireless and I remember often during 1944–5 listening to the 9 p.m. news and then going to the library (where he would sit playing Patience) and I would pass on the headlines to him. Sometimes he would comment that things were 'better managed than in my day'.

Just before Christmas 1943, Tiny fell ill with blood poisoning, and on 21 January 1944 she died. She was only 74, and still full of energy and good spirits until her illness. Ivor was devastated, as were all the family. As a tribute to her memory he determined to have an account written of her life, and a Sussex neighbour, John Gore, was chosen as author. Early in 1946 Gore produced his manuscript, and the biography, which has been referred to several times in this book, was published privately soon afterwards.

Apart from Ivor's and Tiny's strong affection for each other, as demonstrated by the constant stream of letters that passed between them whenever they were parted, there was a bond of mutual interest in many subjects. Ivor had been well aware of the value of such an intelligent and well-connected wife in the advancement of his own career. Back in March 1917, when writing to Tiny about the wife of the Tsar, whom he suggested had 'ungummed' her husband, he added: 'But some of us are lucky and have been literally made by our wives!'[3]

A regular visitor to Little Bognor for many years was Tiny's brother, Charles Leconfield. He would walk over from Petworth in the afternoon, and he and Ivor would have a long talk over tea. Later the chauffeur would arrive with the Rolls Royce to collect Charles and take him home. Potter, who remained with the family for so many years, recounted the story of one occasion when Ivor's brother-in-law happened to be at the house with two other peers. As he was helping them on with their coats, Lord Mersey said: 'Ivor is not hearing very well.' Potter heard Charles Leconfield reply: 'He never did bloody well listen.' Another popular visitor was Jack Evetts, his staff officer from York who had risen to be Lieutenant General in the Second World War. It was said that Ivor's language, which normally remained perfectly correct, could occasionally be overheard reverting to the swearing he was once renowned for in his army days when the two of them were reminiscing in the library.

Potter's story above of the three peers was recorded in some fascinating recollections set down in 1991 by the man who was Ivor's orchard manager from 1947 to 1956, and then remained with the family for the rest of his working life. Some extracts from Harold Watson's notes provide an entertaining picture of his employer in his old age:

> It was Sept. 1947 I first met Gen Sir Ivor Maxse, having arranged an interview for the job of Manager of the Maxey Fruit Co. I still have the letter offering me the post in the General's handwriting ordering me to bring the 'necessary ration documents' and stay a week in the house to see how I got on before bringing my wife and children.

[Ivor chose to use the name MAXEY for his trading company as people had problems pronouncing 'Maxse' correctly, but in the event having the two different spellings tended to increase rather than reduce the confusion.]

Met at the station by Mrs Maxse and taken to see the job and then to see the Gen. It was a very hot day as I was shown into the shady library, I was conscious of 2 eyes rising to meet me and boring right through my head, but lucky for me I liked him from the start; although he was nearly 85 his voice was young.

With the apples he would arrive at 11 o'clock for his days pruning, two rollcut secateurs in one hand and a roll of string on his back, and pot of special water paint and a brush for painting the pruning cuts. He would cut the shoot off and paint the cut straightaway. It never did any good, for most was splashed on his old raincoat, but that was *his* method. And time has proved that none of his theories have been wrong. His adviser then was Raymond Bush who enjoyed his visits immensely, he fared better than a later adviser, when the Gen. said in a loud aside 'look at his ugly mug'. The Gen would not step over that line between his house and the staff house, I admired him for that. Then there was that time when Petworth House was handed over to the N.T. and Macmillan was speaking, and the Gen, then very deaf said to the lady next to him 'Bad luck on you, you have to listen.' He was a different person when talking to me of one of the battles of the great war, there was sadness in his voice as he told me of the 20,000 men who died in a day.

We must not forget his battle that he never won, and that was against brambles in his hedges, he would crawl along the selected hedge with his saw which he would dig into the base of the soil and reveal the base of the bramble and then saw it through and pull it out of the hedge, quite a task. He must have been nearly 90 when he climbed 2 ladders to a flat roof to see what the builders were doing. When I was foolish enough to say he shouldn't be up there, he said 'If I bloody well fall, that is my fault.'

He was lecturing me on tree shapes and the particular value of the Dwarf Pyramid System, which he had used for the bottom 3 acres of the orchard. I put my foot in it by saying the Bush System might have been better there and he angrily said: 'If you want bush systems, then go and work where there are bush systems.' I had failed to appreciate what he had done.

He would lead organised parties around the orchard now and again, stopping at well thought out points to lecture powerfully with racy remarks thrown in. Somebody said that he thought that some of the type IX were scion rooted, to be told 'That's Herbert's fault.' Herbert was his old foreman who was standing at his side with the marker flag. There was great excitement on the day that the first ever tractor was delivered, a Ransome HG5, a tracklaying miniature tractor with cultivator. He chose a Canadian ex-soldier for the driver who was a bit brash, and one day the Gen complained of his driving as 'charging along and knocking down everything before him'. Later he bought a spraying machine to go behind the tractor, when demonstrated the Gen was running along with it to check on the performance, about 89 years of age.

He went to his club in London for a week each year while his room was being spring cleaned. He told me that London was no good now as 'there was nobody up there'.

He and his son asked me to travel with them to Norfolk to see Justin Brook about peach growing. We stayed the night at a hotel at Newmarket and at dinner the Gen surprised me by ordering a pint. From that meeting started off the Gen's last career as a peach grower. He did the planning and I got the work done, I enjoyed that, especially the terracing of the soil and the erection of the iron supports. That's how it's done in Persia he said, except of course their weather was colder at night. I caught him a few years later in a very ungentlemanly position sitting on the ground enjoying a ripe peach, but I pretended not to see him.

When Little Bognor was connected to main water there was a problem because the mains were 2' 6" deep and the house pipe 1' 6" deep, and quite rightly, the water board man refused to connect. Ron Baker, our plumber passed the news of this problem onto the Gen who then took Ron to the phone and told him to ring Greene, who was Council top man (who provided Ron with lots of work). Then the Gen took hold of the instrument to tell Greene in no uncertain terms to order the council plumber back and (being deaf) he then handed the phone to Ron (to listen) he relayed back to the Gen who took the phone and gave Greene another earful, this back and forth went on for several minutes until Greene in desperation sent his man back. The pipe never froze, (it didn't dare).

Before my time he had an engine and pump installed in a specially built brick shed with its own reservoir of stream water. The chemicals for spraying the trees were mixed there and pumped through 2" underground pipes to rubber hoses and lances on the trees. It was in the '30s and the engineer demonstrating the plan told the General that the guard over the long agitator chain had not been put in position, so no one must go round that side yet. The Gen said that anyone who was B fool enough to touch a moving chain deserved all he got. You can guess the rest, the Gen leaned over it and it caught his coat and flung him to the ground where he lay quite winded. After that a very strong guard was erected.

On a rare visit to Kirdford, to Mr Holdsworthy whose hair was white and was aged about 80, the Gen who was at least 86 was heard to say 'Poor old Holdsworthy, he's getting very old, you know.' I saw him arm in arm with the Gen who was pushing him at speed through his own orchard, and at the same time yelling into his ear.

Ivor was 94 when in 1956 a stroke brought an end to his active life. He was moved to a nursing home in Midhurst, from which it soon became clear he would never be able to return to his own home. John decided to sell Little Bognor but to retain the orchards. He and his family moved to a house which they had bought about a mile away. It was at this stage that the massive store of papers that had accumulated over so many years, some as far back as 1780, was divided up and sent to the two places where they can be found today: the purely military documents to the Imperial War Museum in London, and the private papers to the West Sussex Record Office in Chichester.

Ivor remained in the nursing home for nearly two years until he died in January 1958 in the 96th year of his life. His funeral took place at Fittleworth on Monday 3 February and he was buried next to Tiny in the churchyard, near the war memorial.

All the main newspapers carried obituaries, *The Times* giving Ivor two full columns on 29 January. Basil Liddell Hart followed this with a further comment on February. While some of his piece included the usual, slightly over-fulsome praise common to obituaries, one sentence summed up the best aspects of Ivor's character succinctly. It told of '. . . his eagerness for progress, his lively mind, his stimulating effect, his responsiveness to suggestions combined with shrewd criticism, his generosity in giving credit to his assistants, the intense warm-heartedness behind his outward fierceness, and the way he never forgot those who served him.' Even his critics could not deny him these qualities.

Notes

1 Selborne, Lord, Obituary published in *The Commercial Grower*, March 1958.
2 Gore, John, *Mary Maxse, 1870 to 1944* (Rolls House, 1947), p. 110.
3 This letter is in WSRO, file 439.

Epilogue

Throughout his army career, Ivor Maxse was faced with the need to resolve what Major General Eric Sixsmith chose as the theme of his study of British generalship. This is '. . . the apparent conflict between two essential military requirements; on the one hand, the will to stand and fight and the habit of unquestioning obedience; on the other, the need for subtlety and subterfuge, and the necessity to use all possible means of overcoming the will of the enemy at the least cost to oneself.'[1] It is fair to claim that Ivor succeeded in balancing these ostensibly opposing requirements as satisfactorily as any leader of his generation who was saddled with the awesome responsibilities of high command in the First World War.

The unusual and original opinions of his father were a strong influence during Ivor's early years, and were the origin of the enquiring mind which never left him. As his sister Violet put it, the Admiral did not use 'the argument of authority', and his children were left to find 'truths for themselves'. In choosing a military career, Ivor had to accept the limitations it placed on his conduct, but this acceptance of service discipline never prevented him expressing his views on professional matters in trenchant language to superiors and subordinates alike.

He learnt much of his trade as a soldier in the imperial campaigns in the Sudan and South Africa, especially that aspect which Wavell singled out as so important '. . . "the mechanism of war", i.e. topography, movement, and supply'. He also had the opportunity to observe the power of modern weapons, brought out in such a gruesome fashion during the destruction of the Dervish army at Omdurman. On this action two comments must be made. The first, for those whose sensibilities are offended by such slaughter, is that the Khalifa was quite capable of handling his forces more effectively than he did, and had he done so, by for example attacking at night, he would have massacred those who opposed him just as mercilessly as they shot down his men. Mahmud's butchery of the inhabitants of Metemma had shown Kitchener's troops what to expect if they failed to destroy the Dervish army. The second is that the battle taught a lesson which should have been clear to all who witnessed it, but which was not in fact to be learnt until the later years of the First World War. This was that the power of modern, quick-firing artillery, machine-guns, and well-handled bolt-action rifles gave an ascendancy to those in soundly chosen defensive positions against which men advancing steadily in the open in daylight were simply 'sitting ducks'.

When Ivor went to his next campaign in South Africa in 1900 he was not directly involved in the fighting, though this time the British troops were all too often themselves the 'sitting ducks' as they attacked the kop-jes held by Boer marksmen. He was fortunate in the roles given to him, and although he might have selected a posting to a fighting unit had he been given the choice, he had the chance to learn more that would be of long-term, professional value with his transport company and his police force than he might have had in an infantry battalion.

His recognition of how much he owed Tiny in the advancement of his career has already been mentioned. During his smooth progression up the ladder of promotion within the Brigade of Guards from major in 1902 to brigadier general in 1910 her influence was great, and he made good use of it again in gathering the best available officers around him when form-ing the 18th Division. These were the years when 'the brilliant and powerful body', as Winston Churchill described what was known as 'soci-ety', had such influence in British affairs. While Ivor could not have advanced without professional ability, Tiny's personality, allied to her social position at the pinnacle of the fashionable Edwardian world, helped him enormously in achieving the objectives of his ambition.

During the First World War, like most other generals, he found that his fortunes varied. Although he never shared the fate of many who were 'ungummed' and sent home from the fighting theatres, he had his moments when his stock was down as well as the periods when he could mention in his letter that he was 'a blue-eyed boy' – though he always stressed how quickly such a situation could change.

Since his promotion to major general was gazetted whilst with the 1st Guards Brigade in France, he must have hoped for command of a division in the BEF when conditions became more settled after the battles of the Marne and the Aisne. At first, he may have been disappointed at being sent to an apparently less prestigious post at home, but as things turned out his appointment as GOC 18th Division was the most important step in his whole career, and the story of how he raised the division, trained it, and led it in action over a period of two years must be his main memorial as a soldier. Correlli Barnett has written of generalship in war that it 'involves all the intellectual, physical and moral power in a man', and is thus 'the most complete human activity'.[2] Ivor employed his intellectual faculties in several ways: in his original method of teaching practical lessons based on his own knowledge of what actually happens in war and on his understanding of soldiers' reactions to battle; in his readiness to consider new ideas, and adopt them if he thought them sound; and in ensuring that as much information as possible about impending operations was passed to his men; and through his mastery of the French language, in his eagerness to learn everything possible from allies who were so much more experienced during the division's first year in France.

Physically, he was as tough and fit as any man of 51 on the outbreak of war might expect to be, and was always on the move around the units in his division. Among the moral requirements of a general is the readiness to undertake certain harsh and unpalatable duties. These include telling superiors things they do not want to hear; accepting blame when subordinates have done wrong, even though not personally responsible for the errors; dismissing or punishing incompetent subordinates who may be friends, or well-liked old acquaintances; and, worst of all, giving orders to units to undertake tasks during which they are certain to incur heavy casualties. Almost daily throughout the war, a general had to face doing one of these unpleasant things, and the strain broke many of them. It did not break Ivor, but nobody can ever know how much it hurt him on occasions to do his duty, and what the pressure was on his moral fibre.

Although sad to leave the 18th Division, Ivor could not fail to be proud of his promotion to command XVIII Corps. For the first 15 months, from January 1917 to March 1918, fortune favoured him in his new post. During the third long, bitter campaign in the Ypres salient, often referred to as Passchendaele, his corps was successful in most of its battles, and after nearly three months in action he could justly claim to have achieved his objectives with fewer casualties than other corps.

After pulling out from Ypres and going down to the Somme sector again, he soon realised that the impending German attack, which everyone was forecasting, was going to strike before there was time to prepare a defensive line strong enough to hold them. Whatever he thought of his chances privately, he threw himself into creating as impregnable a position as possible, and gave clear warning to all his divisions of likely enemy tactics, based on 'all eggs in the Storm Truppen basket', as he vividly put it.

When the enemy assault was launched on 21 March 1918 it came with a speed and force that surpassed what was expected. The progress of events in XVIII Corps area has been fully described in Chapter 16, but it is, and always will remain, impossible to give a true assessment of Ivor's handling of his command during that perilous week. Between two possible verdicts lies a vast gulf. The unfavourable one, based on the widely held, contemporary view of the whole of the Fifth Army, is that his corps withdrew too far and too fast on 22 March, and thereafter retreated in disarray until being temporarily disbanded by Général Humbert when the French came to save the situation. In complete contrast, it can be suggested that in the circumstances forced upon them by the deficiency of almost everything required for making a proper stand – lack of men at the front and in reserve, shortage of engineer stores, and too little time for preparation – the formations in Fifth Army fought as well as could be expected. Ivor always defended his own conduct and claimed never to have lost contact with his four divisions throughout the retreat, while Gough gave him credit for his action on 25 March which 'saved the Fifth Army, and in fact the whole British Army and the Allied cause from disaster'.[3] Perhaps the truth lies somewhere between these two extremes.

In his perceptive book *Battle Tactics of the Western Front*, Paddy Griffiths puts forward an interesting, though somewhat unflattering, view of how Ivor's next appointment as Inspector General of Training (IGT) came about in June 1918, suggesting it meant that . . . 'he could be moved so tactfully sideways within the BEF when GHQ finally decided to kick him off the fighting line'. Griffiths goes on to say: . . . 'Being every bit as bumptious and outspoken as any senior officer ought to be, however, he realised that he held a splendid Somme reputation and some influential patrons and so he determined to put a brave face on developments.'[4] It has already been claimed that there was not enough time for the IGT and staff to have a great impact on training during the final few months of the war, but against this Sixsmith quotes a letter from General (then Captain) Jack Evetts which describes his '. . . vivid recollection of watching with Dugan the attack of the 9th Division on 28 September 1918, which went like clockwork'.[5] The various good points about the tactics used were then listed by Evetts, all of which show that many important lessons had been learnt about the conduct of operations by this stage of the war, and he at least clearly felt that the doctrine disseminated by the IGT's teams was having a useful effect. In his last thoroughly enjoyable appointment at York from 1919 to 1923, Ivor's main contribution was the encouragement of forward thinking among a number of intelligent young men who came within his orbit. Basil Liddell Hart, the best known of them, may not have been quite the original thinker he spent much of his life claiming to be, but he was an important gatherer of original ideas, and had the gift of expressing what he had harvested in clear and fluent prose.

When his active military career was finished, it was entirely in character for Ivor to throw himself into his new occupation as a fruit-farmer, with only an occasional backward glance at the army life on which so much of his energy and ambition had been centred for the previous 38 years. He passed a further 33 years at Little Bognor, fully employed in satisfying activity until the stroke in 1956, which so incapacitated him that he had to be nursed until his death in 1958. Born in 1862, long before the internal combustion engine was invented, he died in the year when the USSR had already launched the first *Sputniks* into space, and only 10 years before men would walk on the moon. It was a long and remarkable life, lived to the full by a remarkable man.

Notes

1 Sixsmith, Maj Gen E K G, *British Generalship in the 20th Century* (Arms & Armour, 1970), p. 9.
2 Barnett, Correlli, *The Desert Generals* (Pan, 1960), p. 11.
3 Gough, Gen Sir H, *The Fifth Army* (Hodder & Stoughton, 1931), p. 295.
4 Griffiths, P., *Battle tactics of the Western Front* (Yale Univ. Press, New Haven and London, 1994), p. 184.
5 Sixsmith, p. 139.

Short Selected Bibliography

————— ◆ • —————

Only the books which have been regularly referred to during the writing of this work are mentioned here, but a full reading list would be much longer.

Baker-Carr, Brigadier C D, *From Chauffeur to Brigadier* (Benn, 1930).

Banks, Lt-Col T M and CHELL, Capt R A, *With the 10th Essex in France* (10th Essex Old Comrades, 1921).

Bates, Darrell, *The Fashoda Incident of 1898* (OUP, 1984).

Blake, Robert, *The Private Papers of Douglas Haig, 1914–1919* (Eyre & Spottiswoode, 1952).

Bond, Brian, *Liddell Hart: A Study of His Military Thought* (Cassell, 1977).

Edmonds, Brig-Gen Sir J, *Official History of the War, Military Operations, France and Belgium* 1914, Vol I (Macmillan, 1933); 1916, Vol I (Macmillan, 1932); 1918, Vol I (Macmillan, 1935); Vol II (Macmillan, 1937).

Farrar-Hockley, Gen Sir A, *Goughie: The Life of General Sir Hubert Gough* (Hart-Davies, McGibbon, 1975).

Farrar-Hockley, Gen Sir A, *The Somme* (Batsford, 1964).

Fraser, Gen Sir D, *Alanbrooke* (Collins, 1982)

Fraser, Gen Sir D, *In Good Company* (Michael Russell, 1990).

Freyberg, Paul, *Bernard Freyberg, VC: A Soldier of Two Nations* (Hodder & Stoughton, 1991)

Gore, John, *Mary Maxse, 1870–1944* (Rolls House, 1946).

Gough, General Sir H, *The Fifth Army.* (Hodder & Stoughton, 1931).

Griffiths, P, *Battle Tactics of the Western Front* (Yale Univ. Press, 1994)

Harris, Ruth Elwin, *Billie: The Nevill Letters 1914–16.* (Julia MacRae, 1991)

Haythornthwaite, P J, *The World War One Source Book* (Arms and Armour, 1992).

Hutcheson, John A Jr., *Leopold Maxse and the National Review, 1894–1914* (Garland, New York, 1989)

Liddell Hart, Sir B H, *Memoirs, Vol I* (Cassell, 1965).

McCarthy, C, *The Somme: The Day-by-Day Account* (Arms and Armour, 1993)

Macdonald, Lyn, *Somme* (Michael Joseph, 1983).

McInnes, C & Sheffield, G D, *Warfare in the Twentieth Century* (Unwin Hyman, 1988).

Marshall-Cornwall, Gen Sir J, *Haig as Military Commander* (Batsford 1973).

Maxse, Gen Sir F I, *Our Military Problem* (Dent, 1896).

Maxse, Gen Sir F I, *Seymour Vandeleur* (National Review, 1905).

Maxwell, Mrs C, *Frank Maxwell, Brig Gen, VC, CSI, DSO: A Memoir and Some Letters* (John Murray, 1921).

Maze, Paul, *A Frenchman in Khaki* (Heinemann, 1934).

Middlebrook, M, *The First Day on the Somme, 1, July 1916* (Penguin, 1984).

Milner, The Viscountess, *My Picture Gallery* (John Murray, 1951).

Moore, William, *A Wood Called Bourlon* (Leo Cooper, 1988).

Nichols, Captain G H F, *The 18th Division in the Great War (ATN)* (Blackwood, 1922).

Norman, Terry, *The Hell They Called High Wood: The Somme 1916* (Kimber, 1984 and 1989).

Pakenham, Thomas, *The Boer War* (Weidenfeld & Nicolson, 1979).

Prior, R and WILSON, T, *Command on the Western Front* (Blackwell, 1992).

Robbins, S, 'The Ethos of the British High Command in the First World War' in the *Imperial War Museum Review, No 6.*

Shaw Sparrow, W, *The Fifth Army in March 1918* (Bodley Head, 1921).

Sitwell, Osbert, *Great Morning* (Reprint Society, 1949).

Sixsmith, Maj Gen E K G, *British Generalship in the Twentieth Century* (Arms & Armour, 1970).

SIXSMITH, Maj-Gen E K G, *Douglas Haig* (Weidenfeld & Nicolson, 1976).

Terraine, John, *Douglas Haig: The Educated Soldier* (Hutchinson, 1963).

Terraine, John (ed), *General Jack's Diary, 1914–1918* (Eyre & Spottiswoode, 1964).

TRAVERS, Prof T, *The Killing Ground* (Allen & Unwin, 1987).

Index

————•◆•————